David Callahan is an associate professor at the University of Aveiro in Portugal. The editor of *Australia – Who Cares?* (2007) and *Contemporary Issues in Australian Literature* (2002), and author of numerous book chapters and articles on Australian literature and culture, American literature, along with other post-colonial literatures and cinema, he has supported and taught Australian literature in Europe for twenty years. After immigrating to four different countries he has a good awareness of the experiences of dislocation that lie at the centre of Janette Turner Hospital's writing.

rainforest narratives

The Work of Janette Turner Hospital

David Callahan

UQP

First published 2009 by University of Queensland Press
PO Box 6042, St Lucia, Queensland 4067 Australia

www.uqp.com.au

Typeset in Berkeley 11/15pt by Post Pre-press Group, Brisbane
Printed in Australia by McPherson's Printing Group

Cataloguing-in-Publication Data
National Library of Australia

Callahan, David.

Rainforest Narratives: The work of Janette Turner Hospital

9780702237270 (pbk)

Includes index.
Bibliography.

Hospital, Janette Turner, 1942 – Criticism and interpretation.
Women authors, Australian – 20th century – History and criticism.
Australian literature – Women authors – History and criticism.

A820.9

For my children, Nicholas and Kate,
who have had to put up with my working on the weekends
for far too much of their childhood.

Contents

CHAPTER 1

Displacement, interpretation and responsibility

Living is serial, an unending accretion of alternatives.

Thea Astley[1]

Identities in play

In a Toronto *Sunday Star* trivia quiz in 1986 one of the questions was: 'Janette Turner Hospital is one of Canada's leading surgeons. True or false.'[2] While the answer seems flagged by its improbability, 'Hospital' is precisely the sort of name Hospital might give to a famous surgeon, defying readers to deny its appropriateness. Her work contains an American officer accused of atrocities in Vietnam whose name is Slaughter, men called Adam who have relationships with women called Eve or Faith, women called Felicity, Verity or Mercy, an Australian musician named Bartok, and an American father and son obsessed by codes and signs called Mather and Lowell Hawthorne.[3] Hospital's choice of names is not simply playfulness; it demonstrates an attitude that needs to be kept in the foreground when considering her writing: fiction is not a mirror that reflects reality or life, but a created artefact. The writer is not pretending to be an objective chronicler; she is someone with priorities and interests that she wants us to reflect upon. For this reason, readers need to be challenged: they need to be aware that they are being addressed by a writer who demands that they think about what it means to read about moral issues in a type of reality constructed by someone else.

In line with the tendency of modern narrative theory to give a central role to readers in the arrangement of the meanings they derive from what they read, Hospital's work has become extremely self-conscious about the dynamic interface between the writer (or narrator) and the reader. Her books thus disrupt the conventions of straightforward storytelling in order to oblige us to make sense of a plot in which time schemes and information are fragmented and out of sequence. By designing her narratives in this way, Hospital prevents us from slipping into the easy contract of realism, in which we may allow ourselves to be carried along by a comforting narrator, enjoying the story without much reflection. Another consequence of her structuring her fiction as puzzles is that it often has the characteristics of mystery or thriller narratives: working out who has done what to whom, and why, is one of the great pleasures of her work. Hospital does, however, require much more than the average alertness and vigilance of the reader of thrillers, and this book will attempt to offer signposts to what to look out for in this enterprise. It does not claim to clear up the puzzles, but rather summarises the issues involved in each of her books, indicates the principal critical contexts in which they have been considered, and tries to suggest the interpretative practices that might be most useful in making one's own way through her fictional world.

To talk of Hospital's writing as 'rainforest narratives' is to posit a metaphor in which the profusion and entanglements of the rainforest serve as a model for Hospital's fictional strategies. That is, her plots are not straightforward but occlude connections and links until we have made our way into them, and even then they require vigilance and patient deciphering for their sequencing to be made apparent. There is a bewildering oversupply of information in Hospital's books; everything acts upon or lives upon everything else in some way, so that of necessity seeing where one growth ends and another starts becomes an intervention that will be different for every reader. Rather than events ending or starting in any clear fashion, narrative units are brought into relation with others along multiple potential axes, or via different explanatory chains. Links between characters are often obscure, relations between occurrences are unclear, and even identity and time are not as stable as we might expect. Her prose itself has porous frontiers in the manner in which the material and the emotional leak into each other, so that the senses have access to the subjective and the disembodied: in *Borderline*, for example, Jean-Marc claims of his memories of his father that '[a]fter each visit, my clothes stank of him. Literally. An odor of oils and paint thinner and self-indulgence';[4] while in *Orpheus Lost* Leela listens to Mishka playing a Gluck aria and '[e]xtravagant sorrow fogged the kitchen and leaked under the door and down the hall'.[5]

The rainforest is as complex a metaphoric site as it is a complex biological site, so that Hospital's work both invites symbolic exploration and confounds it, just as the rainforest's exuberance can invite physical exploration and confound it. Hospital's work in general does not seek to clear up the many conundra it articulates, nor to suggest easy answers, but to explore things in their connections and the ways in which they implicate each other. Every one of her books is both an examination and a representation of the ways in which strategies of exclusion and simplification are inevitably overcome by networks of connection, entanglements of involvement, by webs and nettings of association which spread ever more widely until one's sense of limits or causality has been thoroughly broken down.[6]

One indication of how the profusion operates is that most of Hospital's main characters show a destabilised and variable identity.[7] Characters generally have different names depending on whom they are dealing with or the situation they are in. This arises partly because Hospital shares the postmodern suspicion of the idea of identity as stable and easily identifiable, and partly as a strategy used by characters to avoid being categorised and controlled by others. Hospital also participates in the post-Rushdie enjoyment of multiple identities, in which the modern cosmopolitan travels to and lives in different locations, becoming a colourful kaleidoscope of identity matter, creatively moving between roles. This can be seen particularly in short stories such as 'Happy Diwali' and 'Queen of Pentacles, Nine of Swords',[8] in which Hospital admires the identity-refashioning energy of Indians in the West. Characters such as Felicity in *Borderline*, Charlie in *The Last Magician* or Mishka in *Orpheus Lost* accrete around themselves varying names and identity positions, albeit with increasingly troubling results. Despite frequent comments by characters as to how they feel happiest in transit (Emily in *The Tiger in the Tiger Pit* or Felicity in *Borderline*), there is at times a melancholy and even a desperation about such characters that undercuts their confidence. In the depiction of the attempts at identity refashioning by Oyster, in *Oyster*, and Mishka, in *Orpheus Lost*, there is also an awareness that the desire to compartmentalise ourselves in the service of manipulating others is more destructive of self and others than creatively rich.

Disjunction between the differing spheres we move in is common, but Hospital grew up with an especially severe cleavage between her home environment and that outside. She refers lovingly in interviews to her family's Pentecostal approach to life, in which there was constant attention to the reasons for our existence, to responsibility towards others, and to the resounding authority of the language of the Bible. She also makes clear, however, that the approach provided such a complete explanation that she came to feel it restricted more than it satisfied, although she also thinks that '[l]iving without radio or television, she developed a sleuth-like approach to events . . . constantly seeking clues "to help her unravel the mysteries of a normal life"'.[9] Many aspects of Hospital's Pentecostal family background can be found nourishing her work, most obviously a love of resonant language that never loses sight of the big issues, and a determination to examine our constant responsibility to interpret the surfaces and appearances that surround us. The presence of the King James translation of the Bible, and of Shakespeare, the language of both of which coursed through her family life, is apparent in what observers have consistently remarked on: 'prose so blissfully shaped that we cannot but see that human genius is somehow itself the fruit of paradox',[10] or writing that 'simply hums and crackles with pace and tension'.[11]

As a writer who belongs in multiple locations, Hospital's career also challenges the tendency to nationalise culture. She can be categorised as an Australian/Canadian/American writer, for whom medieval and contemporary European literature has been central, along with the language of the Bible, Shakespeare and theoretical physics. In addition to the multiplicity of identity sources, Hospital has insisted throughout her career that '[i]n margins and in longings: this is where all homelands begin'.[12] Like many contemporary writers, Hospital has had to battle against the desires of the media and academia to assign her to national or other categories;[13] Lucy's *cri de coeur* in *The Last Magician* surely comes from Hospital's experience: 'to have been born here and gone away is about as good as having been born here of Chinese stock. No known category. Please check "Other" on all forms.'[14] Adam Shoemaker proposes 'that Hospital is in fact "someone else" all of the time, no matter where she is temporally or geographically located'.[15] He goes on to argue that 'a full understanding of her work can only be achieved when one renounces the idea of Canadianness and Australianness as *competing* identities'.[16] Indeed, while Hospital has dealt far more frequently with Australian identities than with Canadian ones, not to mention focusing much more on American identities than Canadian ones, her work is notable above all for its everpresent attention to margins, borders and liminal states. These states cannot simply become the confident identity sites lacking elsewhere, for, like every other category, they are also shifting and uncertain: 'Who decides what is margin and what is text? Who decides where the borders of the homeland run.'[17] People fall through holes everywhere whatever the boundaries, and positive characters are able to make new connections that reach across the dividing lines, whether of nationality (Juliet and Yashoda in *The Ivory Swing*), ethnicity (Cat and Charlie in *The Last Magician*), class (Lucy and the Queen of Sheba in *The Last Magician*), age (Mercy and Miss Rover in *Oyster*) or subculture (Felicity and Gus in *Borderline*). The community in *Oyster* that tries to exist not merely on the boundaries but beyond them ends up tearing itself apart by having no alternative connections through which to deal with disruptive and self-destructive forces. The anxiety over changing occupation patterns in a Toronto suburb in 'Moving Out' has no form of release until two elderly women make contact across the borders of culture and language.[18] Borderlines for Hospital are thus dynamic zones of contact, not ways of shutting everything else out or setting limits to identities.

Living on the margins, however, brings a price along with its relative liberation from the constraints and fixities of a settled existence. Hospital's work portrays a gallery of travellers and inhabitors of liminal realms of one sort or another whose self-proclaimed freedom brings complications ranging from the constant opposition of family members (Emily in *Tiger*) through to violent death (Cat, Charlie and Gabriel in *The Last Magician*, Felicity in *Borderline*, Genevieve in *Due Preparations*). Some characters survive but with their lives in shreds, such as Jess and Major Miner in *Oyster*, Lucy in *The Last Magician* and Mishka in *Orpheus Lost*. Living on or beyond the edge is not an easy proposition; being different often arouses the wrath of others, a pattern that begins in childhood and which Hospital is chillingly good at depicting. 'At seven and eight, we know how to draw blood quickest and deepest', says Charade.[19]

Initially in Hospital's work it is principally women who are punished for exhibiting freedom of movement or difference. It is no accident that the refugee in *Borderline* is a woman; that the principal victim in *The Last Magician* is a woman; that the tyrant in *The Tiger in the Tiger Pit* is a man; that the twinned women in *The Ivory Swing* feel trapped by male-generated structures of power; or that some of her most memorable short stories concern the violence perpetrated upon women by men, as in 'Last of the Hapsburgs' or 'The Second Coming of Come-by-Chance'. Latterly, however, male characters such as Lowell Hawthorne in *Due Preparations*, or Mishka in *Orpheus Lost*, have been the principal objects of threatened or actual violence for stepping outside the accepted patterns. Indeed, a general current of sympathy runs through Hospital's work for those outside society's structures of approval or power, whether men or women: broken old men, prostitutes, drug addicts, the poor, and the dispossessed in general.

At the same time there are several positive characters who are not associated with movement, from Elizabeth in *Tiger*, through Bea in *Charades*, the Queen of Sheba in *The Last Magician*, Muriel in *Oyster*, Zach in 'South of Loss' to Leela's father in *Orpheus Lost*. In some way, however, all of these characters display oppositional stances towards conventional social models that go beyond their supposedly static existence. Elizabeth, Bea and the Queen of Sheba embody a womanly strength that resists male priorities, sometimes directly, at other times more subtly. Zach evokes diasporic Jewish history, at the same time as he is open to the pull of elsewhere in the person of the Frenchwoman who irrupts into his rural life. Among the only successful inhabitors of a realm beyond the borders set up by social norms are people who manage to establish homes in or near the rainforest, such as Bea or Gabriel's mother in *The Last Magician*. The emigré European families in 'The Last of the Hapsburgs' and *Orpheus Lost*, however, have suffered so much on account of the Holocaust that their present peace deep within the rainforest is forever shadowed by the traumas of the past.

Hospital's Australians tend to be displaced, immigrants or the children of immigrants, or in some way different, avatars of her own family's difference. Hospital's family's marginalisation from many of the ways in which white Australian families asserted their identities and common patterns should indeed give pause to those who posit a facile identification between whiteness, British heritage and confident power. While Hospital touches only briefly on the English in England, in the caricatural portrait of Nicholas Truman's family in *Charades*, she writes movingly in her family-history short stories of the displacement felt by British immigrants in Australia, an experience often ignored in contemporary Australian accounts of the dislocation experienced by migrants.[20]

Yet even for characters who stay at home, there is a way to be elsewhere at the same time, and that is through curiosity, reading and interpretation: as Mercy reports in *Oyster*: 'A wandering mind is not something to be ashamed of, Miss Rover says. It's an asset. The great artists and inventors could all be led astray on tangents at the drop of a hat.'[21] At first glance, Hospital's work seems to be cluttered with tangents, and yet not a single apparently throwaway line or allusion or meandering stream of thought is extraneous to either her moral interests or her narrative patterning. This profusion is also of a piece with Hospital's love of medieval illuminated manuscripts, and a type of medieval art and literature in general, in which details and many-levelled meanings are central. Medieval scholar Suzanne Lewis explains the summons that is being made in such art:

> Medieval theory termed the cosmos of Scripture 'difficult ornament' (*difficulta ornata*), whose calculated obscurity elicits an interpretive response in the reader to the extent that the actual process of deciphering the exegetical content of a passage is traditionally regarded as painfully arduous and uncertain. Readers and listeners were conditioned from their allegorical reading of sacred texts to expect that 'the most featureless surface could be made to yield profound significance'.[22]

The endless exegetical energy that accumulates around scriptural texts continues to be lived in Pentecostalism, and is transmuted in Hospital's fiction into a high-spirited determination to activate reading practices – from both characters and readers – that pay attention to the multiple potential meanings called for by everything, down to the smallest detail. As Lewis outlines:

> The medieval practice of glossing and illustrating texts acknowledges the way in which language itself both defies our access to final meaning and inscribes its own ability to keep generating meanings endlessly into the gaps it creates.[23]

Hospital's apparent digressions need then to be seen in this light: as an exemplification of existence as interpretation, in which nothing should go unexamined. From family history and academic training Hospital has been exposed to a view of reality as having been written by God, in which nothing and no possible connection can be without significance, for how could God create anything that was meaningless or insignificant? In such a world, there can be no digressions, because everything means. The task is not to close down meanings but to open them up, even though human perception will always be inadequate to the task.

Representation, language, photographs

The multiple valences of identity, thus, are not so much the *subject* of Hospital's fiction as the *result* of its principal and most dynamic theme: how to read reality, followed closely by how to record one's reading. In the service of these issues, Hospital's work contains numerous figures whose principal activity is that of interpretation. These figures constitute a veritable panoply of the interpretative possibilities open to us, or forced upon us, from Juliet in *The Ivory Swing*, whose cultural displacement has demanded an actively interpretative stance towards the unfamiliar realities that surround her, through to the professional

Intelligence gatherers Mather Hawthorne in *Due Preparations for the Plague* and Cobb Slaughter in *Orpheus Lost*. Characters involved in the Arts provide other models by which realities may be translated into something meaningful, from musicians Emily in *The Tiger in the Tiger Pit* and Mishka in *Orpheus Lost*, artist Seymour and art curator Felicity in *Borderline*, filmmakers Charlie and Catherine in *The Last Magician*, to numerous photographers, from Charlie again to Swann and Odette in 'Frames and Wonders', or the anonymous photographers of atrocities in Iraq in *Orpheus Lost*. Photographs, in fact, are something of a leitmotif in Hospital's work, cropping up in work after work as part of an ongoing questioning of the conditions through which we may represent things, and the part interpretation has to play in the face of certain types of 'evidence'. In a perceptive early article on her work, Deborah Bowen concludes that 'Hospital's fundamental concern is not with the problematizing of representation, but . . . with how to read meaning in appearances',[24] although it can be seen that these are in fact twinned concerns.

The task of deciphering events is demanded of the reader by the form of her novels, in which puzzles, time displacements and differing types of evidence are constantly provoking us to make connections, to decode characters' words and actions and to decide upon what is valuable. As value and moral witness are so central in Hospital's work, the active and ethical role of the reader of appearances becomes dynamically energised in her fiction. Reading a Hospital novel is not something readers tend to be lukewarm about: one either accepts the challenge and enters the heady world in which all types of evidence are questioned, including the evidence provided by the tricky text in front of us, or one rejects the turbulent, provocative prose for reasons which generally range from an aversion to postmodern slipperiness to a rejection of the links between the moral issues raised and the supposedly distracting richness of the language.[25]

In her advice to young writers, Hospital has remarked that 'one of the biggest stumbling blocks for beginning writers is this sticky matter of "the truth"'.[26] To be useful as expression, stories need to engage readers and not direct them overly closely; to do this, stories sometimes need to cut loose from 'those literal events' in order to induce readers to ask questions and draw conclusions for themselves. In Hospital's work the active role of the reader vivifies the relationship between narrator and reader, for narrators are always aware that they are structuring the tale, and that any tale intends to be heard and to be believed. There is no pretence that the reality of events can be transparently perceived through language. The literality of events in fact becomes one of the subjects of her writing, which returns insistently to the ways in which the telling of the tale becomes a reality itself, until the border between any reality other than that of language and the reality of language becomes increasingly problematic. John Tagg states the situation bluntly: 'What exceeds representation . . . cannot, by definition, be articulated.'[27]

The unreliability of language is, however, not its only characteristic. Indeed, the gap between language and the other aspects of reality it gestures towards offers something at the same time as it takes away, for it ensures that language involves the play of metaphor and the dazzling possibilities of invention. Moreover, language is also a tool with which we bear witness to our being in the world and make connections with other people. Russell West writes of 'the strong urge, in Turner Hospital's narratives, to put things in their right place, to understand the world'.[28] The twists and turns of her plots have always involved mysteries whose contours need to be uncovered so that justice can be done. Yet given that we almost never see justice done in terms of wrongs righted – for wrongdoers tend to go unpunished in all of Hospital's books – the justice that is sought is a justice *in the telling*: wronged people's stories need to come out, and these stories need to be duly sensitive to the issues concerned. In order to present anyone's story with the right amount of attention to context, many sides of that story need to be told before the lines of causality and motive can become clearer. The roundabout and manifold nature of her plots is thus not mere technical display but intrinsic to the understanding of the nature of reality as fractal: possessing patterns that are so complex they are difficult to perceive, and, analogously to the discovery of fractal geometries in meteorology, they require special instrumentation and techniques to be made visible. Moreover, simply to see such patterns is not therefore *really* to see reality either. If they cannot be seen without particular instruments and conditions, then those instruments and conditions become a necessary part of the reality themselves; in the case of fiction, this means that language and narrative design become essential elements in any reality that they speak.

Faced, thus, with a perspective on reality that sees it as having as many sides as there are stories told of it, one task becomes that of examining whether it is possible to determine which version is better attuned to the representation that best speaks for principles of moral justice in a world where bullies are all too ready to deny the stories of the weak or different. Allen Thiher divides postmodern writers into two tendencies: those who 'engage in overt dramatization of their works' self-referentiality', and those who do not 'make explicit the meta-linguistic procedure by which the work shows that it is representing itself'.[29] Hospital tends to belong to the first type, for the encounter with language and narrative is part of the stories she is telling, in which a crucial paradox concerns the fact that there is something untruthful about the most straightforward telling of any story, one that makes use of what Jess in *Oyster* refers to as 'those two trollops, those two teases, those tarts, Start and Stop'.[30] Listing events in bare fashion, with linear causal links between them, is often associated in her work with detectives or figures associated with authority in some way, and their versions are invariably seen as limited and even dangerous.

In *Transgressions of Reading: Narrative Engagement as Exile and Return*, Robert Newman writes of 'readers as exiles from an ideal Imaginary state [who] seek to recover that state by wandering the text, only to continually wander into recognitions of their exiled condition'.[31] If we accept entry into Hospital's world, we engage with being exiled, or displaced, for long sections of her novels. Working through the various strands of the plots we find that we cannot, in Newman's formulation of our desire as readers, 'retrospectively impose order by relieving the tensions generated by the plot',[32] because Hospital leaves too many uncertainties. 'Unanswerable questions are the ones that engage us', says Charlie.[33] To impose order is to read like a detective. In fact, arriving at an awareness of the nature of our existence as interpreting animals who are necessarily always in uncertainty is one of the designs Hospital's fiction has upon us. Moreover, trying to assemble a narrative and make meanings, as Jean-Marc does in *Borderline*, leads to a return to a self that has changed, transformed through self-conscious story-telling into a self that is no longer enclosed in upon itself, and the incompletion of this opening out is something morally and imaginatively necessary in Hospital's work.

Stories, in fact, can never be complete. To be complete is to be finished, and to be finished is to be dead. In order to avoid ending up like the dead body entwined in the rainforest creepers in *Charades*, we need to keep moving through Hospital's prose, to break our way through the forest. To mean is to impose, to construct and destroy at the same time; to mean is to interfere, while to become passive in the face of the overgrowth of meaning is to surrender agency. To assume our positions as responsible individuals is to be self-conscious about our interfering activity of making meanings even when we know they involve elements that might be subjective, unverifiable and mutable. Accompanying us through this hermeneutic rainforest, Hospital's work asserts the need for her principal characters to keep interpreting even when the evidence may be unreliable, incomplete and told to them by interlocutors who have their own interests in preferring certain meanings over others. More, the involvement of the reader in the entanglements of her plots ensures that we also reproduce this double responsibility: hacking our way through, never feeling in control, but courageously carrying on nonetheless. We might not be able to follow a very direct route, and we might get scratched in the process, but the multifarious wonders we experience along the way compensate richly for making the effort. When Hospital reviewed Robyn Davidson's novel *Ancestors*, she could have been summarising herself: 'She evokes the hedonism, the self-reliance, the sense of awe and the taste for adventure that rainforest childhoods breed.'[34]

CHAPTER 2

'They are not *my* rules'
The Ivory Swing

The very idea of differences among societies or individuals implies qualities in common.

Tzvetan Todorov[1]

Dislocation and difference

With *The Ivory Swing* Janette Turner Hospital made an auspicious entry into her career as a novelist, winning Canada's Seal Award for the best first novel of 1982. It is easy to see why the book impressed the judges. In addition to its confident and spirited narrative voice, it addressed issues that were highly topical in a period of expanding discussion of multicultural questions in the Canada of the 1980s: the difficulties of dealing with cultural difference; the limitations placed on women by different cultures; and how human beings resort to violence when they are faced with transgressive behaviour or oppositional identities. Moreover, the book was set in what to Western readers was the colourfully tropical world of the south-west Indian state of Kerala, at a time when the Western world was waking up to India as a source of literary material, albeit principally produced by Indians themselves.[2]

Hospital's work is typified by characters who feel that they do not totally belong, and in her later books this dislocation will radiate out to include such existential realities as time, language and identity. *The Ivory Swing*, however, concentrates on the physical and cultural displacement in India of the Canadian Juliet, who is spending a year in Kerala while her husband studies the local version of Hinduism. Her sense of alienation from the surrounding culture becomes the context in which she questions the parameters of her life back in Canada, as well as those values beyond which she discovers that she cannot go in her attempt to relate to the cultural difference of Kerala.

Accordingly, the book begins, 'They did not quite know what to make of each other, Juliet and the [Keralan] boy',[3] and the cultural shocks Juliet experiences thereafter lead her to rethink many of her moral and political standpoints, although not in the end to revise them. The drama of the book arises because even though Juliet agonises over the judgements she makes about a culture with quite different priorities from those she is used to in Winston, Ontario (transparently Kingston, where Hospital lived from 1971 to 1999),[4] she is unable to allow the difference to take its course without herself commenting, and in some cases acting, in ways that defy important aspects of local mores. In general her outrage relates to her beliefs about how women should be treated, as well as her anger over the treatment of the poor. The fact that at the end of the novel the principal representatives of the situation of women (Yashoda) and the caste-bound poor (Prabhakaran) are both brutally murdered justifies Juliet's anger on the one hand, but on the other hand it shows that her intervention on their behalf has not only not worked but has in fact contributed to the murders of the two local characters Juliet cared about the most. The novel thus becomes both a critique of the realities Juliet confronts in India and a self-conscious realisation that the actions of an individual Westerner may not be a force for good in such a context.

Early in the novel the sensation is one of a strangeness that is more abrasive than colourfully exotic: 'There were constant misunderstandings' (10). Juliet is greeted with anger by the owner of the house her family is renting, Mr Shivaraman Nair, when in good pioneer spirit she says she does not need any servants. She, in turn, reacts incredulously to Nair's insistence that they move into the house only on the auspicious day and at the auspicious time calculated by an astrologer. The servant-boy Prabhakaran compounds things by entering and proceeding blithely with his housework when Juliet is naked.

The novel and Juliet will subsequently move in the direction of understanding and appreciating Prabhakaran more than Shivaraman Nair, in line with the novel's support for those whose possibilities of agency are more severely limited by the social system. The chapter finishes with Juliet's admitting that she is treating the servant in ways that are not considered appropriate, a challenge therefore to local customs and a challenge to the local hegemonic forces. It is important that we realise that Juliet is able to perceive the offence that her behaviour causes, so that she is seen as someone who assesses outcomes and makes choices rather than as merely a blundering foreigner. The simplistically exotic never exists for Juliet as mere background or charming otherness, since there is no colour and nothing exotic that is not also constantly asking a moral question of its perceivers. When Hospital was writing this book the enthusiasm for multiculturalism in Canada and the West in general was leading towards a heightened nervousness about criticising other cultures. *The Ivory Swing*, however, in line with Hospital's feistiness throughout her career, will have none of this pusillanimous anxiety about responding to difference. Abstaining from judgement of others because they come from another culture is demonstrating an exaggerated form of respect that has increasingly come to be seen as more limiting than useful. Satya Mohanty sums up the growing suspicion of this withdrawal from the hurly-burly of cultural critique:

> To believe, further, that there can be no responsible way in which I can adjudicate between your space – cultural and historical – and mine by developing a set of general criteria that can have interpretive validity in both contexts (because there can be no interpretation that is not simultaneously an evaluation) . . . is to assert that *all spaces are equivalent*, that they have equal value, that since the lowest common principle of evaluation is all that I can invoke, I cannot – and consequently need not – think about how your space impinges on mine or how my history is defined together with yours. If that is the case, I may have started by declaring a pious political wish, but I end by denying that I need to take you seriously.[5]

The novel thus includes both Juliet's disapproval of elements of Keralan culture (as well as approval of other elements) and a self-conscious exploration of the conditions under which she feels justified in disapproving of, or even opposing, what she sees around her.

Juliet spends a large part of the book attempting to appreciate local realities, but she frequently fails. She cannot ask Prabhakaran to do something, for example, because there is apparently no way of being polite to a servant in Malayalam and she cannot 'bring herself to be peremptory with him' (65). Writing from an Australian upbringing in which history shows a hard-won battle to strip social interaction of the subservience and hierarchical protocols brought from Europe, this would be an act of cultural acceptance beyond both Canadian Juliet and Australian Hospital. The result is disorientation, for Juliet realises that the principal responsibility to adapt is hers, but finds that to adapt would be to abandon some of her core beliefs.

The main contrast with Juliet's frustration is provided in the first half of the book by her children, Jonathan and Miranda, who are enraptured by the freedom, space and discoveries their new life provides. They react to Juliet's fears of the polluted water in which they hunt for pond life with resigned exasperation, and continue to look on everything as a chance for exploration and wonder. Contrasts are later supplied by Juliet's husband, David, and her sister Annie, contrasts which make Juliet's responses more personal and less overly representative of the 'West'.

At this early stage of her career, Hospital's work perceived identity and its problems as principally gendered and cultural. It is a constant property of her fictional world, however, that positions of cultural and personal affirmation are necessarily called into question; people cannot simply be explained or represented as products of a static culture that everybody agrees upon. Cultures contain contradictions, inequalities and inconsistencies – numerous gaps and rifts through which individuals and groups are constantly contesting and realigning priorities and possibilities. This is classically stated in Chinua Achebe's *Things Fall Apart*, where characters in a traditional society attempt to evade convention when it suits them, and in Mulk Raj Anand's *Untouchable*, where the protagonist Bakha's opposition to tradition is seen to arise out of his state of oppression within the Hindu caste system. And it is certainly so in Hospital's work, where she valorises individuals who step outside the patterns laid down for them by either the immediate context of their families or the wider contexts of their cultures.

An implicit question is thus asked repeatedly in the novel: what is the best way to challenge existing conditions? As the book unfolds, Juliet becomes less and less sure of how to go about this, admitting at one point that local people 'have a way . . . of making my democratic instincts seem gauche and clumsy. In bad taste' (156). When she visits the local Christian Matthew Thomas with her children and Prabhakaran, her wish to include the servant boy in the visit makes her host 'confused and deeply embarrassed' and Prabhakaran 'tense and unhappy' (159). By this stage in the book Juliet is not so sure about her approach anymore: is direct confrontation the only way, or the best way, given that it is indeed a way in which as a result 'everyone is suffering', an Indian-English construction that emphasises the presentness of the suffering, its relevance to the here and now?

Ironically, it is when Juliet is groping towards this realisation that matters come to a head. She sees that everything is connected in a functioning system, as she contemplates the meaning of a frond from a coconut palm falling to the ground. It will be used by the local people, things will be made and sold, food will be bought, and everything has a use that ensures the smooth working of the system, so that '[t]o disrupt the chain was disastrous' (164). David also feels that events are connected meaningfully, and that Yashoda's fate and his family's 'brush with death' (205) in a bus accident are not haphazard events. When the restraining wall of a rice terrace gives way and the rice is ruined by the sun, it is seen by the local people not as an accident of nature but as a punishment: 'someone had broken *dharma*' (218). After all, Shivaraman Nair had accused 'the foreigners of . . . causing disasters which would come as surely as planting follows reaping' (164).

On the other hand, the social system scarcely works smoothly, as is evident in the street demonstrations against social conditions and the riotous dissatisfaction of the poorer sectors of Keralan society. Nonetheless, Juliet comes to see that even Shivaraman Nair performs acts that are not economically necessary, such as buying a few handfuls of grass from an old woman who cannot harvest rice any more, and that this constitutes a type of mostly concealed but sustaining solidarity. Just as she is reaching towards this conclusion, however, she learns that Prabhakaran, whom she had been treating almost as one of the family, has been taken away from them because he is supposedly being corrupted by Western ways, and her new-found appreciation of the interlocking harmonies of the social system evaporates in the heat of her anger at this affront to her beliefs and personal connections: '"I won't let them keep Prabhakaran away from us," Juliet vowed' (166).

Swinging and stasis

It is in the nature of Hospital's fictional world that realities leak into each other. Wherever we are is never simply that place but also the comparisons it provides with other relevant realities, and the ways in which different aspects of our lives impinge upon each other beyond our capacity to control them. Throughout the novel Juliet's experiences in India constantly evoke her life in Canada,[6] leading her to question the realities she knows as well as those she does not. Her view of the year to be spent in India morphs into a general summing up of her professional and personal life up to that point, and it is noticeable that she sees her life as a failure to achieve what she had hoped to. In the arena of personal relations, things have become safe and predictable. In her professional life, she has stepped away from the heady excitement and complex challenges of a large city, moving from Boston to provincial Ontario. She feels she is losing touch with a vivid, energetic self, but when presented with the opportunity to make contact with this former existence – having sex with her erstwhile lover Jeremy – she pulls back, saying that what she wants is 'to maintain my balancing act' (18). She regularly recalls Jeremy as a representative of a past free of the constraints of marriage, children and responsibility. Juliet feels caught between these two extremes, and this intensifies the connection she feels with local widow Yashoda, who also refuses to accept the restraints that custom imposes on her by its insistence that she remain withdrawn from society and under the control of a male relative: 'Yashoda and I, she thought, we want everything. We swing between worlds, always in conflict, always looking for impossible resolutions, destined to uncertainty and dissatisfaction' (207). Like the piece of ivory Juliet sees in a local art dealer's shop, this swing is at the same time the opposite of movement, frozen in a representation of movement that is not movement itself, gesturing towards movement but 'going nowhere' (207), a fate Juliet is determined will not happen to her or, if she can help it, to Yashoda either.[7]

The restrictions and frustrations in India are thus made to seem a continuum with Juliet's life in Canada, in which the key restrictions are those of provincial life versus the freedom of large cities 'that heave untidily with history and event and garbage strikes and miraculous chance encounters' (68). The irony of this is apparent, for if there is anything that can be said to characterise India it is that it heaves 'untidily with history and event', and the novel contains numerous 'miraculous chance encounters'. The irony is rendered immediately after Juliet has this thought, when she meets Yashoda disguised as a Muslim (so she can hide her face and go into the street), a chance encounter intensified by the historical contexts that make the veiled figure an object of intense wonder and speculation on the part of everyone in a mostly Hindu and Christian part of India. By the end of the novel the irony will have turned tragic as events pile up with increasing rapidity, until the shattering occurrences that are Yashoda and Prabhakaran's deaths mark the end of the chain of circumstances and the clashes of conflicting wills that Juliet's swinging state of mind has largely precipitated.

This doubled location of the novel – mostly in India but constantly shadowed by Canada – is an early example of Hospital's frequent use of contrasting pairs set against each other, although, as Margaret Schramm points out, this generally takes the form of doubled characters.[8] In *The Ivory Swing* there are two of these twinned pairs, Juliet and Yashoda and Juliet and her sister Annie who comes to visit her in India. Annie represents the apparent contemporary Western possibility of living largely unconstrained by male structures of power and disapproval, to the extent that Juliet exclaims to Annie at one point: 'I want to be you *and* me' (172; Hospital's italics). This is mirrored, in turn, by Annie's envy of Juliet's apparent domestic bliss back in Canada. The most significant twinned pair, however, remains Yashoda and Juliet, Yashoda being introduced much earlier when Juliet is having trouble coping with her vision of her life in Canada as constricted and limiting.

Yashoda is not simply a young widow who is expected to withdraw from society but a mysterious and beautiful woman who could be seen as a Western stereotype of Indian women. Hospital has prefigured her appearance by referencing Radha, the beautiful heroine of a Sanskrit epic, and this activates the meanings accruing to the figure of legend and attaches them to a contemporary person, thus incorporating India's own myths about itself and not simply Western ones.[9] In this sense the connection between Yashoda and the book's title inserts Yashoda into a wider iconography than that of the orientalised beauty, given that Indian culture – as indeed most cultures – also contains the stereotype of the beautiful young maiden. It is this wideness of reference that David summons up when he is remembering her at the end as he looks at representations of Radha in old manuscripts: 'I am everywhere, she said. I am the idea of perfection and of flawed endeavour. I am unattainable beauty. I am the moment of opportunity forever lost' (247).[10] At one point Juliet perceives that 'Yashoda flitted back and forth between the trees like a woman on an ivory swing – translucent, a trick of the light, an artist's fantasy' (132). In even more destabilising a fashion, she imagines that Yashoda drifted through David's mind 'like a *yakshi* on a swing, back and forth, mesmeric, a hypnotist's trick' (141). The swing has here become a sign of danger, where it was initially an *objet d'art*, a sign of beauty removed from a real context. Later in the novel Juliet will imagine her own life in Canada as being 'shackled to a swing that I can't get off' (172), inflecting the trope further with the resonance of something on which women are expected to sit and serve as an adornment, but which they cannot choose to remove themselves from. The swing itself, then, is a metaphor that references its own instability as it calls up the contradictions between traditionally sanctioned myths of sensual contact between men and women and contemporary aspirations for something less restricted.[11]

Women, restriction and freedom

Juliet's fluctuating relation to India comes to a head principally through her anger at its treatment of women. At question in this novel is the potential for agency for women in a world where the possibilities of action have been circumscribed by men in such a way that their acting independently is perceived as transgressing. Hospital shows us representations of female development in both India and Canada stunted by the social boundaries that prevent them from developing along lines they perceive as desirable. Juliet is made to feel that she is secondary simply because she is a woman, and we are quickly introduced to some of the consequences of this in India when she is commanded to prepare tea for the Nairs who are visiting the house Shivaraman Nair has leased to them.[12] When she pours herself a cup and sits down to join in the conversation, the men get up and leave, shocked. Even though this is explained by Nair's son Anand as a cultural misunderstanding, indicating that they know she did not mean to offend them, the fact is that she did know her action would unsettle them. The question here, as elsewhere throughout the book (not to mention throughout the contemporary world), becomes: to what extent can we accept the protocols of others when they enter into direct conflict with our own most cherished beliefs? To what extent can we accept cultural norms that appear to relegate women to a secondary position?

One response to these questions is to realise that cultures are not homogeneous, and that not everybody within a culture supports all of its features. As Nair and the uncles move disgustedly away from the house, for example, they see Yashoda, who has also defied local customs. Already upset by Juliet's behaviour, one of the uncles takes it out on Yashoda, throwing a stone at her 'as a landlord throws a stone at scavenger dogs' (42). Given that Yashoda presumably cannot approve of having stones thrown at her, we are reminded that so-called cultural norms may not be norms at all, in the sense of being practices accepted uncomplainingly by all sectors of society; rather, they may be expressions of power wielded by elements of what we call a culture, and which have as their aim the preservation of aspects of the status quo that buttress the ability of those elements to maintain and enjoy their power: in the case of the novel, the power of men over women. Customs that Juliet has flouted are also flouted, in different ways, by Yashoda, and these customs are versions of male power, something that runs through the structures of power in all cultures. The desire to transgress these customs does not occur just in the area of what might be considered as a selfish personal freedom, but, for instance, when Yashoda accepts milk from the low-caste Prabhakaran, 'an act that would be considered a form of ritual pollution' (63). The suggestion in these moments of conflict with custom is that it is not merely because Juliet is foreign that she outrages, both deliberately and accidentally, the milieu in which she finds herself but that there are women in all cultures who resist the flagrant or veiled protocols of social control that disempower them and introduce division between the genders. *The Ivory Swing* has an ethnocentric character at its centre, albeit one who strives to respond thoughtfully to the alien environment in which she finds herself. However, to presume that a novel chronicling the encounter of a Canadian woman with Kerala could exist in some realm outside ethnocentrism is to presume something unresponsive to lived realities. In anthropologist Marc Augé's words:

> By trying too hard to avoid ethnocentrism, we have run the risk of removing all substance from the others' reality, of remaining unaware that their questions are also our questions (and vice versa) and that their responses are therefore not arbitrary or exotic in a way that might make them forever foreign or derisory to us.[13]

In this case, the book implies that Juliet's questions and those of Yashoda are related, whatever the differing rituals and prohibitions surrounding them. As Juliet says of the treatment of Yashoda by the Shivaraman Nair family: 'It frightens me. It threatens me. It threatens *me*!' (99; Hospital's italics). This is also brought home in reverse when Yashoda visits the market disguised as a Muslim but finds that she 'was not expecting such tumult, such staring' (89), something Juliet experiences each time she appears in public. Yet while Juliet may complain specifically about the treatment of women in Kerala, the book asks the same question as the 4000-year-old statuette encountered in an art gallery in Toronto: 'Well? demanded the haughty eyes. Do you think you're any smarter after four thousand years? Have you figured out a better solution?' (70). Later, Juliet will come across an old woman in the street, and:

> It seemed that all understanding passed between them, the knowledge of all women who braid their years into shackles, who weave with love and resentment the silken cages of their lives. Then the woman shrugged. Her gesture said: We make whatever adjustments we can. We turn to whatever is available. (158)

Hospital's work is sympathetic to the weary endurance of the oppressed, but cannot approve of this as a permanent solution in any wider sense; an individual woman may need to resign herself to the limited options her circumstances give her, but a better solution would be society's changing the likelihood that such circumstances would occur.

In any case, neither Juliet nor Yashoda wants simply to be 'free', in the sense of being completely independent, for they share a taste for the flamboyant which feeds off the restrictions that surround it. Moreover, their rebellion has significant differences. Juliet rebels against being considered simply domestic, an adjunct of her husband, with no intellect or intellectual interests of her own. In Winston, she is expected to conform to a stiffly limited vision of the role of 'wives', and her own academic activities are discounted. Yashoda, however, wishes to have 'love' (109), and to be able to display her beauty as well as her finery in what might seem an acceptance of women's status as principally that of a visible object. There is no sign that Yashoda wishes to develop her intellect or be respected as a person with opinions and knowledge that are worth attending to. It is in part to guard against women's being treated as nothing more than sexualised objects for men's gazes that the restrictions that apply to Yashoda exist, although it is only being treated in a certain manner in public that they prevent, for the firmness of the restrictions is a clear sign of the intense sexualisation of women at all times. Yashoda exists as a particularly flagrant example of this in Shivaraman Nair's eyes, as he imagines that her 'thoughts wander after men, straying in all directions like the roots of the banyan tree' (129). By desiring her freedom in the same terms as those which restrict her, that is, by constructing what she means principally via her sensuality, Yashoda is enacting a different sort of rebellion from that of Juliet, one which confirms some of Graham Huggan's suspicions of the orientalising aspects of the novel, in which the Western woman is intellectual (Culture) while the Eastern woman is physical (Nature).

In the second half of the book the main contrast on Juliet's side of the cultural divide is provided by her sister Annie, who arrives when Juliet is particularly anxious about Yashoda's position. Annie is delighted by India, a delight that, in Juliet's eyes, seems insensitive to the operations of power and the differentials of equality; for example, Annie is enchanted by Yashoda's cabin, which she sees in terms of Euro-American cultures, through Thoreau and Yeats, when to Yashoda it is merely a prison. Then again, Yashoda muses about the love she yearns for in terms of the conventionally canonical Western texts *Romeo and Juliet* and *Wuthering Heights*, situating the meaning of the West for her as liberation and passion, even if the books she has chosen ironically speak centrally of doomed love, of love that offends local rules and leads to rupture and violence.

Annie may serve to provide a challenging contrast to Juliet's domestic Winston self, but the contrast with Juliet's Kerala self is to highlight what extreme Western indifference to local realities might look like, and to make Juliet somewhat less representative. Annie also needs to be brought in at this point because Juliet now knows too much about local culture to feel comfortable flouting it any more, having reached an awareness of the force of cultural constraint that brings with it 'the knowledge of loss and the awareness of evil and the possibility of harm' (139). One does not need to believe in the explanations given for particular customs to feel 'the power of the society that believes' (139). Annie now utters the types of confident denials of Indian conventions that Juliet had uttered, to some extent, in the first half of the book. Annie's brash assessment – 'why should Yashoda submit to that nonsense? And what can he do?' (163) – her incorporation of Yashoda into her lifestyle and her breezy dismissal of local mores reveal the shallowness of her claim to 'love' the country. Taking what suits you and thoughtlessly violating the rest provides a model of presumptuous cultural insensitivity that enables Juliet's anguished battles with India to appear more responsible.

Social justice

The patterning between characters is not the only axis upon which the drama of difference revolves. More generally, the book chronicles Juliet's encounter not just with the individuals who relate to her own issues of dependence and freedom but with a whole gallery of South Indians: street vendors, student demonstrators, antique dealers and servants. She is often tempted to see South India as unchanging, inert, 'the palm trees limp with the stupor of centuries' (198), but every time she lazily feels this she is jolted into the turbulence of the present. In this process, every interaction is troubling to her. They all involve learning new rules, which Juliet accepts in principle, though many of the rules continue to vex her. The egg seller who charges her more than other people bothers Yashoda more than it bothers Juliet, for whom the difference is small: why should commerce operate on a principle that all buyers are the same, when manifestly they are not? While Juliet appears to accept the rudimentary equalising action here, it enacts her main objection to social interaction in India – the high level of negotiation needed at all moments of one's day. Whether buying an expensive antique or a few eggs, Juliet is caught up in complex human transactions in which what is being negotiated is not simply price but also justice and recognition.

The concept of justice is activated more sharply after these two purchases by a brief conversation with a demonstrator, Prem, who accuses Juliet of being an 'imperialist' (26). Justice in his view will consist of sweeping aside the current power arrangements in which privilege ensures that some children will never lack while others will die of hunger. Juliet is made nervous by the stark truth of this unfairness, unable to excuse herself from complicity as a beneficiary of the global distribution of power (and unable not to take advantage of it when she jumps the queue and barges in on the Air India office manager and threatens him with her husband's 'powerful friends' [52]). It is the personal contact made with Prem that saves Juliet and her children later in the book when their taxi is caught in a rowdy street demonstration. In the sort of coincidence that Hospital uses increasingly in her later work, the same man who had upbraided them at the market is there to help when the taxi driver abandons them. Later still, she runs into him again on another visit to the city, and again, when a bus she is in rolls over as a result of violent street demonstrations, Prem is one of the people helping passengers out of the bus.

Coincidence like this is not simply a narrative shortcut but functions throughout Hospital's work in basically two ways. In the first place, like the patterning between doubled characters or situations, it reminds us that Hospital is not trying to be a social-realist chronicler; rather, her work partakes of some of the characteristics of parables in which protagonists and events enact moral issues in ways that make them both individual and representative. In the second place, for Hospital the world is a place that confounds our attempt to force linearity and logic on to it, and she incorporates an ever-surprising patterning of events that offers the world to us as a place where coincidence forces characters to contemplate justice and agency. We are both challenged to accept the idea of our responsibility for events and led to marvel at the consequences that nobody could have predicted or controlled. Later in her career she will thread through her work references to chaos theory and the butterfly effect, but at this early stage these aspects inform the narrative without being directly theorised.

As Juliet moves towards an appreciation of features of the Indian system of tradition, she is able to stand up more to

Prem. His arguments and accusations had left her feeling guilty and responsible in the first half of the book, but by later in the narrative this too has to be recalibrated. The simplistic assigning of guilt for inequality that before seemed reasonable, now seems to pay too little heed to the complex entanglements of culture, gender and class, in which responsibility splinters and touches everyone, leaving few people or sectors of society unaccountable (apart from children). Prem can now be shocked and intrigued by a perspective that from one angle aligns him with Shivaraman Nair, in this case in his disapproval of Prabhakaran's eating with Juliet and the children in a Western-style ice-cream parlour. Still, however, she cannot convince him that his desire for equality and fairness has anything to do with Yashoda's situation. Both tradition and revolution are articulated by men, and in both contexts women are relegated to a secondary position. Only later does he realise that the control over women's daily lives masks the possibility of the ultimate control, the determination by men whether a woman should live or die.

Prem introduces the wider political currents in Kerala and India into the novel, but he is not simply a mouthpiece, for he also changes and learns as the book progresses. After the bus accident, Annie and Prem work side by side to help passengers get out of the overturned vehicle. This throws them together in ways that could not happen with married Juliet. Annie, exhausted, accepts his offer to rest at his place. She moves to kiss him in the morning, untrammelled by convention, but he does not know how to respond, and has conflicting politicised references that categorise Annie as a representative of the system that ensures that the only food the women of his family often have is the water in which rice has been boiled. The personal and the global lock him in indecision and the moment passes, but after ablutions and breakfast Prem concludes that '[i]t was so pleasant to work with her, to have breakfast with her, to talk with her as an equal and a friend. Not to think of her as a woman and a Westerner' (195). Annie had been accused implicitly and explicitly for her complicity in the unequal distribution of power and resources, but had come to the conclusion that, even though she agrees about the inequity of global arrangements, she does not want 'to waste her time making endless futile apologies for being white and western and middle class' (200). Such generalising accusations are broken down by personal contact, the best way in Hospital's world to deal with the injuries of categorisation. Annie is attracted to Prem, and he is attracted to her. When he asks her to stay with him, and she agrees, the barriers that are being surmounted are not simply those that prevent people from having sex outside marriage. Nevertheless, this is an awkward passage in the novel, criticised in no uncertain terms by Mathew Zachariah as 'a silly resolution of one of the most significant issues of our day, namely, the empowerment of oppressed people'.[14]

Men on the margins

In a novel that is so concerned with women's agency, many of the issues are stated by way of their relation to the various men who inhabit the narrative. Juliet's husband, David, for example, is at first largely removed from the picture, mostly absent doing his research, and treated quite differently by the surrounding Keralan society. His occupation frequently gives him the role of explicator of the surrounding culture to Juliet, though this does not align him with what Rana Kabbani reminds us is the 'commonplace of Orientalism that the West knows more about the East than the East knows about itself'.[15] For a start his knowledge is not mostly 'sustained by a long tradition of Western scholarship, by other Western texts' but by a study of Indian material.[16] The fact that he is attempting to learn from local scholars and through the local university suggests that his interest is more respectful than the eurocentric perspectives on the East associated with the term 'Orientalism'. When he visits the Shree Padmanabhaswamy temple, something for which he has to get unheard-of special permission as a non-Hindu, his perceptions are genuinely admiring and not filtered through Western scholarly references. When the temple priests explicate elements of Hindu symbology to him according to Indian hermeneutic custom, David feels 'thoroughly familiar with the poetic and interpretive traditions being expounded' (150). His interest is, however, detached; he is not a believer, and he admires aspects of the temple as art rather than as theological representation. Ironically, explanations of the symbolic yearning of the soul for union with the divine set David off into a consideration of his responses to physical women and his desire for union with Yashoda. Like his rejection of the temple priests' explanations, this sequence casts him as the superior Westerner, above the absurd disputations of believers; and yet there is nothing in the characterisation of David that suggests he would consider the priests of any religion, Eastern or Western, any differently. Certainly, he is able to connect quite genuinely with ritual in the temple at one point, when we read that: 'David soared to the heart of the mystery . . . David bowed his head in the presence of a great wonder' (154).

In general, though, one might legitimately consider a rational, mostly art historical, approach to religious iconology as Western, inherited from the traditions of Western rationality and opposition to the metaphysical, and here we are returned to one of the book's insistent questions: does respect for difference mean that one is unable to affirm one's own positions or to adopt critical positions towards other cultures and their traditions? David is himself returned to this question as he attempts to square his knowledge of what the priests are telling him with the circumscribed position of Yashoda. On the whole, his ability to connect with these elements of Indian cultures may be part of what makes him more impervious to the aspects of local life that so exercise Juliet. On the other hand, his light reading of the incident with Yashoda in terms of the mythical *yakshi*, an avatar of the succubus figure who drains men of their purpose and purity, reduces the serious matters of hierarchy and control not just to the exotic ways of the East but to age-old conventions in which women exist as temptresses and distractions. David, as a man, is an avatar of the Nairs himself, part of the problem, for not only does he make light of Yashoda's being controlled by the men but he also has no sympathy with Juliet's desperate desire to get away from Winston, musing to himself: 'We'll stay forever, if necessary, he told himself. Her discontents will fade like a photograph left out in the Indian sun' (45). His transgressions of local custom are not framed within the same moral economy as Juliet's, given that, possessing power as a male, he may choose to enact that power or not, while a woman cannot choose to claim more power. For all of his ability to appreciate ancient mythic resonances in the life around him, he is unable to perceive that atavistic patterns of male control continue to reverberate in Canada as well. By feeling the impact of the issues on her own possibilities, Juliet understands their relevance in ways that the scholar does not, until the end of the book.

After David, Shivaraman Nair and Prem, there is another significant male character, who is introduced as one more vector of Juliet's frustration with local realities, with her dealings with officialdom, in this case in the local Air India office. While fuming over waiting for three hours simply to find out if she can pick up a parcel, Juliet meets Matthew Thomas, a local Christian, and therefore a test case with respect to the operation of male hierarchy solely in terms of religion as opposed to either a wider Indian cultural patterning or an even wider relation between men and women in all cultures. The narration enters Matthew Thomas's thoughts, the first time it has entered anyone's other than Juliet's (later it will enter David's as well).[17] Immediately, we are in a calmer place, for despite having more reasons to complain than Juliet (he had spent all the previous day in the office standing, before he had discovered he had to write his name in a book to be called; he is making an enquiry for a cousin, not for himself), he 'simply accepted such little inconveniences' (48). Notwithstanding the attempt to represent this event from another perspective, the result is rather to ridicule his thought processes, which appear naïve and submissive. He accepts waiting many hours in the office, rather than wishing that the procedure paid more respect to people; and his vision of Burlington, Vermont is represented as pathetically limited. Although he may be functioning as an attempt to show Juliet from a perspective other than her own, his assessments of her seem not only patronising but to operate within a male vision of womanly beauty and propriety that speak once again to mechanisms of male control as well as of women's supposed responsibility to present themselves according to decorous conventions associated here with men's requirements. Thomas also fits the Western stereotype of the quaint, innocent Other,[18] even when most of his basic impulses are generous: he is generously giving up his time for his cousin; he generously worries about his daughter in Vermont; he generously goes to help lower-caste fisherpeople; and he generously contemplates Juliet, even if after his first appraisal he cannot approve of her.

Again, when he later meets her on the beach his impulse is to try to place her within a context that would make her strange appearance and behaviour more understandable, something he is able to do by imagining what his daughter must have experienced in the United States when she emigrated there. By doing this, he regrets having been irritated by her at the Air India office, illustrating that ways of perceiving people sympathetically can exist between people from such different backgrounds, once the thread of connection is found.

From sex to death

The principal form of connection that introduces tension into the novel is sex, a major issue in *The Ivory Swing*. It is an important factor in the relationships of almost all the major characters, both enabling and epiphanic on the one hand but also destructive and destabilising on the other. Juliet dreams of wild abandon with Jeremy, but enjoys David's lovemaking as well. The most explicit sex scene is that between Annie and Prem, partly confirming Annie as the most sexually generous of the characters, and partly constituting a cathartic moment in Prem's ideologically rigid view of the world.[19] Yashoda's fate also is connected to the control of her sexuality by the men of her culture. David is unsettled by her, and makes love to Juliet thinking of her, having to sublimate his desire through pounding rice with a pestle on another occasion. Shivaraman Nair is excited by her and jealous of what he wonders might have passed between her and Prabhakaran, working out his frustration by kicking a calf away from the boy, a sacrilegious action in a religion where cows are sacred. He sanctimoniously decides to have sex with her himself to calm her down and save the family name from further scandal. Matthew Thomas, who does have sex with her, is also destabilised by her after their meeting on the night of the bus accident and helping to look after the disturbed children together. Passion is felt to be something that needs to be controlled by most of the people in the drama, something powerful but with the potential for great disruption, a perception that is, after all, at the heart of local restrictions on contact between the sexes.

Once again there is a twinned pair in their relation to passion as something to be pursued and enjoyed: Yashoda and Annie. Where Annie sees sexual passion cut loose from romantic love or sentimentality, Yashoda conflates her sexual desires with romantic yearnings. Their different fates are inflected not only by their cultural origins but by their relation to their desire. Indeed, almost everyone who feels the clutch of sexual passion suffers for it. It animates the image of Krishna and Radha, an inspiration to Indians and Westerners alike, but people are unable to manage it comfortably; people's sexuality is only semi-controlled, like the profuse and exuberant nature that Juliet experiences in Kerala, with a sense of wonder and anxiety.

All of the characters and events come together in Yashoda's fate. Owing to the Western tutoring she has had, the foreign travel, the opening out of her experience provided by her father while she was unmarried, she is perceived by Shivaraman Nair as having been corrupted by foreign influences, as being in some way a mixture of Indian and Western. She herself comes to the conclusion that '[t]here is too much danger living between your world and the old world' (235), and events prove her right. The inauspiciousness of a burst levee is felt to be connected to the death of a Nair family member. In the consultations of the men of the family as to what is to be done to punish Yashoda for being the cause of these calamities, it is revealed that someone must have been visiting Yashoda at night. The novel at this point swings back from an appreciation of interlocking and balancing features of the social system to angry sarcasm about the chain of reasoning that leads to the conclusion: '[a] woman not in the custody of a man is an abomination' (219). Despite the sympathetic character of Anand, Shivaraman Nair's son, who defends Yashoda, the value system of the majority of both men and women condemns Yashoda, and by extension all women. To respect this is a step too far of cultural relativity for the novel.

The destructiveness of conventions and customs designed to control women's sexuality is underlined by the deaths of both Yashoda and Prabhakaran, beaten by drunken workers hoping to curry favour with Shivaraman Nair. Prem's high-minded separation of the problems facing Yashoda and those facing the poor is shown to be limited in its understanding of the complex currents of power and oppression in his society. He comes to know 'that there were other wrongs and other griefs besides hunger and poverty' (243). Moreover, the fact that the two are murdered by harijans, who in Prem's view of society are seen only as victims, indicates the fragmented nature of power distribution and enforcement, in which the oppressed along one axis are capable of ensuring the oppression of others along another axis, and in which the socially disadvantaged do not see that the gendered disadvantage of women is part of a system of hierarchy and authority of which they are also guilty. That the servant boy is also murdered confirms the confluence between the operations of power upon women and those upon the lower social classes, along with the punishment the system exacts when solidarity appears to be forming between these two groups. Shivaraman Nair may have had the murderers arrested, but the source of their violence is in a system of values that he upholds and represents, and that the murderers were trying to interpret through their deed, imagining it would please him and be useful to them within the values of this system.

At the end of the novel all of the characters are left to ruminate upon their parts in the events and how those events have affected them. Nair realises that he is one of the causes, indeed the main cause, of the deaths. Matthew Thomas, in turn, feels that he has caused the disruption, while David also feels partly responsible. Some characters claim they will change, but Juliet sees in Annie's resolve as she leaves, 'the long arc of a swing that would never be still' (246). David decides that keeping Juliet in Winston against her will will not work and suggests that she move to Montreal where he can visit her on weekends, to which she assents, albeit with an ambivalent 'guilty eagerness' (251). The symbol of this freedom, however, her former lover Jeremy, has been cast adrift from her thinking on these issues by her tossing a letter from him into the water without opening it. Prem is left, discarded and hurting, by Annie, a symbol of inconstant and selfish Western intervention in India.

The novel finishes with Juliet and David holding each other, kissing timidly, and even though the novel has constantly counterpointed Juliet's life in Canada with her life in India, the drama of their wider existence is overshadowed by the events that have happened. Despite the attempt to relate Yashoda's life to a series of linked exclusions with which women are faced everywhere, the attempt is not completely successful. Juliet's anger over not having enough of cities and passion seems excessive when compared with the real lack of options facing Yashoda, not to mention Prem's mother. Moreover, as she has children she has responsibilities that Yashoda did not have, and her acceptance of the plan to move away from David implies removing them from their father. A tradition of women's writing, particularly since Kate Chopin's

The Awakening (1899), would argue that a woman's personal happiness comes before duty or responsibility; but as this novel is centrally about the necessity of responsibility to and solidarity with others, the assent to the removal of children from a parent seems somewhat casual.

Just as it is easy to appreciate why *The Ivory Swing* won the Seal Award, it is also possible to see why Hospital would say that '[t]here's quite a bit in that first book that embarrasses me'.[20] When pressed, she refers to 'all sorts of unsolved artistic problems and a lack of structure',[21] but, despite having '[m]entally (and, I'm afraid with naïve arrogance) . . . appointed myself as some sort of . . . mediator between east and west',[22] she defends herself vigorously against criticism of her representation of India.[23] Nonetheless, the experience did lead to her becoming 'increasingly cautious about the difficulties involved in writing about someone quite "other"',[24] as will be seen in later books. Her next novel, *The Tiger in the Tiger Pit*, focuses exclusively on white New Englanders and a white Australian. In addition, *Tiger* displays a much greater attention to structure, and a sophistication of point-of-view and the use of time shifts that mark a significant step towards the trademark destabilisation of narrative certainty and linearity in Hospital's work from *Borderline* on.

CHAPTER 3

Anger mismanagement *The Tiger in the Tiger Pit*

. . . memory breathes revenge as often as it breathes reconciliation, and the hope of reaching catharsis through liberated memories might turn out to be an illusion.

Avishai Margalit[1]

Streams of family consciousness

After the success of *The Ivory Swing*, Janette Turner Hospital signalled by producing a very different book that she was not going to allow herself to be pigeonholed as a writer of the drama of intercultural dislocation. *The Tiger in the Tiger Pit* has an elderly couple at its centre and is set in Massachusetts. It is even a determinedly occidental novel, in the sense that it deals with notably WASP characters and begins with a quotation from that central Anglophone icon, Shakespeare: 'Anger's my meat, I'll sup upon myself.'[2] This quotation sets the scene for the family drama of the narrative, in which seventy-three-year-old Edward Carpenter and his wife Elizabeth examine their lives as they prepare for a family reunion to celebrate fifty years of marriage.[3] Although *Tiger* is very different from *The Ivory Swing*, continuity can be observed in the attention to family politics, to the unstable nature of understanding, and to the destabilising power of the erotic and the burden of love.

At first glance a less ambitious novel than her others, *The Tiger in the Tiger Pit* has been unjustly neglected in critical work on Hospital's novels, and may have fallen foul of the geographical politics of writing that have taken hold of the critical consideration of literature during the rise of post-colonial and identity studies. That is, after beginning as a 'Canadian' writer, Hospital's next novel eschews Canada or Canadian characters for the most part, leaving it marginalised in the contemporary desire for the reflection back at us of national identities.[4] Although the novel received enthusiastic reviews in both the United States and Canada,[5] this does not guarantee attention from academics, curriculum designers or literary historians in any sustained way. Perhaps also, the novel's concentration on bourgeois New Englanders does not accord well with contemporary scholarly interest in minority or marginalised voices.

This is a pity, for *Tiger* is the first of Hospital's novels to exhibit what will become her characteristically intricate plots, drawing the reader into a lively game of supposition, intellectual challenge and surprise. She refers to the book as having the twinned structural schemes of the wheel – 'with Edward and Elizabeth at the hub and this constant moving out to the periphery and back again' – and the fugue – 'the constant motifs played in different keys'.[6] These motifs, broadly speaking, are the tension between versions of the past in the service of power struggles within the family, the articulation of traumatic experience within psychic economies dedicated to its obfuscation or denial, and the pressures that ethical responsibilities undergo as family stories about the past contend with each other in constant mutation. No wonder Canadian biographer Elspeth Cameron describes the novel's tone appreciatively as recalling 'Bergman's darker films: reflective, slow-paced, tortured, stylistically ornate'.[7]

The tiger in the tiger pit is on one level the patriarch Edward,[8] the first of the series of autocratic fathers in Hospital's work, as he is also the first of the series of absent fathers, albeit absent affectively rather than physically. He is enclosed by the restrictions imposed by his aging body, but these in turn are metaphorical of a more generalised frustration that Edward feels in a world where others do not do his bidding or see him as he would like to be seen. He spends his life watching feverishly for the signs of his existence in the events that happen around him, while his family adopts various strategies to try to minimise the damage inflicted by his ego and his rage. Rage is central to Edward's emotional life, and not for nothing is 'anger' the first word, typically a word in quotation, as if he cannot live his emotions without the support of canonical citation. His son Jason sneers at him for his tendency to bracket every experience with quotations from Shakespeare, although in general this is the rattled authority of Shakespeare's thwarted heroes.[9] The key word in Edward's angry relationship with the world is betrayal, his ire at the beginning of the novel directed at the fact that he has a grandson whose existence was kept from him for five years.

In Edward's world, everything resists him, including language itself. Even when he has shattered the hopes of all those around him, when his fury has led him to suffer a heart attack, he is aware that all he has to do is to utter a few words: 'if I could say *Adam*', but 'words were not pliant to his bidding. They went their own way as his children had done' (127). The textualisation of Edward's life becomes further apparent as he imagines that he needs to edit his life, to 'compose a variant past' (14), which not only relates to the past but also to the future, to the desire 'to approach death from a different direction' (14). In his revision of that past he fumes over moments that he let slip, significantly moments of attachment, as when he failed to bond with his daughter Emily when she finally presented him with Adam, or more importantly the erotic opportunity with Marta forty years previously that he did not take up out of the sense of rectitude that he believes has diminished the majesty of his life. With typical self-centredness he is considering this intensely as the day approaches celebrating fifty years of marriage to Elizabeth, whom he treats with unyielding scorn and contempt.

The second chapter reveals that we will be exposed to different voices, in this case Elizabeth. Ironically, after being presented to us by Edward as uninteresting and plain, we see she is working on composing a family symphony, a metaphor for the rich form of the novel itself.[10] She is also in her seventies, but, where Edward is consumed with fury, she is 'infected with hope' (18). Where Edward feels life as separation and conflict, Elizabeth experiences it as connection and suturing: 'Anything calling for action, for transposition into beauty, this is her credo. Stay busy with birth and mending' (130). She also quotes from and alludes to books, but her intertextual allusions are to folk tales such as 'Little Red Riding Hood' or to sunny lyrics. The Shakespearian connection she feels is to Prospero, her desired magic that of bringing the family together, at least physically.[11] Elizabeth's focus, like Edward's, is on the relation of family to self, but where he feels trapped she perceives opportunity and richness. For example, the blood of the cut caused by the shaving bowl Edward had smashed captures the violence of their relationship, but the playful manner in which she draws with the blood on herself indicates the way she turns injury into play. More than this, there is a contrast between her veering away from the past when it appears damaging and Edward's probing and prodding the past to buttress his wrath. Near the end of the book, Elizabeth confirms that '[t]his is the problem: nothing is settled in the past, it is a shifting region of fault lines and instability' (249). The drama of the book lies in the contention between these two approaches to memory and to life, and, in Charlotte Clutterbuck's summary: 'Ultimately Elizabeth's hope saves the family . . . Because she can accept past guilt and continue to live in the present, she has the courage to take risks, believing that damage can be remedied.'[12]

The third chapter brings in another of the players in the family drama, daughter Emily. She is also a refugee from the wars of the affections, in her case displacing her feelings on to music and fleeing from connection. Emily is one of Hospital's many examples of dislocation and movement as positive and creative, whatever their costs in destabilisation: 'Only in transit did she feel at ease' (132). Emily's movement and transience are strategies for dealing with the choking tendrils of attachment and the power that it has to make us suffer: 'love is visceral and vicious' (229), she thinks. Like Juliet in *The Ivory Swing*, Emily craves the anonymity of the city and the chance encounter, being unpoliced and unwatched, along with the possibilities of uncommitted passion that this offers. The western Massachusetts town of Ashville (another version of *The Ivory Swing's* Winston, Ontario) epitomises entrapment and the stifling of individuality. When connections go wrong, when men make demands, or when lovers want her to belong to them, even New York seems 'to shrink, to resemble the small town in western Massachusetts from which she had fled' (135). Escape is thus paramount for Emily, but the trouble is that, while she can escape physically, memory ensures she never escapes entirely.

Rage against the memory

In a novel dedicated to reconstruction and memory, naturally the question of different versions of the truth arises. In line with a strand of modernist and postmodern writing running from Marcel Proust through Virginia Woolf, Jorge Luis Borges and William Faulkner to Peter Carey, Hospital is fascinated by the way in which any story that is told, whether to others or even to ourselves, is not simply a transparent mediation of events but a shimmering mixture of verifiable references and subjective selection, of self-promotion and self-delusion, of other narratives and buried allusions. One way of depicting this is to have different characters reporting on the same events, and Hospital mentions being influenced by Virginia Woolf in her use of several different points of view.[13] Another way is to cast doubt on characters' testimony so that readers are put on their guard, interrupting their tendency to follow passively what they are being told; and from this novel on, Hospital will make increasing use of this strategy. Accordingly, Edward concludes an outburst about how he tamed Bessie by saying: 'None of this is true. None of it. The medication makes me maudlin' (51). He is being provocative here, lest readers feel they have him pinned down, but ironically his denial will be confirmed as the story unfolds, for one of the novel's central ironies is that he did not tame Elizabeth at all.

Despite this truculent admission, Edward claims that 'it is important to reconstruct objectively' (67), a possibility that is challenged constantly in Hospital's work. Nonetheless, if objectivity is impossible, that does not free us from striving to order our memories so that they represent what 'really happened'. Edward admits that his narrative is a version, but one that he assesses as 'a fair account' (73), an assessment that raises the possibility that other accounts may also be fair, or even fairer. Indeed, Edward immediately says that reconstructing objectively is achieved by conducting 'research from different perspectives, looking for clues' (68). This is an area he will return to often, given his assertion that 'I am too old to deceive myself' (83). Objectivity will be most challenged in the novel by his treatment of the story of Marta, a defining reference in his life, all the more unsettling because of the clash between his concern for rectitude and his desire to feel he has lived or could have lived a grand passion.

Edward believes that he has forgone the opportunity to live his passion for Marta, but that even at this late stage it might still be experienced in some way if Marta comes to the party. The wife of a former deputy principal, Marta provided a note of extravagance in the staid New England town, displaying colour and ornate jewellery in an environment of decorum and containment. Unsettled by Marta, Edward moved in the direction of enacting his passion, but refrained when he discovered that Elizabeth was pregnant with Jason. The significance of his contact with Marta remains strong many decades later, a memory that sidelines others, 'a relic in the sacristy of his mind' (119); and yet, paradoxically, he also burns with the desire for others to recognise both the intensity of his passion and the nobility of his renunciation. He imagines others referring to his courage, the sacrifice he made for Jason, when everyone could see that the atmosphere around Edward and Marta was electric with desire, for '[h]e could not even allude to the Wilsons for fear the air around him would catch fire' (89). Despite Edward's attempt to represent his emotional life as vast and powerful, the echoes of Prufrock multiply, an explanation of the self that keeps shading into bathos the more it insists otherwise. As he sways back and forth between present raging at Elizabeth and past memories of Marta, a hypothetical tense creeps in: 'it must have been a party' (87). This is then amended to: '[t]here had been a party' (87), back in 1942, the first summer of America's direct involvement in World War II, a loss of collective innocence that is counterpointed with what we discover is Edward's ignorance of what really happened.

When Marta arrives at the fiftieth-wedding-anniversary party, she encounters Elizabeth first, and we realise with a shock that the passion had been Elizabeth's, that Elizabeth had had an affair with Marta's husband, that Marta had been with Edward in the gazebo on the night of the famous party in 1942 only with the intention of commiserating over their both having been betrayed. The principal axis around which Edward has constructed the history he might have participated in, the overwhelming erotic love he feels for Marta and the belief that this is the context of their connection, is revealed to be pathetically false.

This revelation is, however, a double-edged device. On the one hand it reveals the untrustworthiness of story and the need to have multiple versions, while on the other it suggests that there is a right and a wrong history after all. This is one of the most productive conundra in Hospital's work: a metafictionalist's commitment to the multiplicity of reality in constant tension with the moralist's need to combat the lies and self-delusions that obscure the realities of power and violence. The fact that it never becomes an either/or choice makes it all the more disconcerting, one of the most potent sources of Hospital's troubling mixture of intellectual playfulness and ethical seriousness.

The interplay of ethics and memory is further activated in the versions of Edward's children, who know nothing of their father's dilemma and who reconstruct history quite differently. Choosing how to relate to the past is something we see all of the characters constantly attempting, confronting us with the fact that memory does not simply assail us unbidden but that we also interact with it, manipulate it, summon it up, reject it. Explaining and trying to make things clear is what all of the characters are engaged in, and naturally the more we read the clearer many things become, but absolute clarity is not reached, nor is it possible when we are dealing with human beings. The multiplicity of explanations and the jagged, personal nature of memory work to make the latter both a clarifying function and one that complicates the possibility of clarity. For example, after we have been exposed to a damning depiction of Edward as tyrannical and unbearable, we see Jason facing the possibility that, in his implacable refusal to send back any of the postcards his father had thoughtfully mailed to him already stamped and addressed to be sent back, he is even more guilty than his father of wilful rejection. In this family, everyone has played a part in the hostilities, but the comparative assignment of guilt is not an exact science. Who is more guilty?, asks Jason. This is the type of question that families generate and that people answer all too readily; but in *The Tiger in the Tiger Pit* it is one whose answer is deferred while the skein of memories is unpicked.

As the memories are disclosed, different causal factors are added. What at first was merely personal, a matter of temperament, is built on until the factors become more and more confused. Edward insists, for example, on the role of history. World War II had estranged fathers from their children and damaged husbands' relation with their wives, to the extent that Edward's absence during the war, as well as his exposure to fear and death, meant to him that the 'war' (113) at home was lost. His efforts to make contact with his children founder against the inevitable centrality of Elizabeth in their life, leaving him embittered. Elizabeth's significance to the children, on the other hand, can be seen as a result of the loosening of male authority occasioned by the war.

As with all explanations in the novel, these contain some truth but it cannot be the whole truth.

Also casting a shadow over Edward's vision of his elevated dignity is the issue of class. Hospital has a sharp outsider's eye for the pretensions of Americans to an egalitarian society, particularly in New England, where old money and family origins lead to none-too-subtle gradations of social acceptability. In this, Edward relates to another common theme in Hospital's work, that of the class outsider who believes he is scorned or marginalised by the establishment. In his vision of accession to the Boston Brahmin class, the gazebo in the garden of the headmaster's house in Ashville serves as a metaphor for the values Edward hopes to associate himself with, a symbol of social ease, grace and comfort. Gradually, however, by means of the dense network of hints and echoes that Hospital knits into the novel, we will become aware that the gazebo is linked to something terrible, too terrible even for the optimistic Elizabeth to face in memory. When Elizabeth approaches these recollections she recoils, even cries, her attempts at 'binding up' are 'not enough' (82) in the face of this traumatic history.

Dysfunction and disturbance

Central to the significance of the gazebo is the family's eldest daughter, Victoria, but once again Hospital withholds information from us, something she does repeatedly in her novels from *Tiger* on. All we are told initially is that Victoria is disturbed in some unspecified way. When we see her in an institutional ward she is able to quote Poe, and to read and write; her authority is that of the observer who has not been smoothed out by social protocol or propriety. Victoria's thoughts and poetry reveal experiences and sensations that are private and painful, a realm of hallucination, dream imagery and anxiety. When her words periodically enter the novel they operate as the cutting wisdom of the court fool. The rules of discourse and sequence are abandoned in favour of a stream of association, quotation (generally from the same disturbed Shakespearean characters as her father), direct accusation and incantatory intensity, often revealing a sharper vision of family realities than the others admit. Victoria lives in a world where her vision of the cloth-cutting and temporising of the world is so acute that she is unable to operate in it as others deem appropriate; as Emily explains, 'nothing makes her feel safe' (193). She has evinced a strangeness that has led society to control her, a control that leaves 'her rages and poetry cured' (102). Her rage is an echo of Edward's relationship to the world, and her situation is a warning that we are all potentially avatars of New Zealand writer Janet Frame, liable to call down the incarcerating impulses of others if we become excessively sensitive.

Initially, Victoria appears to be somewhat extraneous to the plot, just one more example of dysfunction in this crippled and ruptured family. However, even apart from the awkward relevance of many of her meanderings and articulations of panic (which bring to mind the prickly and penetrating New England sensibility of Emily Dickinson), she assumes an iconic significance for her siblings Jason and Emily. Emily later claims that her own inability to connect or to believe in emotional interdependence is linked to Victoria's letters, testaments to the psychic depth of the chains that bind them. Emily in turn wounds Victoria deeply by refusing to answer the letters, testifying to their unanswerable rhetoric, to the family claims that cannot be denied and cannot be written away.

For Jason, in contrast, 'love and passion . . . were absolutely matters of illusion' (32), meaning not that they are not real but that 'they had to be played against a backdrop of danger and betrayal or they did not exist' (32). This aspect of life is then to be set against the backdrop of the order of daily life, a contrast necessary to provide the energy of the illicit and a challenge to the restricting authority represented by Edward who, ironically, is crushed by his sense that he failed to respond fully to the 'danger and betrayal' represented by Marta. Like Emily's attempt to escape from commitment, Jason's escape from commitment is unsuccessful. He continues to have dreams in which he is trapped in small spaces, and the network of references in the novel evoking entrapment of one sort or another is overwhelming, from the provincial smallness of Ashville, to Victoria incarcerated, to Edward trapped inside his failing body, indeed, to being trapped inside marriages or relationships or roles generally. The tiger in the tiger pit appears on the one level to act as a metaphor for Edward, but eventually radiates out to include the whole world of the book.

Dreams are frequently used in Hospital's work as an abbreviated introduction to a character and her or his concerns, tending to reveal anxiety and panic, the disturbed grammar of a fragmented reality. Even the optimistic Elizabeth has a nightmare, in which she loses the children and they are never found again. Significantly, Jason's dream of enclosure morphs into his observing Victoria, oversized, overexposed, her near-naked body in bed suggestive of the nakedness of her responses to the world but also of failure, a recurrent theme in the book, that of the wrong turning, of promise denied. In Victoria's case her present obesity is a failure of the beauty she possessed when younger, 'a beauty so stunning that people were almost afraid to look' (97). The theme of the road not taken supplies dramatic density to the narrative, but it also relates to Hospital's interest in the mysteries of causality – the way in which cause and effect can be explained reasonably if we look at them in one way, but if we look at them in another way they seem altogether more inexplicable. Indeed, Hospital's fiction mimics this duality, in that one of our defences against the vertigo of causality is the created order of fiction, and yet fiction is one of the most potent means of inducing that vertigo as well. The novel thus appears as both a depiction of the intensities and outrages of a specific family's dynamics and an awed examination of the general fractal complexity of causality.

Space, time and Australia

Along with the dizzying tracery of time, Hospital's writing is centrally concerned with space, with how we situate ourselves in relation to places. Places are intense sites of meaning and not just background or locations we pass through. In *The Ivory Swing* the exuberant vegetation of Kerala became highly suggestive of the entanglements of social interaction and the difficulties of separating out the personal from the social, from the political, from the gendered. The visual referencing of location in *Tiger*, however, is less insistent, and in general Hospital's work does not celebrate the cold places she has lived in for long periods. With the exception of the late short stories 'Unperformed Experiments Have No Results' and 'Litany for the Homeland',[14] and occasional passages in *Borderline*, Canadian locations are almost entirely absent as meaningful visual sites. In New England, Boston has a special resonance in *Borderline* and *Orpheus Lost*, and especially in the pseudonymous *A Very Proper Death*. By far the most evocative places in her writing, however, are Australian, whether the combination of brooding menace and glowing paradise at Cedar Creek Falls in Queensland, the shimmering suggestiveness of far west Queensland, the tropical richness of far north Queensland, or even the seedy edginess of Kings Cross. Australia may not be the focus in this novel, but Hospital introduces the country by way of the period that the restless Emily spends there.

Australia is here the Sydney of the early 1970s, before the election of Gough Whitlam in December 1972, and this locates the novel's criticism of many of the country's social arrangements of that time as an anti-nostalgic critique of the nation's conservative traditions. Along with the country's violent and racist past (the present is perceived by Emily as better),[15] the pages dealing with Australia concentrate on the relations between the sexes among the chattering classes, Australian men being represented as breezily arrogant, the women as able to give as good as they get. Overall, nonetheless, is the joy provided by the sun. Emily observes to an Australian that 'you must grow up with the goodwill of the universe in your bones' (40). The first extra-family member of importance is Dave, a sunburnt Aussie from the outback who introduces Emily to the less lucky-country aspects of the city and then the bush. These include the routinely derided suburbs, inhabited by what Dave assesses as 'the world's most bored and unhappy women' (41).[16]

Dave sums up Australia as 'parochial, isolated, sun-blasted, and full of beer-punchy [*sic*] Philistines', yet admits that he 'loves it with a bigot's passion' (42). Not only does this seem a fair summary of Hospital's own relationship with the country, but it hints that the rounded personality in the novel is aware that objectivity is impossible. When Emily later muses on how she felt when in Australia, she remembers contemplating either the ocean or 'the never-never of cracked brown earth and ghost gums' (185) and feeling finally free, capable of writing to everyone in her family, even to her father and sister. Dave, and Australia, as the first step outside the claustrophobia of the family, takes us into meanings of connection and attachment, both to him and to his own attachment to place, so different from the disjunction Emily feels. The connection here aches with the longing of the expatriate, the description of swimming in the surf for example, along with the repeated references to the ever-present and brighter, southern-hemisphere sun. Personal connection at this point is nonetheless still something that Emily thinks has to be broken; so although she has sex with Dave, she warns him against expecting commitment. Dave, however, is a connector. He helps to connect Emily back with herself, and he has a view of family dynamics that rejects the extremism and denial that undermine Emily's connection with her origins.

The theme of the positive value of connection is carried further through Adam, Emily's son, whom we first see as a schoolboy in England. Adam fences warily with other boys because he feels different. Hospital has a keen eye for the patristic ferocity with which children classify each other, which she will expand upon frequently. Adam feels displaced from Australia, allowing Hospital to develop further her sub-theme of the meanings and sensations of the country for an expatriate. For Adam it is important to be connected, which he feels he is to Dave and to the glorious Australian sun, sand and surf; even the rain is more dramatic and intense than anything he observes in England. The predictability of some of this nostalgia is diluted by having it mediated through the consciousness of a child, and it is to be expected that a child removed from a home and a father-figure would experience Australia in terms of loss and yearning; 'he grieved for them as for the loss of a paradise' (55).

This experience of loss is spliced in with a school outing to Roman ruins, where Adam's class is given a lesson in the fact that history inevitably moves on. At the same time, the survival of the ruins testifies to the fact that something always remains as well. There is no absolute past and thus no absolute present. For Adam this is small consolation, as it reminds him even more of the absence of people and places he misses, despite Dave's trying to teach him that even if everyone goes away they 'come back eventually' (195). Through Emily's life Hospital valorises movement, but always underneath lie the loss and anxiety of Adam: 'Was there a place in history where he could just be still for a little while?' (58). Embracing the sundial as the rest of the class wanders round the museum, Adam notices the movement of the sun, and it occurs to him that, whatever grown-ups say, time does not move on, it moves '*around and back!*' (61, Hospital's italics). In fact, leaving for New York the day after to see Uncle Jason and his grandmother proves that whenever anyone or anywhere is taken away it does not mean that they will not come back. If time is always moving, that also means that it can move us back to where we started, that we are not fixed where we are in an endless series of loss. Like the magnificent Blue Wanderer butterfly, a symbol for Emily, that flies off but then comes to rest on another leaf, we exist in a ceaseless dance of movement and alighting, which may bring us back to the same leaf, to similar leaves, or to somewhere as yet unimagined.

Symptomatic of the book's focus on this dance, the first chapter not named after a character is called 'Converging'. Adam and Emily are flying over the Atlantic from England to Massachusetts, while Emily fills in another element in the puzzle by recalling her time in New York and Montreal. Her memories widen the aperture from the family by recalling the social turbulence in the 1970s in both the United States and in Montreal with the Free Quebec movement. As in *The Ivory Swing*, Hospital sets personal dramas in the context of social agitation. In *The Ivory Swing* social unrest provided a background that cast into question the conclusions that Juliet was reaching. In *Tiger* the concerns of a violent protest movement suggest that Emily's absorption in the personal, in music, may be seen as self-indulgent in a world where there are larger issues to be fought over.

Self-disgust and others

When Hospital deals with wider social issues in the West, she does so with a vigilant suspicion of institutions of control. Individual figures of authority do not appear to advantage in her work, and even less do the organisations through which authority is managed, the courts, the police, and governments in general. Myths of social decency on the part of Western cultures are seen to be unachieved, with little people trampled upon when social protest becomes urgent or unruly. As Sasha, the son of her soon-to-be lover Sergei, tells Emily, 'Due process doesn't apply' (142), an accusation that Hospital makes repeatedly throughout her work, whether it is set in Canada, the United States or Australia. A personal consequence of this is captured in Emily's self-questioning: 'Where was there safety from guilt? And from self-disgust?' (144). This is a theme that will be taken up and expanded brilliantly in Hospital's next novel, *Borderline*, but for now it is a question Emily cannot answer, can only attempt to sublimate in music. At this point the authoritative answers appear to be given by Sergei, a type of worldly wise, confident male who occurs with some frequency in Hospital's fiction, and here as a wealthy, benevolent, elegant older man. Despite Sergei's certainties, the nature of power is ambiguous and compromised in Hospital's fiction, and unless it feels the call of moral coherence it is suspect.

The Free Quebec movement, for example, is not seen as admirable even though it opposes the rigidities of entrenched authority. Its yearning for ideological and cultural purity echoes that of the Keralan militants in *The Ivory Swing*, who were agitating for greater social justice. Hospital's work is full of radical groups whose vision of bettering society involves the urgent systematisation of a program allied to violence when their vision is not met. The ironies of the rhetoric of social justice becoming associated with violence, and the legitimising of the death of opponents, recur throughout her work, providing a theme that could hardly be more urgently topical.

It is a theme taken up not just in relation to Emily but also in relation to Jason, through the traumatised state of one of his patients, Stephen Wall. Wall had gone idealistically to support the Allende communist regime in Chile, only to be caught up in the brutal collusion of the Chilean Right with American interests in the 1973 military takeover by the barbaric General Pinochet. Wall's experiences lead him to ask basic questions in Hospital's moral universe: 'Where is logic? . . . The problem . . . is how to *atone*. And how to go on' (164–5). The depth of Wall's emotional involvement in the fate of others is counterpointed here with Jason's petulance over being dumped by his lover Jessica. Wall feels a sense of responsibility for something; he is desperate that priests who are dismembered and nuns who are tortured by 'Christians' must not be forgotten, while Jason is locked into a self-centred world in which everything has responsibility for him and he has responsibility for no-one, including, ironically, his patients. Wall's panic interrupts Jason's self-regarding anger and occasions his melancholy perception of the uselessness of attempts to make a difference, to enable goodness: 'It has always been this way, hasn't it? Mere flickerings against the night' (166). Or, in Jason's partner Ruth's surprised words when Emily asks her if she feels desolate: 'Doesn't everyone?' (183).

Jason is brought into increased focus as a version of Sergei, a man who takes up with women when he has no intention of committing to them, and drops them when tired. It is principally women who are hurt in the book, devastated even, by male self-centredness. Accordingly, Hospital enjoys pinpointing men's vanity and their self-delusional observation of themselves as fine and clever. The most common way of deflating this vanity is through revelations that women are not as dependent as the men think they are, so that when Jason is loftily considering how cleverly he is dumping his lover Jessica, she has pre-empted him by moving out of her apartment without his knowing. Once again, Hospital is both dissecting social behaviour and making a larger point concerning our interconnectedness: people are not exchangeable counters, time-fillers, or mere backdrops to our identity manoeuvres. In sparring with Jessica at a party when they meet, Jason is told that therapists 'manipulate. They're power freaks' (159). Hospital is withering about professional caregivers whose sense of decency and moral coherence is as solid as puff pastry. Rarely does a therapist come out positively in her work; indeed, rarely does any professional appear admirable. The most estimable characters in her world tend to be either humble people, such as the fatherly taxi-driver who cares for Jessica after Jason has had sex with her to satisfy the turbulence caused by Stephen Wall, or creative people, such as Emily, who are committed to their art and who do not treat other people as screens on which to project confirming images of themselves. For all that Emily abandons lovers, she does not pretend she will do otherwise.

Stephen Wall's connections are not only outside his family but outside his culture, providing a lesson that, if only safe North Americans were exposed to the injustice, brutality and severing of the bonds of solidarity he had experienced in Chile, they too would find their daily lives altered irremediably. His visceral reaction to this sense of responsibility contrasts immediately with Jason's selfishness, but also with Emily's cutting herself off from her family. In a world where things happen as happened in Chile, what indulgence is it to dismember one's own family as this family does? In general, erecting barriers or fleeing are both extreme actions of separation, so that in a way the radically purist vision of society associated with both Right (Chile) and Left (Quebec) finds an avatar in the various forms of purist analysis and response demonstrated by the triangle of Edward–Jason–Emily, to which are opposed the binding visions of Elizabeth–Victoria–Adam. The latter have each suffered such extreme types of dislocation that rejoining becomes more important than a hard or proud separateness. Compartmentalisation and an attempt to control the wild energies of the family are shown in Jason's exclusion of Ruth from the planned family reunion. We see again how ironically flawed a therapist he is, how unfitted he is to receive Stephen Wall's declaration of responsibility when he is unable to take responsibility even for Ruth, whom he not only cheats on but refuses to offer the succour of connection owed to a partner.

The impossibility of evading the power of the family is inexorably revealed as the family members move back towards each other, and admit the depth of the connection, a connection into which Stephen Wall's word – atonement – enters. 'We're very big on atonement, aren't we?' realises Emily ruefully (197). This strength of attachment is what each of them, apart from Elizabeth, has been attempting to evade, evasions that bring a corresponding augmentation of guilt when separation removes the possibility of being able to atone. Jason claims that he has 'come to believe in the supreme importance of redemptive actions' (198), something that reverberates throughout Hospital's work. Given that we cannot expect permanent coherence from ourselves or others, we can either cut ourselves off from others or devise mechanisms by which failures can be atoned for, can be dealt with, so that we may remain connected. Jason's self-regarding coldness allows him to recognise how imperfect he is, but he is still capable of perceiving the importance not only of redemptive acts but of people who seek to be redemptive, who connect and heal wherever they go, or who at least move in that direction. At this point Jason is able to see for others what he cannot manage for himself. He can see, for example, that Emily's response to her father has led to others getting burnt in the consuming fire of family dynamics, namely Adam and Dave. Jason, moreover, has caught Elizabeth's fervour for the reunion, searching for the possibility of being able to love his father before Edward dies. For despite the large part of the book given to different family members, it is Edward's rage that constitutes the focus of the family's disconnection and the assorted kinds of damage they all feel. In Adam's words: 'So it's Grandpa everyone is afraid of, and so am I' (203). As a child he is able to break through the disjunction by refusing its logic and hugging his grandfather when they meet; all the tension goes out of Edward, allowing them both to cry and hold each other.

'Convergence' is followed by 'Prelude', and it begins with Edward the next morning, symbolic of new beginnings, feeling that something has changed. If there should be any doubt about the level of Edward's monstrosity, he remembers laughing last night with Adam but cannot remember the last time he laughed, unless it was when Emily was born. Jason wonders when the last time was that he had felt content, and is not even able to recall a single occasion, feeling that his part in helping to bring Adam and grandfather together might be the 'act of unambiguous benediction' (208) that could serve as atonement for his destructiveness. In Edward's imagination, '[t]he smell, the touch of a grandchild, was like an armful of hyacinths' (206), a moment of epiphany.[17] It is a genuinely affecting moment, but something dark begins to creep back into his recollections as he remembers having sent a telegram to Marta, the symbol of his failure of nerve, of the injuries to his sense of self caused by choosing control and responsibility over passion and pleasure.

Notwithstanding the overriding importance in Hospital's world of connection, the option to cut oneself off is one she can appreciate and respect, being unwilling to judge harshly the options we may choose in order to cope with the damage and difficulty of others. There are numerous characters in her fiction who have chosen to try to step aside from involvement, and one book – *Oyster* – has such characters as its focus. In a way, absenting oneself validates the power of connection, of involvement with others, a power so strong that in certain circumstances we are unable to cope with it. The family in *Tiger* illustrates one such circumstance, the danger of concentrating family power in the hands of one figure whose options override all those around him, who damages everyone else's ability to believe in connection itself.

Despite Edward's moment of bonding with Adam, the regnant atmosphere remains one of fear, intensified by the slightest family memory, such as Edward hurling the bust of Beethoven that Jason was whittling out of soap through the window when Jason nicks the table a little. Emily asserts that '[s]ome things shouldn't be forgiven' (218). This brings the revelation from her mother that she has been corresponding with Dave, in this case evidence that '[p]eople do terrible things just by lifting a finger . . . If we didn't understand that, and didn't forgive it, we'd be savages' (218).

Elizabeth is pointing out that Emily did something terrible to Dave when she disappeared out of his life and yet he forgives her. Everyone is capable of brutality in manipulating others to serve their own ends, and the novel shows us that this capacity exists even in as positive a character as Emily.

Fates in the water

The chapter entitled 'The Tiger Pit' signals a point towards which the narrative has been heading. The reunion is finally in full swing, and the swirl of guests reminds Victoria of another night in which there had been a dinner party. Beginning the chapter with Victoria allows her fears and heightened sensitivity to provide a troubling augury for the evening. Like a character in a Janet Frame novel, Victoria feels the pressure of every little social interaction to such an extent that it becomes impossible for her to cope with anything multiple or complicated. It all seems too threatening, all the signs are harbingers of doom. Moreover, Victoria's memories introduce the shimmering memory of a connection she had made herself, with a young man she calls Gabriel, a figure who brought her 'absolute peace and safety' (226).

At the moment when Edward's story is about to be shattered by Marta's revealing to him the truth about the former bond between them, Victoria, who has been hiding under the gazebo, senses something is not right between her father and Marta and turns the hose on them. Although a link between this event and an earlier occasion involving the gazebo has been hinted at throughout the novel, we still do not know what it is. Even Edward's scream that he had been trying to save Victoria and to keep her 'pure' (239) remains enigmatic as Edward blacks out. The justice of Victoria's action is finally made clear in the revelation that at an earlier teenage party Edward caught her and Gabriel naked in the gazebo and turned the hose on them, in full view of the rest of the party-goers and the family. This had snapped something in Victoria's sensitive being. With Victoria's act of soaking Edward in the present, many of the clues, hints and puzzles of the novel move into focus, and we see that the result is an apparently symmetrical justice, a vision of cause and effect that promises some form of equity, which in reality can never be realised. The symmetry at the level of act cannot be equated with justice, for how can Victoria's lifelong despair be considered equal to Edward's dousing and the lost opportunity to make the connection with Marta he has dreamed about for decades? Given that the connection he imagined, a sustaining fiction as much as a corrosive one, was illusory, by being soaked by Victoria he was spared the knowledge that he had deluded himself pathetically all these years. As she contemplates the madness of her passion for Marta's husband Joe, Elizabeth imagines that '[f]or every moment of passionate elation there is an equal and opposite cost' (255), and in her equation the cost of the elation was Joe's death in World War II and Victoria's slipping over the edge. Again, the equation appears punishingly unbalanced; indeed, Victoria had witnessed Elizabeth and Joe *in flagrante* when younger, but had revealed nothing. There are, after all, no absolute equivalences in human experience, and justice in human affairs is erratic, to say the least.

Nonetheless, the family reunion is cathartic. Emily announces that she will call Dave – remaking a connection. Jason comes to the conclusion that: 'I really think, from now on, I'll be able to *do* something. With his life he means, with his patients' (247). The final section, however, belongs to Elizabeth. What had begun with Edward, arrogating centrality to himself, finishes with his wife, the true centre. Elizabeth continues to propound a philosophy of hope: 'Simply the growing, she thinks, the movement from day to day, ruptures old forms and is violent with beauty' (246). The challenge is the apparently straightforward one of passing from day to day without damaging those around us; when, after all:

> The greatest mystery, Elizabeth thinks, is the wildness of the beast within us. At any moment we may move in some primal way, take a mere step in the direction of private desire, stretch an arm: and our claws have left blood in their wake (246).

On the face of it, this is a strangely fierce way for Elizabeth to sum up what has happened, despite her having been unfaithful to Edward. The tiger in the tiger pit may not be simply Edward after all but the beast Elizabeth is referring to here, a beast that we all harbour – the capacity to wound cripplingly those we should care for the most. Thus it is that Elizabeth strokes her arms 'and is surprised to feel flesh. She realises she was expecting something coarser, the pelt of a tiger perhaps' (249).

What Elizabeth refers to as life's 'inexhaustible offerings of irony' (249) are endlessly fascinating to Hospital. The simple hedonism of opting for passion is not simplistically opposed to a bland responsibility. Hospital has been able to make responsibility, connection and family also appear intense and satisfying, as if she were writing against the valorisation of passionate excess in *The Ivory Swing*. In the end, Edward does not realise that his construction of his life has been false, Elizabeth does not understand what he has been going through, and yet they are gently together: 'It has sung itself well, she thinks. She likes this ending' (256).

As Margaret Schramm notes, the sense of resolution reached by Elizabeth at the end of the novel, however ambiguous, is unique in Hospital's career.[18] For the most part, however, *The Tiger in the Tiger Pit* indicated the direction that Hospital's writing was to move in, a direction in which almost every element was to increase in complexity. The step up in narrative intricacy from *The Ivory Swing*, involving the manipulation of different points of view alongside the intertwining of ethical responsibility with the destabilisation of memory and causality, will become spectacularly more sophisticated in her next novel, *Borderline*, the work that really brought Janette Turner Hospital's work to the attention of observers of contemporary literary fiction in English.

CHAPTER 4

Tuning the telling
Borderline

. . . a catastrophe that is experienced will often seem eerily like its representation.

Susan Sontag[1]

Borders and narrative

Borderline marked a great step forward for Hospital. Highly ambitious in the philosophical and political issues it deals with, and the teasingly challenging literary form it employs, this third novel garnered widespread critical praise and was the major catalyst in the elevation of Hospital as a significant writer.[2] The explosion in the recognition given to literary fiction from outside the British–American axis that occurred in the 1980s and 1990s, along with Hospital's focusing in sophisticated fashion on one of the key concepts in this growth of interest – borders – combined to produce a leap in the respect she was accorded. The foregrounding of Hospital's concern over what she explained as 'the essential *unreality*, for us in the safe and insulated North American middle class . . . of many real and verifiable and quite horrific events which go on daily all around us in the world'[3] gives the book a wider resonance than the essentially family politics of *The Tiger in the Tiger Pit*. In addition, Hospital's fascination with questions of representation had become much more self-conscious, challenging her readers to follow the struggles of the narrator with his material in such a manner as to prevent us from relaxing into the familiar conventions of linear realism.

The incandescent first page certainly helped. Hospital had given much evidence of her ability to contain a suggestive combination of concepts in a short phrase, often a pithy yoking of the concrete and the metaphorical, or the particular and the vast, like the 'knives and shadows'[4] that the protagonist, Felicity, will need to hide from as the story develops. Thus we read in the first line that '[a]t borders, as at death and in dreams, no amount of prior planning will necessarily avail' (11). The chilling realisation follows: 'control is not in the hands of the traveller' (11). Time has further confirmed the truth of this, as the post-9/11 world increases the vigilance and mechanisms of control at frontiers everywhere. At the same time, this applies to the readers who are entering the country of the book; we are crossing a border as well, and for us also control is uncertain. To cross a border is to allow one's right to be somewhere to be determined by others, and this brings an existentially disturbing anxiety in itself. When the decision to let us pass the border or not may have consequences of life or death, the stakes are raised terrifyingly high at the moment the border is approached. These factors come together when Felicity drives up to the border between the United States and Canada (New York State and Quebec on I-87), but in the structure of delay, and the fragmented accumulation of detail that characterises Hospital's work, we are soon removed to another time, and to the beginning of the complex explanations of causes and effects that so fascinate Hospital. Paul Roberts pinpoints this effect as 'a curious ability to keep shifting from a strong story-line and deeply personal obsessions to a compassionate treatment of themes of universal concern'.[5]

The novel constantly moves backwards and forwards across many of the borders by means of which we situate ourselves and are situated by others. This is not simply a metaphor, however, given that our presence on one or other side of these borders can determine whether we live or die. The woman from El Salvador who is trying to cross into Canada at the beginning of the novel is attempting to escape death, but in the process she has become 'La Desconocida, the unknown or unknowable one' (11). Preserving her life she has lost her name, her identity, her family, even her voice. She never has a voice in the novel, but will be given a name later – Dolores Marquez (134).[6] 'Dolores', as Elspeth Cameron notes, 'meaning "grief" – is the other half of Felicity, or "happiness"'.[7] Like all of Hospital's borders, however, this one is permeable; borders are human attempts to impose demarcation on a reality that mocks our efforts to classify and control it. The woman from El Salvador does cross the border, but this does not save her; for neither she nor any of the others in the novel are safe wherever they are. As the El Salvadorean character, Angelo, says, '[n]one of it's possible . . . None of it's real. But it happens' (211), glossing Hospital's concern with respect to the ignorance of most comfortable North Americans about the wider consequences of American economic and political power.

The activation of what will become a widening spiral of dislocation occurs immediately, in the novel's second chapter, where we learn that both Felicity and 'La Desconocida' have disappeared, proving that a privileged American can become one of the *desaparecidas* just as much as a nameless Latin American. One of the consequences is that Felicity's story is being narrated by someone else. She is the object of a man's narration, that of her ex-lover Seymour's son, Jean-Marc, and this objectification produces a distancing that situates her as other even in her own story, a mark of how our own stories are not our own stories in any simple fashion at all.[8]

As both subject and object in her story, it is no surprise that Felicity has 'often overheard herself described as a painter's dream' (17). To complicate matters still further, this painter was her lover – teasingly named 'Seymour' (see more; Alistair Stead adds 'seemer' and 'seamer' to the possible echoes[9]) – so that Felicity speaks from beyond multiple borders, multiple framing discourses, that are not her own. The link between Seymour's production of her in terms of images of elsewhere – 'the view could be South India or the Queensland coast of Australia' (19) – and her crossing the border as an escape from being elsewhere, is activated by her dream character's escaping from a painting, but being turned back at the 'border' and pasted back on to the canvas. In addition, she is an art curator/art historian, her profession one of arbitrating upon and placing art in spaces, so '[s]he knew better than most people how simple it was to rearrange the past' (131), depending upon curatorial, critical or commercial choices.

In this persistent questioning of identity and the narrative conventions of the subject position, Hospital has moved from the inflecting of identity with culture, albeit not unproblematically, in *The Ivory Swing* and some of the early stories to a notion that links it with more personal things: memory and memory's explorations of those cracks that allow the real to be always already dislocated by its magical shadows and tributaries. Helen Daniel summed up the result by referring to Hospital's 'passion for chimerical borderlines' in which 'hers is a baroque consciousness, her vision polyphasic, containing rivalries and revenants, each of which might break away and incarnate in a different context'.[10] Hence Hospital's assertion that 'the shadowy interplay of reality and unreality (and its political, social and moral dimensions and implications) is the major theme of the book'.[11]

There is one further, central anxiety in the novel which contributes to the energies of all of Hospital's narratives, and that is the anxiety concerning not just the extent to which reality is mediated but the responsibilities that this mediation allows or renders difficult. Jean-Marc begins by telling us he has not heard from Felicity for a year, that her disappearance is connected with that of someone called Augustine, but that he still hopes to hear from her. The whole narrative is therefore a mixture of memory, investigation (Jean-Marc trying to follow Felicity's tracks) and re-creative fabrication. Not for nothing does he soon begin talking about Felicity's dreams and the importance of dreams to her, something that has absolutely no possibility of external verification. Right from the start the dizzying ways in which circumstances lead to unforeseen and distant consequences are referenced in an anecdote about how Felicity's having made up a dream to tease a counsellor at school many years ago led, 'in a way, to her disappearance' (13).

The butterfly effect fascinates Hospital and provides much of the allure of her work, and, in order to demonstrate the complicated paths causality takes, her narratives develop in highly non-linear fashion. Typically, there is an oversupply of apparently disjointed information at the beginning of her novels, before we have worked out who the characters are or the relation between them. At the beginning of *Borderline*, for example, we do not know who Augustine (generally referred to as Gus) is, or who Kathleen is, or the importance of the Old Volcano (Jean-Marc's father and Felicity's lover, Seymour), so the reader has to accept a certain degree of initial puzzlement. This corresponds to our general hermeneutic situation: we are perpetually faced in all of our interactions with criss-crossing signs, links and references, and we need to decide how we will negotiate them when from the outset we know we will never make all the connections or decipher all the signs. As Felicity says, 'There are only three possible defences: the first is not caring, and the others are irony and art' (14). Given that not caring is not one of either Felicity or Hospital's defences, this leaves irony and art, and while we can see that art is clearly Hospital's principal defence, irony is also ever-present within her story world. As was evident in *The Tiger in the Tiger Pit*, given the mismatch between the stories we tell ourselves and the stories others tell, irony suffuses human relations. Moreover, Hospital's work is unashamedly ironic about such things as the hypocrisies of public figures from teachers to politicians to literary critics. Felicity collects clippings of the terrifying ways that human beings devise to oppress and silence others, an activity she terms the collecting of 'ironies' (95). Nonetheless, Hospital is not ironic about life in the overarching sense of feeling the mismatches between human aspirations or beliefs and what they actually do to be so depressing that all of our efforts and all of our philosophies are merely futile. The paradoxical relation between her moral drive and her ironic perception of the fissures between narrative and verifiable realities energises much of her ethical and aesthetic economy.

Jean-Marc, however, is not Janette Turner Hospital. If his sex did not give us a clue, the fact that he says he distrusts art (14) might suggest that his position as storyteller lies athwart Hospital's own. That is, he does not simply represent the opposite of her point of view, but rather exists as a type of doppelgänger to enable her to think about, and to make us think about, the nature of the contract between anyone who tells a story and anyone who listens to it, coupled with the central issues of bearing witness and of intervening. The crucial nature of this device to the novel is not apparent to everybody, and there are readers who feel it interferes with the tale of suspense, semi-official violence and the unravelling of clues that the story of Felicity becomes. Clearly, Hospital's New York editor wondered about this too, and she had to plead: 'I cannot emphasize too much that J-M's chapters are *anything but* trimmings added to the "main" plot line.'[12]

Disappearing into stories

Felicity, who becomes the centre of the story, is another of Hospital's characters in the vein of *The Ivory Swing*'s Annie and *Tiger*'s Emily, someone who 'felt at ease in airports and in the hearts of great cities' (14), not solely on account of the anonymity and ebullience of the metropolis, but on account of being with 'other people who don't belong – my closest relations' (14). Felicity feels herself to be an outsider: 'My entire history. Nobody even believes it's real' (22). Jean-Marc muses that there 'has always been a quality of absence about her' (18), so that her disappearance becomes one more in a series of ways in which Felicity is unable to be pinned down. Margaret Schramm notes that *Borderline* is Hospital's 'first work to include the postmodernist element of absent subjects',[13] an element that takes various forms in the novel, including missing people, missing identities (Dolores), errant fathers, and subjectivities that are told by two different layers of narrator (Jean-Marc and Hospital). Schramm even suggests that Felicity's quest to aid Dolores is in some way a filling in of the emptiness in her life left by her father, who also disappeared, albeit at sea, linking the novel more firmly to the absent father theme in much of Hospital's work.

Jean-Marc is, however, more concerned with Felicity's role as his famous father's lover and model. Another mode of representation, painting, is shown to be no more capable of fixing her than writing, thus allowing the son to dilute some of his dominating father's authority. Seymour is also one of Hospital's doubles, twinned with Felicity's dead father, who had been a friend of Seymour's when young. Representing opposed approaches to the mysteries of existence – art and religion – their debate is rather one-sided given that Seymour's words are often reproduced but Felicity's father's only rarely. This suggests that the artistic approach is privileged, and that is true of Hospital's work as a whole. For all of Seymour's maddening egotism and self-belief, his art is high-spirited and brilliantly coloured, and anything less is inappropriate, even unbefitting, given the multifarious and bewildering nature of reality.

Competing with his father, Jean-Marc frequently steps backwards to talk about himself, frustrating the reader's desire for a clear and sequential story. As in many postmodern books, the teller is a part of the tale, and Hospital makes sure we do not lose sight of this, forcing us continually to confront the constructed nature of what we are reading. Jean-Marc claims to be patient and methodical, and is supposedly therefore a reliable narrator. In explaining his profession of piano tuner, however, he has to admit that, despite the mathematical basis of tuning a piano, there is a space in which minor adjustments are made that are beyond the strict dictates of mathematical precision. This process, called 'tempering', is based on ear and experience, and for this '[t]he absolutely accurate is too narrow; it is false and imperfect. I am after something more organic: the truth . . . the whole of it, the messy unpresentable fantasies' (25–6). Like tuning a piano, telling the story is something that must proceed 'note by note' (26);

it cannot be rushed, and has to be listened to attentively to hear 'the patterns, resonances, meanings' (27). Jean-Marc will return repeatedly to this theme, aware that the teller of the tale is necessarily battling with the 'imaginative sympathy of the onlooker', given that 'truth must be tempered because mere accuracy was false' (189). In this sense it is more important that he begins 'by guarding not only against error but against the spirit of error' (189). Telling the story aright, as all through Hospital's work, is not only a matter of obvious things like detail and accuracy but of witness, of being responsible to what is most significant, not only in our own story but in those of others. At one point Jean-Marc quotes a newspaper piece about the events at the border, and this is introduced after we have been exposed to the beginning of his reconstruction. Inevitably, the newspaper report comes across as limited and flat, and Jean-Marc asks the question for us: 'With what voice can such a newspaper item be appropriately interpreted' (50). In writing history – 'and history is what I'm writing' (131) – an intertwining of teller and tale, or of present and past, inevitably takes place.

Music is often referred to in Jean-Marc's account as an explanatory tool that helps him to articulate his understanding of the events he is narrating, as of the world in general. Music is based on mathematical precision, but at the same time on non-measurable individual hearing, analogously to the mysterious individual and cultural preferences that drive motivation. The modulation of these two opposed impulses leads music to represent a human desire for both the shared precision of notation and the individual variation of interpretation or reception. There is not one without the other, so what seems to be a digression – Jean-Marc wittering on about himself – is central to the book's interest in how stories get told. It is also relevant that he is a piano tuner and not a pianist, for this is a profession that he believes exempts him from the intrusions of the ego or from having to make decisions about his relation to music: he thinks he simply follows the taste and directives of whoever employs him. In the course of the narrative he will find that it is not so simple, and his discovery that our every action is an interpretation and an intervention serves as an example to the reader: we do not simply follow the directives or taste of the writer, for our relation to the story is always one of interpreting and intervening. Even to turn the page is to express a relationship to a narrative, and the constant 'interruptions' in Felicity's story remind us of this.

Solidarity, sinning and survival

To complicate matters further, we are introduced to Gus: another, very different, major character. Gus allows Hospital to bring in a different set of issues from those surrounding Felicity. He is a Canadian, allowing attention to be paid to Hospital's land of residence at the time. He is a Catholic, permitting Hospital's interest in religion to be introduced. And he articulates a whole series of topics to do with relationships, faithfulness, guilt, and moral survival in the front line of capitalism. Silvia Albertazzi relates him to the book's title by describing him as a '*bourgeois* on the border between the religious upbringing of his past and the loosened sexual mores of modern society'.[14] Gus is a travelling insurance salesman and a sequential adulterer (turning him into another form of absent father), and as he approaches the US–Canadian border he runs through the anxieties and pressures that ensue from his mix of business and pleasure. Ironically, being in insurance provides no insurance whatsoever against making a mess of his personal life or coping with the unexpected that is about to occur. It is at this point that the disturbance happens that shatters his and Felicity's lives – the border officer opens a meat van and exposes a group of illegal immigrants.

This draws Felicity and Gus together, even more so when the official drives the meat van away, a beef carcass falls out and a woman emerges from within it. Without thinking, they decide to harbour her in Felicity's car. Gus may represent the ordinary, those who go unquestioned at borders; but the safety of such people has already been denied by the detention of a group of weekend fishermen in the car immediately ahead of the meat van. At the border there is no ordinary, everyone is a suspect, as the contemporary world has come to know only too well. Moreover, Gus's generalised guilt over his failures as a husband, inflected by a diffuse Catholic sense of guilt over everything, makes him always feel suspect. His befuddled anxiety melds the border patrol officer with a priest taking confession, and the questions at the border with questions about his transgressions, but he and Felicity nonetheless make it through safely.

Felicity's connection to the woman is imagined to be related to her memories of the loss of her father in a fishing accident, so that the woman becomes not simply herself but, like everyone we interact with, a border between ourselves and the other. Deborah Bowen summarises this interaction: '[Dolores] is identified with whatever is unattainable in significant others. For instance, she represents the unattainableness of Felicity to the narrator Jean-Marc [and] the long-suffering of his wife to Gus.'[15] In Hospital's fictional world we subsist only through frontiers after all, for our selfhood exists in the multiple borders we cross between ourselves and those who surround us, borders we cross daily, hourly, in action and memory. In *Borderline* the principal characters are imagined by the narrator to be attempting, to some extent, to evade intervening against the grain. Both Felicity and Gus are imagined as feeling themselves slipping out of their 'real' lives and being dragged into realities that are increasingly opaque as they become involved in the attempt of the Salvadorean woman to cross the US–Canada border. This reading of the characters' involvement, however, is constructed for us by Jean-Marc, who will discover, ironically, that his attempt to bring Felicity to life for himself results in constructions that are in fact interventions of his own, frontier zones between his memories and desires. His attempt to mediate the memories and desires of other people becomes an unstable border between himself and others.[16]

Responsibility is accordingly constantly interwoven in the book between the imagined anguishing over their responsibility for what they are doing, on the part of Felicity and Gus, and Jean-Marc's responsibility for their story, along with a third level of the reader's responsibility towards the text. Felicity and Gus thus constantly discuss the rightness or wrongness of what they have done. Felicity claims that compassion is instinctive; Gus feels befuddled, nervous and guilty. Gus's guilt is centrally focused on his sexual unfaithfulness to his wife, and the possibility of absolution is a theme that follows him throughout the book. Here, Gus feels he needs a framework to explain his repeated infidelities to himself, for he is aware he is hurting his wife. Because he is aware of this, his guilt feels appropriate to him, and absolution undeserved. Gus is imagined as inflecting all of his actions and perceptions through his Catholic faith, envisaged as an intense and constant system of weighing and valuing everything. His Roman Catholicism is returned to frequently as an overarching scheme through which everything is filtered, and there is frequent byplay in the book between depictions of Felicity's stern puritan aunts and French-Canadian Roman Catholicism. The church of Our Lady of Sorrows in Central Square, Cambridge, arouses feelings of solidarity with sufferers, an appreciation of 'a tradition that could sustain, at the very core of urban dissonance and flux, such a sanctuary to the inner life' (248). Even the elderly priest, Father Bolduc, whom Felicity appeals to in the middle of the night for help with La Magdalena, and who is 'obtuse as only the pure in heart can be' (80), is considered with wry tolerance, in spite of his retrograde ideas about women. Gus's belief in miracles is a further link with Felicity, who thinks of the Salvadorean woman as La Magdalena, in the painting by Perugino in Florence's Pitti Palace. By following such thoughts Gus comes to the realisation that he will look after the woman, both as an unacknowledged form of absolution and out of a need to produce a miracle himself.

Gus and Felicity are thus thrown together as representatives as much as individuals in Hospital's strategy though which everything becomes a drama of symbolic positions. Felicity is the manicured, glamorous, artistic woman, while Gus is a hard-drinking, low-culture insurance salesman, a person figured as a negative type in high culture, and accordingly a type of other every bit as alienating as national or ethnic others.[17] Hospital's use of an insurance salesman as a positive figure is transgressive of the conventions of intellectual fiction and the frisson between Gus and Felicity provides further moral drama, echoing the relation between Leopold Bloom and Stephen Daedalus in Joyce's *Ulysses*. Restlessly calibrating and examining his life in lachrymose yet optimistic fashion, Gus echoes Bloom clearly when, for example, he examines an egg in a frying pan, experiencing its materiality intensely but also connecting this with 'receiving the Host at Mass' (98), or when he links the 1437 times he has mowed his lawn in the last decade with the number of his transgressions. As with Bloom, everything means something to Gus; things are portents or signs that radiate out in unexpected directions.[18] This means that the events concerning the Salvadorean woman cannot be shunted aside, for everything has a meaning that must be processed in Gus's ledger of transgression and atonement.

With Gus so fixated on his guilt with respect to his marriage, he is constantly exploring where he went wrong, and what he might do to make things up to his wife, Therese (again ironically, the insurance payout after his death is the only useful thing his being in insurance has done for his family). This allows for Hospital's interest in the operations of memory and the way it slithers around, adjusting itself to our needs at the same time as it carries out a complex campaign of accusation and a nostalgic measuring of loss. One of Hospital's common effects is the use of the bathetic, the build-up of an emotional register only to have it deflated by the intrusion of some plain or ridiculous aspect of daily realities. Generally relating to an individual's hopes or self-image coming up against resistant contexts, there is a prime example when Gus, radiant with the guilty drunk's belief in reform and changed habits, approaching his front door quietly so as not to wake his wife, steps on the cat. Not only does the noise wake her, the ugly shrillness of the cat's protest metaphorises the protest of reality at his ludicrous vision of a renewed future. Self-deluding characters are rife in Hospital's work, although, as here, her general approach is both to reveal the self-delusion and at the same time to provide such detailed contexts for its occurrence that the reader is not faced with simple disapproval but a degree of amused forbearance.

Indeed, the challenge of representing someone who does not fit in to Hospital's intellectualising world is a challenge over which hangs the suggestion that such people represent something more solid and at the same time more mysterious than artistic or intellectual people. We see this when Felicity wants to wish him well:

'"And for you too, all the best with . . ." – she was obviously uncertain about the aspirations of insurance agents' (127). When the book deals with other people in the business/insurance world, it treats the meretricious shallowness of their commercial relationship to life's objectives with scorn. Gus, however, is excused from this by being the salesman in the company with the largest number of clients but the smallest sales per client, the insurance salesman who believes in insurance for the little person, a battler for people like himself. Elizabeth Perkins even suggests that '[b]ecause Gus does not represent a successful figure in patriarchal society he can hear the voices of the wounded women'.[19]

The main undermining factor in Gus's life is his philandering, and here also Hospital is attempting something perhaps even more difficult than making an insurance salesman a central figure in a serious novel, and that is making a philanderer and a lecher a morally complex and forgivable figure in a novel put out, in one of its editions, by a feminist publishing house (Virago, in the United Kingdom). Gus's perpetual indiscretions with women are not cast as macho conquests or cynical scoring but as a wondering appreciation of the ultimately unreachable otherness of women's bodies along with the promise of (momentary) release from the anguish of coping with responsibility. That the release only intensifies the sense of failed responsibility highlights the paradoxes of human motivation. As Gus thinks when contemplating the tangle he had got himself into with La Desconocida: 'It was impossible, impossible, to untangle right and wrong. Existence was rust-riddled beyond repair, a pockwork of errors' (109). Gus's stolen moments of contact with a woman in a florist's, for example, are seen rather as an articulation of Gus's dreamy hopefulness than of any patriarchal oppression of women, an expression of desperate lack rather than an assertion of oppressive male presence.

Detection and detail

The plot thickens when Father Bolduc reports to the police how Felicity had taken him to the cabin in the woods but there was no woman there. His explanation is that Felicity had been raped and had displaced her trauma on to this story of another woman. When characters other than Felicity and Gus are brought into the story, we are moved out of Jean-Marc's imagination into his detective work, for he has followed up leads in the search to discover what had happened to Felicity. Not all of what Jean-Marc writes is unfounded fabrication, for not only does he have access to the recollections of such figures as Bolduc but he had also seen Felicity during the period of the events in question: she had called on him in Montreal after driving from the cabin, had explained what had happened, but had disappeared when he awoke in the morning. On other occasions she leaves a message on his answering machine, or rings him, even visits him, so that there is some real evidence for Jean-Marc to base his story on, and for us to accept that he has some authority to be telling it.

Concrete leads also appear to be provided by Felicity's aunts in Beacon Hill, the classiest part of old Boston. As usual, it appears as if Hospital provides an excess of detail about the aunts and their fussy, patrician habits, holding back the mystery, interrupting the narrative. There can be no excess of detail in Hospital's fiction, however, for part of its energy lies in reading the codes, the minute signs, that surround us, and we never know which may be the detail that we will need. Moreover, Boston is a crucial element in Hospital's visual and emotional economy, and attempting to read its signs is something she returns to often. The city and its history, its powerful institutions of learning[20] and its class contrasts provide much moral stimulation in Hospital's world, all the more so in the frisson between the Pentecostal background of Hospital's childhood and the severe Puritan history and inheritance informing the history of Boston and Massachusetts.

The aunts also exist in terms of their class position, an assertion of superiority through the rituals and the expressions of taste, whether in tea or music. Their fussiness over such details as the cream in the cakes indicates precisely the acuity of Hospital's perception of how removed many North Americans are from the realities of horror and oppression, an extreme example, perhaps, but all the more chilling in the chasm that separates the aunts from the experiences that a close family member has just been through and which they refuse to credit. This brings us up against an inescapable conundrum, as Felicity avers: 'Whether you look at them the right way or not, there are certain things, certain intractable things' (115). Reality is not just a matter of perspective. People *are* being oppressed and murdered, and to suggest that this can be read in any way other than outrage, sympathy or a desire to help is to deny something basic. At various moments in the book Gus or Felicity says, '[a]nyone would have helped her. I did it without thinking' (108), or something similar. Yet how can doing things 'without thinking' be accepted as a moral guideline? Jean-Marc's hermeneutic problem, Hospital's hermeneutic problem, returns insistently: if reality is something we must decode constantly, if reality consists of a series of interpretations and versions, then how can we say that one version or interpretation should prevail, how can we say that something so apparently unproblematic as the things happening to La Magdalena are wrong? Just as we are being enveloped in the cosy security of the aunts, for whom all is in its place and all manner of things will be well (alluding to Dame Julian of Norwich, as ironically as in the story 'The Last of the Hapsburgs'), the narrative rug is pulled out from under our feet once more. This is Jean-Marc telling the story, and he admits he never met the aunts; this is not even a reconstruction on the basis of known scraps of conversation.

Further questioning of the nature of evidence occurs when we read that two supposed detectives arrive in Felicity's Boston office and show her photographs of a murdered woman, a body found in the woods near Felicity's cottage. They try to connect Felicity to the woman through supposed political links. Unimagined links appear to make the connections real (as will be seen whenever detectives construct narratives in Hospital's work): the sheltered aunts donate to Central American social agencies; Felicity's clippings of horrific events seem to point to political activism; her demurrals in terms of Escher, Magritte and Borges drawing blank stares from the detectives.

The presence of detectives, whoever they really work for, and the murder inquiry are not mere plot enhancements on Hospital's part. A murder inquiry is another way of piecing together events, a particular relation to history and interpretation that is set alongside other approaches to interpretation in the book. Felicity explains her clippings by observing that 'the desire to understand is itself absurd, isn't it?' (138). Several shards of meaning break off and splinter in different directions at this observation. In the first place, the detectives' piecing together of events is revealed to be absurd by what we know; but in terms of what they know it is not only not absurd but serving an appropriately non-absurd desire: the desire to understand who murdered someone, and who is involved in the processes of political and dirty violence that led to the woman's brutal killing. This is a desire that Jean-Marc's narrative and the novel share, and, by implication, anyone concerned about the 'many real and verifiable and quite horrific events which go on daily all around us in the world'.[21]

The connections made by the detectives between Felicity and the Salvadorean refugees activate her sense of the irony of the world, the sense that in fact such connections *can* be made, that reality really can be construed in nightmare combinations. It is not that the detectives are not reading the signs reasonably when they connect her to political activism. The bizarre reasonableness of their conclusions is underlined by the coincidence between Felicity's file of clippings of violent events around the world and her later meeting the son of an El Salvadorean sewing-machine businessman about whom she had clipped an article from a newspaper. The detective serves Hospital's purposes well, for he has to deal with conjunctions of circumstances that disturb his sense of what might be possible or not. Being a detective and seeing the surprising things human beings do has led him to claim: 'I don't even think about what seems real and what doesn't' (141). The detective has to discover the supposed facts, and yet in order to do that he has to enter narrative, interpret, and reconstruct events, so becoming an avatar of Jean-Marc, and ultimately of the reader, as we also piece together evidence and choose what to believe or not, form hypotheses, and are surprised or not by the version displayed before us. The popularity of the detective story in fiction and in film relates to the decoding urge that is part of the human condition, an urge that Hospital links to the wider human need for significant patterns, a need that entwines detective stories with religion, with art, with daydreams, music, stories, lies and language.[22]

In Hospital's writing the presence of such concerns in the lives of her characters is often referred back to their childhoods. She writes disturbingly and brilliantly of childhood in many sequences of her novels and short stories, and characters are apt to remember or allude briefly to childhood events at any time. The intensities and fears of childhood above all are apparent, childhood being a time when her characters feel isolated, apart, marginalised in ways that the fierce hierarchies of children make even more brutal than anything experienced as an adult. The horrifying treatment of Felicity's childhood friend Hester, whose leg and hip were disfigured from polio, reveal an unsentimentality about childhood as well as about any supposed caring solidarity among girls. Nonetheless, whatever the degree of girls' taste for tormenting anyone who is different, the violence and hatred demonstrated by boys surpasses it. Hester is raped by older boys, and Felicity is saved from a similar fate only by the bloody result of what the boys have done to Hester. Hester claims she could imagine her vagina was made of wood so she did not feel anything. By denying her sexuality she denies men's power over her to a limited extent, but this is to deny herself and her story, as the two girls do by never telling anyone until Felicity tells Jean-Marc many years later, when he is a frightened child.

By including this story from Felicity's childhood, Hospital reinforces several things at the same time. First, she highlights the depth of the impulse in human beings to harm and discriminate against anyone who is different, and in particular the ugly revenge of males against girls or women who oppose their power in any way, even unintentionally, as in the case of Felicity's being made to humiliate lumbering Grade 8 boys in class. In addition, Hospital shows that violence is not restricted to undisciplined or third-world environments, that the horror of human nastiness also exists in the putatively idyllic Queensland schoolyard. Indeed, it is not only manifested by El Salvadorean death squads (from Left and Right) but can be found in the centre of probably the greatest concentration of higher-education activity in the world – Cambridge, Massachusetts and adjacent areas of Boston. Finally, we see Felicity, who is called monkey-girl at school on account of her Indian connections, defending an even more marginalised person than herself, and we see that there is a cost involved in sticking up for the underdog, in admitting one's difference, in being courageous. Living one's difference presupposes the likelihood of damage.

In writing about Felicity, Jean-Marc has the benefit of having known her since he was a child, since she became his father's lover. In Gus's case, however, Jean-Marc is inventing more, and inventing the thoughts and anxieties of someone who is radically different from himself, although they did meet. Jean-Marc is aware that there are large doses of wish fulfilment in his narrative, that the central character might be nobody but himself after all, that our ceaseless decoding means that '[w]e impose our own lives on the world: the self as template' (171). At the same time, he feels sure that he is not being untrue to Gus in representing him as panicking on account of the feeling that 'his life made no sense' (171), for in Jean-Marc's eyes this is common to all of us, whatever the process by which we arrive at that point. Whether this was how Gus inflected his experience or not, it relates to the central theme of 'making sense': whatever we are doing we are entangled in the procedures of making sense, and by this time there is a readerly entanglement with the narrative, Jean-Marc's entanglement with his narrative, and Felicity and Gus's entanglement with the events they struggle to understand. Jean-Marc further characterises his enterprise as that of constructing the perfect lover, as Dante constructed Beatrice, though Dante could only immortalise the search for her, never reaching the representation of the sought-for perfection, the one who would make everything mean what it means and nothing else. Hospital often refers to Dante, and especially to being lost in the dark wood, the position Dante finds himself in at the beginning of the *Divine Comedy*. Undeterred, Dante sets out with Virgil as his guide through dizzyingly complex and crucially interlinked scenarios, each of which adds more meaning to the mystery of creation. Noticeably, however, it is to the state of being lost and embarking on the search for meaning that Hospital refers, and not to the culminating explanatory circles of the *Paradiso*.

Saving the text

When Felicity finally manages to evade the watching detective with his ominous name, Hunter, and go to Central Square, the address she has been told to look for also appears elusive, fictitious. It is symptomatic that an aged and enigmatic Holocaust-survivor watchmaker appears to be the guardian of the place Felicity is looking for, El Centro Salvadore (it should be Salvadoreño in Spanish, but Hospital's version more clearly references 'saving', what Felicity had hoped she was doing for La Magdalena). In answer to why she helped, Felicity says again: 'It was instinctive. Anyone would have done it' (183). This is an answer that explains motivation not by recourse to argument, logic or reasons, but to sympathy, to something vague and beyond rational explanation, an answer that pleases the watchmaker, and that articulates the solidarity that the world needs if it is to act outside personal advantage and self-interest, outside calculation. She is directed to another address, to a gaudily kitsch Hispanic barbershop, from where she is led back to Massachusetts Avenue, and left to wonder about the meaningless run-around she is being given. Threatening and harassing young men turn out to be sympathisers; nothing is what it seems.

This goes for the story as a whole, of course, and whenever we are caught up in the mystery back comes Jean-Marc to remind us that he is stage-managing everything. Now he admits that perhaps, after all, he has not been searching for the known and surface facts or even for emotional accuracy; he has fallen in love with his creation, as 'one rather enjoys playing God' (189). Perhaps, he thinks, he is better at telling Felicity's story than she would be herself, that he has 'begun to dream her dreams' (189). We are not able to measure this, of course, but we do have his reporting that Gus's daughter Kathleen has complained about the way he has depicted her father. He claims not to have a sense of responsibility like Felicity, but he constantly reminds us of his responsibility to the tale. He even defies our desire to identify with the characters by pointing out that, since he is telling the tale, ultimately Felicity is him, that Felicity's continual referring to her father is a displacement of his own sense of his father's absence. This is the literary contract, he tells us; Beatrice *is* Dante, Rosalind (in *As You Like It*) *is* Shakespeare, for whose voice can it be coming from their mouths? At the same time, 'all this conjuring is both true and not true' (192), writers do inhabit their characters, there is a leap of imaginative power, and as readers we have to live with the ambiguity of the space over which this leap occurs. If we slip towards investing too much in the writerly contract – being carried along by the writer – then our own contract as readers is diluted, rendered less challenging. Desiring us to live the ambiguity of this space, Jean-Marc – that is to say, Hospital – keeps returning us to it so as not to allow us to slip into either the comfort zone of unproblematised identification or the zone of alienation from the pleasures of narrative. It is in this borderline that the dizzying possibilities of the contract between writer and reader become most active, but to stay on a borderline is difficult, for we have to be continually pulled back from driving off with one of the characters.

There is a lot of driving in *Borderline*. Hospital is interested in all sorts of transitional states, from that between writer and reader to the practical presence in contemporary Western life of movement. Movement occurs constantly in her writing as she explores the hypotheses of escape and translocation, along with the equally ever-present hypotheses of surveillance and control. In this novel also, Hospital activates a porous location between French Canada and Anglo America, a place close to the major population centres of both countries and easy to move back and forth between for comfortable North Americans. Hospital is intrigued by the operation of national borders in a manner that may reflect the fascination of the native of an island nation for the existence and nature of borders that one can cross by car, even on foot. Hospital's fictional world is one in which people are on the move, and it is in the nature of her mixture of suspicion of power yet delight in people's subversive inventiveness that this movement offers more possibilities than restrictions, so long as people are vigilant and do not stop reading the signs around them. As illegal immigrant Angelo tells Felicity: 'He who trusts least, lives longest' (205). Hospital's favoured characters, like Felicity, are happy in crowded places where people are coming and going with myriad purposes. Globalisation can bring damage, as can be seen in the reach of supposedly local Central American oppression into Cambridge in this novel; but violence hardly originated in globalisation, and Hospital's approval of the turbulent mixture of peoples and ideas that modern cities evidence ensures that her writing places the responsibility for oppression elsewhere.

Even an anxious character like Gus, caught up in a puzzling and dangerous event, and feeling that he is hurting his wife even more by his strange behaviour, 'inhaled optimism' (194). His daughter Kathleen reports to Jean-Marc that '[h]e never felt lost, he was an eternal optimist' (204). His Catholicism, his desire to believe in miracles and his restless reaching out for the women he comes into contact with all come together in the vision he has of La Magdalena when he revisits Felicity's cottage. He believes that this has changed him, that he will not cheat on Therese any more; but there is a suggestion that he drinks so much that his visions are alcohol-induced, with an admixture of guilt to bring them on as well. With Hospital's enjoyment of twists in the narrative, Gus arrives home to find that Therese has left him, the irony being that she thinks Felicity's phone calls have to do with Gus's extramarital affairs.

The operation of irony mocks Gus's belief that he has derived the right meanings from what is happening to him, but it also works to sharpen our vigilance. Hospital's novels challenge us repeatedly to ask ourselves how it is that we find or make meaning for ourselves, given the presence both of things that should not happen but do (having to give birth by the roadside while being chased by armed killers and seeing the baby die) and ironic conjunctions that defy any simplistic notion of cause and effect. Jean-Marc keeps wanting to deny the presence of meaning but is driven to continue to produce it, to tie events together, to imagine links. And as he does this he makes them as well, his links become part of the story, they alter the shape of events. Elizabeth Perkins points out that 'Jean-Marc may also contribute to Felicity's death through his refusal to pass on to her Gus's message that he has found Dolores Marquez'[23] until after she has revealed information to Father O'Dowd which leads, it is suspected, to the dismantling of the underground refugee network. Jean-Marc tells Gus that La Magdalena has been murdered, for

Felicity had told him this over the phone; and he tells Felicity that La Magdalena is still at her cottage, for Gus had convinced him that his vision involved her material presence there. This criss-crossing of information sends them both back there to a fate in which Gus arrives at the cottage to meet two hard-faced men, from whom he flees in a fog of fear and images of cloven feet. He ends up in a mouldy boarding house in Montreal, where he descends into a dark night of the soul assailed by nightmares, visions and presages of doom, a furious swirl of Gothic motifs and emotions that Jean-Marc knows are gaudy but which Kathleen feels might be appropriate as a way of writing her father after all. Jean-Marc meets Gus's sixteen-year-old daughter when she visits him on the track of her father, and she charms him so much he becomes concerned for her, ironically moving into related territory to that of his father whom he had vilified for taking up with young women.

Throughout the book Jean-Marc has been obsessed with Felicity, whom he has loved since he was a child, and he is enraged by the fact that she had been his father's lover, confusingly turning Felicity into Jean-Marc's de facto stepmother.[24] Seymour is represented as a self-obsessed devourer of women, a user-up of young women especially, while neglecting his son. Father figures recur in the book, Felicity's dead but missed, Jean-Marc's alive but in practical terms absent and dismissive of his son as a 'parasite' on music. In writing this book Jean-Marc realises that he is empowering himself as a creative artist at the same time as he is a 'parasite' on events, even as he attempts to be true to what happened. The writer's type of creativity is not that of the musician, although each may stimulate the other to reach towards the other's strategies and effects.

Beyond the border of control

Just when enough time seems to have passed for Felicity's life to have returned to normal, she sees the increasingly suspicious 'detective' Hunter on the subway. Her sense of responsibility assails her, while Jean-Marc is annoyed at her for reading the signs in such terms. Felicity is accused by both father and son of being too much like her father who wanted to save, heal and salve. The problem, according to Jean-Marc, is 'a very perverse understanding of the random' (244), a belief that there are no simple coincidences, and that reality is something that demands to be decoded and pieced together, and that moreover we should act upon the meanings we find. In such a world there is no such thing as the random; there are only connections, and it is up to us to follow the chains and make sense of them. Felicity finds solace in confessing to a Catholic priest, and hands him the photograph she has been entrusted to get to La Magdalena. That is, she hands over her meanings to another, gives up responsibility, for which she feels relieved. In Hospital's world, however, giving up responsibility to another is always problematic, if not dangerous. A rigorous focusing of responsibility on the self and on the self's reading of the signs characterises her work; but this exists in tension with a concern for that sense of responsibility being responsive to the needs of others. Given that the individual who assumes responsibility for everyone else can be dangerous – as will be seen in *Oyster* – we are left with the need to articulate our responsibilities with the help of others, to define them with and against others, and with constantly having to decide on which side of the balance to place our belief, in the contexts of others' necessarily differing understanding of the issues or courses of action to follow. Felicity hands over information to the priest, but it transpires that he is rabidly opposed to any form of liberationist ideology, and despite having received the information in the confessional, albeit from a non-Catholic, he may have turned it all over to the authorities, leading to Angelo's being deported and shot. This appears to be the only explanation for the underground network's links being broken, although, in a book that radically questions all explanations, it may be one more paranoid conclusion on Sister Gabriel's part, or perhaps on the part of Jean-Marc.

Hospital has said that readers tend to deny that Felicity dies just as Jean-Marc denies it,[25] even though he provides enough evidence for us to accept that this has happened, and even though Hospital thought she had written enough to convince us that Felicity had indeed been murdered. After all, Jean-Marc tells us that he is writing his 'own hunt through a maze of riddles for a woman who has been missing for a year' (192). As if being missing for a year were not conclusive enough, her death is suggested in other ways as well: in the fact of Felicity's being thirty-three years old, the age of Christ when he was executed for assuming that he could save others, the age of Christ when Mary Magdalene came to him. Another is Sister Gabriel's telling her that they needed a lay worker to go to Central America to help 'the thousands of homeless and hungry children' (254), but given that even nuns have been murdered this is not a mission that one could be optimistic about surviving. There are also the facts the police present Jean-Marc with: Felicity's burnt-out apartment building, several bodies, her car parked outside, Gus's car consumed by fire in an accident,[26] two bodies (the implication being that they are Gus and La Magdalena, although Gus's feeling that he had found her may be an alcohol- and guilt-induced delusion). On the other hand, we need to be attentive: we have had the nature of fact destabilised for us on different planes throughout the novel, both in terms of the ways stories are told and information stitched together and in terms of the ways information is manipulated by forces who want us to believe they are interlocking in a certain way. Felicity had not driven her car for months, while a supposed sighting of her entering her building is no guarantee at all. In any case, the suspicious connections generated by the police lead to the same results as the emotional and imaginative connections generated by Jean-Marc: 'They know no more than we do' (268).

Among the many possible resonances of this narratorial relationship, one is that it is not possible not to intervene, not possible not to assume responsibility. In Elspeth Cameron's words, Hospital 'here offers hope that man's impulse to care for others is as strong as his instinct to gratify himself'.[27] Even the distanced piano tuner cannot avoid imaginative sympathy, or an awareness of the pleasures and dangers of intervening, that is, of the pleasures and dangers of wielding responsibility. As Jean-Marc proceeds with his narrative, he comes increasingly to realise the attractions that making narratives holds, and ironically reproduces to some extent what he perceives to be the megalomania, the wish to control, of his father. He approaches an understanding, finally, in Deborah Bowen's view, of 'the image's representation of the past as a magical site of potential transfiguration'.[28] Where his father has always tried to fix people in his paintings, Jean-Marc realises that by telling this tale he wants 'to be the official biographer, the final authority' (256), but also that he 'got carried away by the performance' (282). In this way, the novel carries out a simultaneous representation of two public interventions, or what Margaret Schramm calls their 'questing for some form of redemption':[29] that of Felicity and Gus helping someone they do not know in the face of danger and death, because 'that's what anyone would do'; and that of Jean-Marc reconstructing this to the point where he understands that the personal realm he thought he inhabited is not enough.[30] Naturally, there is no 'final authority'. Jean-Marc's father paints a series of paintings based on Felicity's story, enraging Jean-Marc when one of his inventions coincides with one of Jean-Marc's. This sends Jean-Marc off into one more of his tirades at the manipulative and parasitic behaviour of his father, for which the only defence is to manipulate right back, to take on his father at his own game, to dream his father, to have the last word. Given this allusion also to the controlling strings of the author Hospital, who is dreaming Jean-Marc, it is one of the delicious ironies of the book that both Jean-Marc and many readers refuse to believe that Felicity is dead. Just as Felicity and Gus struggle against the forces of control, in the version of a son who struggles against the controlling power of his father, so also do readers fight back against the controlling power of the author. In this sense, their denial of what Hospital had thought she had made clear is both a confirmation of and a compliment to the success of the novel. By insisting on the slippery nature of narrative authority, Hospital has convinced some of us so well that we take up Jean-Marc's position, we continue to write Felicity. After all, in the borderline between the work and the reader strange things happen, for 'at borders there is never an ordinary course of events' (11).

CHAPTER 5

Out of the comfort zone *Dislocations*

. . . the snag is no more how to discover, invent, construct, assemble (even buy) an identity, but how to prevent it from being too tight – and from sticking too fast to the body.

Zygmunt Bauman[1]

Homeland insecurity

After publishing three novels in four years, Hospital had achieved a high enough profile to publish a collection of short stories, a genre publishers are generally wary of, in 1986. *Dislocations* declares its focus in its title: the experience of disjunction that arises from being located outside the familiar. This takes many forms in the seventeen compressed short stories that make up the volume:[2] from contemporary diasporic displacement to the adjustments of facing up to the presence of immigrants; from coming up against the shock of others' perceptions to the jolt our perceptions of ourselves undergo when confronted by the unexpected. Hospital interprets her title widely, underlining Brian Castro's almost contemporaneous suggestion that 'more people are beginning to realise that we are more free when we struggle, more free even when we encounter friction between cultures, than if we wrapped our lives in cotton wool'.[3] Accordingly, Hospital makes the experience of dislocation central to contemporary experience in general, whether or not we are spatially or internationally dislocated, and to this end she incorporates a readerly dislocation as well in her constant recourse to puzzling situations and narrative surprises. Her own approach to the short story may be appreciated in her dismissive comment on:

> the familiar minimalist turf of much American short fiction, whose tone and style are so relentlessly and assertively modest: no syntactical complication, no splashes of imagery please; improprieties such as symbolic allusion or the faintest whiff of metaphysics will not be tolerated.[4]

Hospital's writing delights in flouting all of these conventions, in being what Canadian writer Barry Dempster called 'vivid with techniques':[5] often immodestly abrasive or overtly symbolic; and certainly concerned to question the neat schemes by which we manage our daily activities, including the activity of reading. Graham Burns aptly synthesises the volume's designs upon us: 'Fiction, Hospital seems to say, cannot be a mimicry of life, since the order it achieves amounts to yet another dislocation of the disorderly truths of experience.'[6]

Hospital's publishing career began with short stories,[7] and they have earned consistently high praise; in Lucy Frost's judgement, for example, Hospital is nothing less than 'one of the most gifted short story writers publishing in English today'.[8] The genius of the short story has always been to articulate that moment of disruption when the apparently tight world of the tale falls away to reveal that what we thought to be the case was a matter of perspective, an illusion or even perhaps a delusion.[9] Hospital's stories delight in the complicity of such formal conventions with her examination of the ways in which we understand or misunderstand the world around us, particularly when it involves people self-righteously convinced of their place in the scheme of things. Moreover, in *Dislocations*, as Martha Ann Mueller remarks, '[t]here is a "wholeness" to having these stories in one place. It provides the opportunity to note facets of the author's intentions which might otherwise remain unseen when each story is read in isolation'.[10] In the first place, on the thematic level we have a volume dealing with what Mueller calls 'the main theme of mental dislocation',[11] which generally occurs when characters are confronted by people who challenge their sense of themselves in some way, but may also result from some shock to one's view of the order of the world. This shock gives rise to the expected disjunctions in perception and behaviour that such challenges occasion. Hospital manages this type of estrangement brilliantly, but even so it is only an antechamber to other moral concerns, for the estrangement occurs on two planes as it were. That is, estrangement provides the *background* for most the stories, in that characters are moving through a world that resists or surprises them in some sense from start to finish, while the *moment* of estrangement is related to something more focused and less dispersed than the unease produced by perceptual dislocation. This other moment relates to fundamental tendencies in Hospital's world view, to a moment in which fantasies of purity or control are challenged or subverted. Seeing where and how these moments of general and particular estrangement collide with and interact with each other provides for a large part of the moral excitement of this volume.

It might be said of all the stories in the volume that, as for the characters in the first story, 'Happy Diwali', 'only exile and isolation unite us' (10).[12] Whether we are looking at Indians in

Canada or a professor who deludes himself about his place in the scheme of things (Hospital likes to purvey such wild exaggerations about the vanity of university professors), the principal characters are all dealing with the ingenious ways human beings devise to separate themselves from those around them. As they struggle to retain their sense of themselves in the face of change, characters may attempt to hold on to solid reference points when it is these that have failed them. Despite the loss of bearings occasioned by the disruption experienced by some characters, Hospital pointedly began the volume with a strong story centred on the wisdom and growth that displacement can facilitate.

Lost purities and edgy solidarity

In 'Happy Diwali'[13] physical and cultural dislocation provide the background against which a myth of lost purity is placed, setting the consoling story of a pure India that many of the immigrants cling to against the climatic otherness of the Canadian winter outside. Even though the emblematic figure of the gathering, known as His Highness, perhaps waits on tables in another city, the spell of his authenticity must not be broken by speaking of it publicly. Gentle irony is directed here at the manoeuvres made to shore up nostalgia, which is seen to contain the human need for connection at the same time as it is inflected by the human capacity for wilful self-delusion. In any event, if we do not pick up Hospital's indirect hints, the idea of the blend, the mixture, is directly appealed to by Perpetua, the culturally complex Goan narrator, who approvingly observes the celebration of Diwali in Canada: 'It is an eclectic mix that strikes me as just right for the occasion' (13). With its Portuguese–Indian history and traditions, Goa is a location that appeals to supporters of the commingled (as can be seen in Salman Rushdie's *Midnight's Children*); but 'Happy Diwali' acknowledges that in fact all of India is dynamically impure and multiple in ways that some migrants choose or perhaps need to overlook. In this story, the pious expectations of the reader who reads postcolonially are punctured, for it is not a fantasy of lost cultural purity at all. We are not reading solely an indignant exposé of the way in which Indian immigrants are treated in Canada, or a melancholy reflection on how we lose parts of our culture and our being when we are forced to emigrate by economic realities largely established by the West.

Perpetua thus stands as a person who actively confronts her transnational condition, refusing to be rendered a passive victim. In her observation that the Western view of things as essences or defined presences elides the connected multivalence and shading of things, Perpetua indicates that Indian and Canadian cultures are not incommensurably opposed but connected along the axis of the human condition. Her example is the impish one of 'foreplay', which she claims is a typically divisive Western concept, erecting the notion of a separate activity from that of the supposed real thing, as though lovemaking (like everything else) were not all one flowing continuity. Indian eclecticism holds a great attraction for Hospital, and it is strategic that this story comes first in the book, with its double-edged critique of the Western essentialist as well as of those characters in the story for whom the absent India has become a nostalgically fixed presence. Moreover, the fulcral moment of estrangement in this story is not that of any of the characters, but that of the reader. It is we who are gently, implicitly, reproved for leaping too readily into the discourse of lost purity, when we realise that Perpetua and His Highness have a very knowing awareness of the compromises their dislocation calls for. They have adapted, found ways to take advantage of their transnational lives rather than merely complaining about and rejecting the place in which they find themselves. In this, Hospital participates in a strong current of contemporary reflection on the rewards to be gained by being elsewhere than home,[14] as well as on a 'shift from ethnicity to diaspora as master tropes of social diversity and migration', as argued by Vered Amit and Nigel Rapport.[15]

Nonetheless, despite its approval of the eclectic, the story acknowledges the real sense of loss occasioned by expatriation. In several of the stories Hospital is attentive to the stress that accompanies emigration. Nowhere is this attentiveness more apparent than in the last three stories, in which details of Hospital's own family background are refracted. These more autobiographical tales reprise the concerns of her other more overtly fictional stories and novels, so that there is no gaping fissure between her autobiographical stories and others that are apparently less so, and indeed Selina Samuels finds the stories set in Australia to be 'her most effective'.[16]

Hospital's territory is one in which memories come up against the quiddity of the past. In the three final Australian stories, for example, that quiddity adheres to the contours of family members: one grandfather, another grandfather, and parents. In Samuels's words: 'Hospital often evokes place in the form of a representation of "home," which is located in memories.'[17] Yet Perpetua's very name in 'Happy Diwali' both mocks and celebrates the nature of the past and memory, which survive within us always and yet vanish in the moment they are lived. In this sense, a lost purity is not so much cultural as temporal, associated with individuals and their trajectories rather than with the obstensibly fixed essences of places or cultures; that is, what cultures are is what the individuals who inhabit them are, and individuals inevitably change. While her characters, as in 'Happy

Diwali', might be tempted to live via constant emotional reference to an essentialised homeland, the story's surprises deflect such fixity, for if there is one thing all of Hospital's works invest in, it is the belief that everyone who is in a place has a stake in the cultural flows that occur there. There should be no unitary culture for locals, relegating immigrants to a zone of exclusion. There should not even be a separating multiplicity of cultures (locals and immigrants in rigorously different boxes), for, in Nick Couldry's words, '[t]he idea that there are "cultures" attached to a particular location underpins the idea that cultural differences correspond to ethnic differences and (usually also) differences of "race"'.[18] Hospital is certainly interested in and sympathetic to cultural specificities, but ultimately her sympathies incline so strongly towards solidarity and making connections that her work often explores strategies to cross over and link the synapse between cultures rather than rehearsing their incommensurability. She wants to believe that human beings are not just determined by and restricted to the patterns they are used to, that we can escape the scripts that have been written for us. This is affectingly represented in the commonalities of the woman from the long-established white Canadian family and the recently arrived Chinese woman in 'Moving Out'.

'Moving Out' is a story of belonging, rendered through Mrs Phillips's suburban anxieties about propriety, and the nervousness associated with the presence of sudden difference. In this case, the difference is not simply that of ethnic difference, for Hospital cleverly indicates that this is a distraction, and that the most crucial difference between human beings concerns their sense of responsibility to and solidarity with others, particularly others who are vulnerable or fragile. The axis of sympathy in this story thus becomes one of generations, of age, which cuts across the expected difference of ethnicity. The pushy Chinese-Canadian male becomes aligned with the selfish Euro-Canadian students, while the presumably more different older Chinese woman is able to establish a bond of sympathy with the fearful older white Canadian woman, crossing the ethnic divide. At that moment, Mrs Phillips discovers that the proprieties and the calibrations of belonging and loss that the rest of the story had dealt with melt away in the solidarity of loss that comes with age, whatever our culture. The selfish and the young commit violence on the elderly in this story, but also enable the latter to establish connections that had been nonexistent before. In this way, one of the refrains of the story becomes animated with more than the irony it had appeared to possess, as the long-resident white neighbours exclaim: 'We should have done this years ago . . . it takes a crisis . . . we must do this again' (48, 51). What had been imagined as the purity of belonging has actually masked the neighbours' wariness of each other, not the ease of interiority and connection at all. The Euro-Canadians had not formed any particularly warm community, but lived in their own separate interests until these had been called into question by the immigrant presence. The outsiders have had the effect not of destroying community but of enabling it, even if the community that is thus activated is more interested in excluding others than in welcoming new members. Nonetheless, crotchety Mrs Phillips's poignant moment of togetherness with the elderly Chinese woman who cannot speak English implies the possibility of positive change. In this case, the relation of the generation they belong to, and of their relative, and gendered, powerlessness, operates more meaningfully than the simple details of residence and long-term proximity.[19]

Solidarity, however, can be misplaced. In 'Ashes to Ashes' Hospital has been stimulated by a report from a newspaper in

Trivandrum, an article entitled 'A spooky crematorium', which she reproduces before her story. The article is a droll piece about an apparent jinx attached to a new electric crematorium, detailing sudden deaths and illnesses among anyone attached to the project, so that when the time came for its official unveiling, there was scarcely anyone from the press brave enough to attend. The central character in Hospital's story is Krishnankutty, who has returned home to Kerala after spending time at MIT, and from the outset the story adopts an amused, superior tone that could read somewhat uncomfortably as Western amusement at Indian habits, although it should be noted that it is picking up on a similar tone used by the local newspaper reporter. Krishnankutty's new wife, Saraswathi, for example, 'had a college degree in English literature and was an avid reader of Barbara Cartland, Victoria Holt, and other English novelists circulated in paperback among the well-born young women of Trivandrum' (69). Western superiority extends to Krishnankutty's having to learn about the *Kama Sutra* from his American friends, while Saraswathi, who has not even heard of the text from her own cultural traditions, thinks that her husband's sexual prowess reveals 'the glorious mysteries of American sex' (69).

Positioning the story's protagonist in this register establishes Krishnankutty as ridiculous, so that his brave interest in transferring the decorum and efficiency of an American crematorium to Kerala seems doomed from the start. Before long, however, Krishnankutty's American friend John is introduced, and he too is portrayed in the same register, with the difference that his half-baked interest in Indian exoticism is not an attempt to better his community. Further, where Hospital is affectionate towards Krishnankutty she is downright sarcastic towards John, whose 'family had so much money that it was only natural he should turn from things material to things spiritual' (72). John's vision of India wants it to remain fixed according to his ideas of Indian spirituality, while Krishnankutty's is fired up with enthusiasm for Western technology. As the project advances, John is increasingly absorbed in the cultural differences until he goes off to an ashram, while Krishnankutty's project is hit by mysterious deaths and accidents. Their two fates diverge and yet converge as John's rejection of the body ends in illness and imminent death, after which he hopes his dear friend Krishnankutty will light the traditional funeral pyre on the banks of the river.

The story chronicles a series of mismatched enthusiasms in which the dilution of cultural imperatives through contact with another culture has resulted in disaster. The sophisticated compromises and strategies of denial of 'Happy Diwali' are nowhere in evidence as Krishnankutty and John simply transpose values from one setting into another, refusing to ameliorate or mix their desires. Both are absorbed in dreams of purity that do not contextualise what they are doing in terms of the muddied interaction of difference, until both John and Krishnankutty's projects are doomed. Learning from other cultures, the story suggests, does not mean adopting them wholesale and rejecting the culture one has come from. The search for perfection through total abandonment of the always already imperfect originary culture is as ill-fated as any other search for perfection.

Perfection and fantasies of control are linked, and they do not become apparent only in translocation from one culture to another. Whether dealing with people who move from one side of the world to the other, or with people who scarcely move from their homes, Hospital repeatedly exposes the ways in which human beings attempt to hedge their lives with controlling structures. In 'The Dark Wood', social worker Dr Angela Carson maintains herself unencumbered in her personal life, believing it allows her a perfect situation from which to comfort the dying and to lead them as positively as possible towards death. Her will to control is emblematised also in her domination of the highways, in which she evades following cars, and anyone who tries to get too close; but this is seen to be a dangerous tactic on the road, metaphorising the danger of attempting to avoid others in one's life. Human beings cannot be evaded in the same way, for even if she brushes off a lover for having introduced the complexities of his relationship with his children into their lives, she cannot deal as smoothly as she imagined with the dying. The dying have the advantage over the messiness of daily life of knowing that they will soon be removed from further complication, an awareness that leads to an intensity and a questioning that renders Angela's patronising care emptily superficial. Angela's vainly assumed compassion is thus revealed as a desire to control connection, not to feel it. When Beatrice, an elderly patient, resists her well-oiled strategies, Angela begins to unravel, and she is now unable to face the freeway. Her strategies of evasion fail her when Beatrice's resistance opens up a form of connection, thus demonstrating the desirability, as well as the mysteries, of connection that lie at the heart of Hospital's world. As Angela loses control, she enters the vulnerable world of her patients and becomes more human as a result. In Gina Goulder's summary: 'It is difficult for anyone to face their own ineffectiveness against death: it is impossible for someone who really believes she has triumphed over it daily.'[20] Only by admitting there is no triumph can death become real.

The vertigo of lost comfort

Death serves as the motivator of desperate questioning in Hospital's work, pushing us to consider the nature of such large concepts as causality, pattern and justice. In 'Some Have Called Thee Mighty and Dreadful', the protagonist is obliged to contextualise to her two young children the sudden and apparently random death of a friend, with whom they had just been playing in the park, and one of the children has reached the age where consoling explanations are revealed to be illusory. The fragmentary nature of the story, with two dream narratives, anguished thrashing around for explanation, and a framework within which to see the irruption of catastrophe, in addition to awkward and unsatisfying conversations with the children, all indicate the impotence of the woman in the face of traumatic disaster. The nature of apparent chaos and fate will exercise Hospital repeatedly throughout her work, and she will move towards contextualisations in terms of chaos theory, as well as towards a greater degree of awed fascination with the operation of chance and time. Here, however, the narrator is left anguished and adrift, unable to face the possibility of nothingness after death, but equally unable to hope there might be something meaningful that would help to explain the injustice of sudden death.

In contrast, the type of death represented by being abandoned by one's partner has a devastatingly destructive effect on the unnamed protagonist's hold on reality in 'After the Fall'. We are led through a day in her thoughts as she tries to capture on paper the exact characteristics of the fall of a dead amaryllis flower, but what has fallen is her notion of the contours of her life, and, activating the echo from Genesis, she has fallen from innocence. In denial over the fact that her husband left her for a lover, unable to remember that her children are a lot older than she thinks, that it is summer and not winter, she herself demonstrates what she thinks she is attempting to reproduce: 'the inexorability of self-destruction' (101). She has displaced on to her relationship with representation what she is unable to cope with in her daily life: 'the essence of change' (102). Involved in the precise fixing of a moment in the death of a flower, she has allowed the important connections in her life to become vague, unaware of where her children are or what they are doing with their lives. Here the character has found something that helps with the injustice of sudden disruption caused by her husband's leaving; but it is not to search for meaning in or through the event, but instead to evade it; and the picture Hospital presents is one of intense loss, the gain of the woman's relationship with her art hardly figuring as compensation for the loss of her hold on her own past or present, the loss of those human connections that Hospital values. The damage done by the husband cannot be drawn away by art. Sometimes there are no consolations.

Severe disruption is also at the centre of 'Golden Girl', in this case the destruction of a young woman's features after a barbecue fire that kills one of her sisters and deranges the other. As Cilla moves back through her memories to acknowledge what happened, she keeps everyone at a distance, her former beauty and self-assurance enabling her to face the future with a certain confidence, despite the anguishing dreams of fire and separation from her sisters. The story prepares us for the removal of the bandages on Cilla's face and her inevitable dismay, but that would be too simple a fable of pride going before a fall. Justice is not meted out in banal fashion in this tale or in any of Hospital's work, which in general challenges our desire for a neat rendering of accounts. The good and kind sister, Christina, dies in the fire; the timorous and unconfident sister, Wendy, remains mentally disturbed and blames herself even though it had been on Cilla's instigation that she had added more lighter fluid to the fire. Cilla, however, although she has lost her former golden looks, retains her belief in herself and accepts the twist of events, or perhaps the two things go together. Yet it is a self-belief that is vain and hard, and the tale takes its place in the book's series of desperate reflections on fate and injustice. Our pretensions are mocked by what happens, and perhaps a thoughtful sensitivity only leaves us more vulnerable.

Hospital's work contains many characters, principally women, whose sensitivity renders them ill-prepared to deal with people who do not share their bookish approach to life. The second story, 'You Gave Me Hyacinths', pointedly jumps from the snow of Canada and the intercontinental dislocation of 'Happy Diwali' to the heat of tropical Australia and the intranational dislocation of the protagonist. It may be the same nation for her, but the school amidst this tropical exuberance seems like a 'brave outpost of another civilization' (23). 'You Gave Me Hyacinths' is also a celebration of this place, of the pungent and fertile tropical landscape that suggests to Hospital the intertwined complexity of the world. One of the ironies in the story, however, is that this symbolic richness of place is not reflected in the lives of the local inhabitants. As if providing a deliberate contrast with the expected culture clashes of the first story, in this story most of the schoolchildren characters are faced with the injuries of the local. Their estrangement is actually from their own potential, and this is insistently gendered as well, dovetailing with Perpetua's inability to escape completely from the protocols of a place half a world away from where she is. For women, even radical dislocation in terms of place may not relocate them from their subservience within social systems.

Accordingly, Dellis, the teenager who is counterpointed to the metropolitan teacher, is constantly telling the latter that she spoils things, that the questions she asks are the wrong ones or should not be asked in the first place. In this encounter, Hospital is reprising the Lawrentian confrontation between an educated narrator and the putative unreflective immediacy of the rural, in which the superiority of the teacher is shaken by Dellis's easy access to her pleasures and impulses. This tension will recur throughout Hospital's work: uneducated characters will cast doubt on the mental procedures and literary connections of educated characters, and in general these uneducated voices will be respected. This duality will not be resolved in this story. Here, the teacher holds on to the pleasures that words and poetry give her, and is able to relate Dellis's appearance at her door to the appearance of the hyacinth girl in *The Waste Land*.

In typically self-deprecatory and colonial fashion, when called on to say what a hyacinth is, the teacher does not know, and can only imagine a Cooktown orchid. On the surface, this is a comment on the imperial nature of the references that education in Australia used to be full of; but at the same time it is a demonstration that the pleasures of language can float free from concrete experience, that words are experiences themselves. Lack of referentiality, ultimately, is not seen to be important: the teacher connects with Dellis and Dellis responds to the teacher, despite their differences. As with the tropical forest, connection occurs anyway, in however confused and tangled a fashion.

The story 'Mosie' provides an even more concentrated version of the experiential fissure that lies between the teacher and Dellis, the speaker of the story being a black cleaning woman in a Columbia University apartment block. At the centre of the tale lies Mosie's practical knowledge of the ways of the world gained through the manoeuvres and allowances that poverty and menial labour necessitate. Her chief observation is that educated people are not flexible: 'Their minds are so full of education, there's no room for give' (157). While on the surface this is a homage to Mosie's forbearance and patience, she is claiming that we should be patient with nothing less than harassment and aggression. In *The Last Magician*, this opposition will recur in much more complex form in the shape of the wise prostitute the Queen of Sheba and Lucy, where the Queen of Sheba will repeatedly say of Lucy and her friends Gabriel and Charlie that they do not know the realities of the world and that it is not a good idea to rock the boat. While she is a positive voice, and will even be proven right in that Gabriel and Charlie disappear, giving in to bullying and violence is generally to be resisted in Hospital's writing.

The third story also deals with the split between the educated and the supposedly uneducated. Its title, 'The Inside Story', points to the revealing of a truth, something that only someone in the know has access to, but the narrative soon casts doubt on the knowingness of the narrator, for the 'Inside' referred to is that of prison, where the teacher, she who carries knowledge, is revealed to be the one who clearly has things to learn. The primary 'knowledge' that she had brought to her job relates to her belief in prisoners as oppressed souls whose condition can be elevated to the tragic, victims of the unforgiving and harsh treatment that society metes out to wrongdoers. The purity of bodily suffering had appeared to underline their status as martyrs, about which she naively tries to lecture them. As it happens, her knowledge of bodily suffering is derived from books, and the inside story is the one communicated to her precisely by those inside. It is a story about human resistance, survival and sense of self in the face of attempts to break it down. It is also a story about the insidious self-damage the system encourages the prisoners to inflict on themselves, echoing the self-damage the narrowed horizons of the Queensland country town lead the locals into enacting in 'You Gave Me Hyacinths'. In the end, the woman, who is nameless (it is the prisoners who have individuality, the humanist has none), is forced to leave the job, but her assertion that she was only doing it for the money rings hollow. Her estrangement is from her ideas of how to judge human beings, the story ultimately evincing sympathy for the inmates and unable to criticise them. The murder of Jed, one of the most sympathetic of the prisoners, confirms his own previous assessment of the synapse between motive and action that prison conditions can bring about. Human motivation is revealed to be as impure as that of the teacher herself: claiming to be only doing it for the money, but revealing her sympathy for and movement towards the prisoners at the same time. This is the case with the inmates also, whose tales of motivation continually surprise her, from the meditative bank robber, to the gentle giant with an explosive temper, to Jed the worldly-wise analyst of human irrationality. The inconclusive nature of the stories in *Dislocations* works to estrange the reader from certainty, and this story does so more than most, making it one of the most troubling and one of the strongest in the volume.

In many of these stories the moment of narrative surprise is revealed as a character's mechanisms of control are shown to be inadequate. Those characters who perceive this, like Mrs Phillips in 'Moving Out', or like the teetotal father in 'After Long Absence' who takes a couple of sips of wine, are seen to be changing, and thus, within the moral economy of the stories, accrete positive meanings to themselves, however discreetly. Peter Williamson, on the other hand, in 'The Baroque Ensemble', soliloquises a relentless vision of his narcissism and lofty dismissal of others in the name of what he imagines to be 'the purity of it!' (113). This purity consists of a minimalist affective décor, translating into the pleasure of the empty auditorium, the deserted cathedral, the refusal of emotional contact. After his self-satisfied contemplation of what he imagines to be the awe and wonder with which people regard his elegance and aloofness, a man with standards in a fallen world, he overhears students talking about him: 'Williamson . . . he's so pathetic . . . Poor old sod', and: 'can't help feeling sorry . . . so embarrassing, isn't he? . . . nothing one can really do' (121). Nevertheless, after a moment of shock and vertigo, he resumes his self-satisfied inner monologue, proving the truth of the student's statement that there is nothing to be done. The moment of estrangement has not been translated into an adjustment of his values; his notions of purity are shaken but not altered and he remains pathetic.[21]

In opposition to Williamson, we have 'The Owl-Bander', set directly after 'The Baroque Ensemble', in which businessman Nick Stewart is living a breakdown from all of his previous values, reassessing family relations and memories, and working his way through them by means of empathy with creatures with whom he cannot communicate.[22] By hoping not to catch any owls when he removes himself to the forest, Nick claims that it will enable him 'to believe in the possibility of defying categorization' (124). He is searching for a world in which meaning will reverberate along the axis of connection rather than along those of economic or classificatory rationality, schemes that rely on separation, hierarchy and competition. As Hospital is an author who is not just highly respectful of 'science' but fascinated by and supportive of the eloquent and imaginative responses it generates to the mysteries of the universe, the activity of charting the banded owls is doing duty as a metaphor here not for 'science' but for an attitude towards fixing the universe that is inimical to the emotional connections that are important to human beings. At the end Nick feels, in direct contradistinction to Williamson, that nothing is explained, that meaning is as inscrutable as an owl's face, that the Western symbol for wisdom cannot provide any. Nick has lost certainty, the certainty that he had possessed as a businessman and inheritor of the family motel chain, and, as in most of the other stories in the volume, this certainty is not replaced at the end by another certainty. Characters who are growing in Hospital's hermeneutic universe are necessarily left uncertain, but they continue to ask questions, to try to make connections, to look at things differently. The reader is not offered tidy resolutions, but is left in the same uncertainty as these characters, left perhaps with hints such as those at the end of 'The Owl Bander' where we read that '[t]he pine needles gave off that musky smell of decay and germination' (133), that is, the ceaseless round of natural processes, paralleling the ceaseless round of interpretive manoeuvres that characterises a properly responsible stance before the owl's face of the universe.

Dislocated at home

The first (Canadian) edition of *Dislocations* finished with the story 'Port After Port, the Same Baggage', paralleling 'Happy Diwali'. The opening story dealt with Indians in Canada, while the final story ended with a Canadian in India. A gentle piece with an elderly woman travelling the world on a cargo steamer, 'Port After Port' comes to rest with Doris watching Kathakali dancers in a Theosophical Hall in Cochin, Kerala, holding the hand of an expatriate English woman. Despite this solidarity between older foreign women, a solidarity of interest in and an acceptance of difference, the title features as a line in the text when Doris is in Morocco, where misunderstandings and hostility occur between Doris and a gay passenger on her boat as well as between Doris and local Moroccans. Travel brings disruption and pain, but also the opportunity for unexpected connections and learning. Without losing sight of the former, Hospital strives to emphasise the latter, hence the bonding with the English woman coming at the end of the story and the volume, not to mention the last word, 'triumph' (179), the triumph of good in the world, achieved cross-culturally, as the women watch, by the Indian epic hero Rama.

The acclaimed neurologist António Damásio has reflected eloquently on the nature of our sense of reality in *The Feeling of What Happens*, where he proposes the loss of homeostasis as the foundational moment of consciousness: 'I propose that we become conscious when the organism's representation devices exhibit a specific kind of wordless knowledge – the knowledge that the organism's own state has been changed by an object.'[23] Extrapolating from this model, the awareness of having been altered by contact with something or someone different can be aligned with nothing less than the basic model of the operation or the existence of consciousness itself. Put another way, to be conscious is to have admitted difference into the system. To be conscious is to be impure from the start, and, by implication, to remain impure.

To be aware of change is necessarily linked to the power and the survival of memory, but memory is subject to continual reassessment, and Hospital is adept in all her work at chronicling that moment when the present is defamiliarised precisely because we perceive something about our past that we had not before. The nostalgia of presence is destabilised, in the sense that memories are a presence but they always enact an absence, the more so the more we try to wring their presence out of them. When there is a catch in Grandfather Turner's voice in 'The Bloody Past, the

Wandering Future', as he feels the fissure between the present and the past, all he can do is hug his grand-daughter, a representative of both the present and continuity. The story itself is a catch in Hospital's voice, and accordingly it is also writing an embrace that holds on to Hospital's Australian past in both its pastness and its presentness as memory. The gap between the event and its recreation means, nonetheless, that presence is constantly subverted, is swallowed up by the gap, can only be searched for and lamented but never found, except as that restless search itself. And such estrangement is ironically the most intense presence we are heir to, available only to those who are, precisely, conscious of their estrangement in the first place, their inevitable impurity.

'Morgan Morgan' deals with a version of Hospital's other grandfather, a twinkling, story-telling, hail-fellow-well-met Welshman, in which the grandmother complains that the child will never be able to tell the truth from lies, a hint as to Hospital's future career as a writer of fiction, a teller of both truth and 'lies'. Morgan's stories help him to deal with past disappointment, and make his conversation magically colourful to the young girl. The news of his brother's death shakes him momentarily, while Hospital's grandmother pronounces the 'fact' that the brother 'has gone straight to heaven, and that is the simple truth' (198); but he recovers and credits his grand-daughter's vision of doves with gold wings in church, for there are many ways of being true for Morgan.

These twinned reminiscences are followed by 'After Long Absence', a transparently autobiographical representation of returning to her family in Brisbane after many years away. The grandfathers had to cope with memories of translocation, of trajectories not followed as well as the surprising ones that were followed, and now it is Hospital's turn to deal with the past both in and absent from the present. Finishing the definitive Australian edition of *Dislocations* with this story removes the hopeful 'triumph' from its status as the optimistic last word in the book, and gives us a more troubled piece, in which elements of the past can be embraced but others must be rejected, even at the cost of paining people one loves, in order to be true to the self one has become. The teetotal father sipping wine is a massive gesture of 'give', to use Mosie's word, but the daughter will not reciprocate by reading from the Bible at dinner. The cost of emancipating herself from the evangelist values of her family has been too great for her to deny who she is now, even to please them. After all the examples of characters in the book who have 'give', and the general disapprobation of those who do not, there is an irony in finishing the book by depicting a representation of her own narrative self as lacking in 'give'. The last words now are 'black gargoyle wings' (210), deflecting the authority of the 'bright demanding wings' of the 'Holy Spirit' (210) that the narrator's parents invoke as an aid for those facing spiritual difficulties, and it may be that, as Selina Samuels says, this experience 'teaches her something very important: she cannot go home'.[24] Taken along with the other stories in the final triptych, however, it may also suggest that home has been recalibrated through the experience of dislocation to the extent that the narrator rejects many of her parents' values in favour of her commitment to the mixture of more widely referenced, nuanced, colourful and personal truths suggested by the conjunction of her two grandfathers, other representatives of home but, importantly, fellow dislocatees as well.

Home, in fact, can always and yet never be reached, because for people who have undergone disruptive change, it is located above all in memory, given the absence of continuity in space with the time of the past. In the words of His Highness in 'Happy Diwali', '[w]e love best what we have lost forever' (21). The loving here takes place in memory, but memory, as a form of history, is always being rewritten. For Proust, the directed act of recalling is an inferior type of memory, 'the memory of the intellect, and . . . the pictures which that kind of memory shows us preserve nothing of the past itself';[25] it is the involuntary component of memory, working beyond conscious control, that connects more authentically with the past. Nonetheless, for Marcel in *In Search of Lost Time*, the involuntary presence of memory needs to be processed in the present by the self-consciously shaping imagination for its lessons to be learnt; it needs to be translated into art, in other words. For Hospital also, nostalgia, home, memory, summed up as the past, will stun and cripple us without our active involvement in recasting them, and this is all the more necessary for those who 'live at the desiccating edge of things, on the dividing line between two countries, nowhere' (184). Hospital's stories, accordingly, for the most part deny narrative linearity or the certainties of philosophical systems in their insistence on representing the trade back and forth across the dividing line of involuntary memory and the processing sensibility, a liminal mental space in which the properly reflective individual dwells, with dislocation, in many guises, constituting something inherent to the human condition.

CHAPTER 6

Particles, waves and stories
Charades

Horns, what a waste of effort it has been
To give you Creation's vast and exquisite
Dilemma! . . .
We have wasted paradox and mystery on you
When all you ask us for, is cause and effect! –
A copy of your birth-certificate was all you needed
To make you at peace with Creation. How uneconomical
The whole thing's been.

Christopher Fry[1]

Grand unified theories

If *Borderline* was bursting with ideas about responsibility and art, along with narrative strategies complex enough to do justice to Hospital's views on the nature of representation and an ethical stance in the world, *Charades* is even more effervescently engaged with Hospital's intertwined interests in how to act responsibly, how to represent the universe in ways that do justice to its complexity, and how to profit from the operations of personal and cultural memory despite their inherent instability. In articulating these interests, the novel is fascinated by twentieth-century physics, particularly Heisenberg's Uncertainty Principle, and the ongoing search for a Grand Unified Theory. Such theories, in turn, relate to Hospital's preoccupation with our experience of causality and pattern in general, along with the consequences of a postmodern displacement of the certainty of reality or history, in which the test cases here are the nature of the original British encounter with Australia and the apparently very different but ultimately related status of the Holocaust and Holocaust deniers. Interlaced with all of these themes is a celebration of tropical Queensland, which comes to do metaphorical duty as an emblem of Hospital's narrative practice and of her reading of the profuse nature of reality in general.[2] This profuseness is reflected in the construction of both *Borderline* and *Charades* as, in Alistair Stead's words, 'conspicuously hazy hybrids, perpetually evading clear generic classification'.[3]

The novel begins with an eminent MIT physicist reading, his first words being '[t]he grand unified theories'.[4] We soon discover that, while theories may be grand because they attempt to unify explanations of reality, they are difficult to verify in practice. They remain attractive, nonetheless, because they illuminate our understanding of reality in stimulating and intriguing ways, something that could equally well be applied to the explanatory value of stories. The book will consist of the ramifications of this confluence of theoretical physics and fictional storytelling as played out in the contrasting lives and quests of the scientist, Koenig, his lover Charade, and Charade's wider family, principally back in Queensland. As their stories are told, we will see that they are anything but unified in any clear sense, but that they do all belong to a dizzyingly complex unity that perhaps the resources of story are uniquely able to access. Hence the title's echo of Scheherazade, the woman who told tales to save her life and ultimately to change the history predicted for her.[5] In the course of Charade's stories (over the 366 nights she spends with

Koenig), it will be found that the rapidly expanding universe after the Big Bang may be able to be theorised about elegantly, but the rapidly expanding universe of our personal histories from the moment of our conception (a personal 'Big Bang') requires somewhat more unruly narratives.

The first page sets Koenig against Charade, who is cross-referenced with Hospital's previous novel when her eyes are described as 'a kind of borderline blue, intense' (3). And once again we find ourselves in the territory of ambiguous zones, frontiers and blurred margins; between ideas, between identities, between nations and between supposed reality and non-reality. Charade mentions in quick succession the trial of the Holocaust-denier Ernst Zundel in Toronto, Koenig's ex-wife Rachel and Charade's aunt Katherine; and while Koenig is rubbing his eyes in shock at how this unknown woman relates to such personal references, she disappears. Grand unified theories are after all of limited use in the emotional hurly-burly of daily life, where things happen that cast doubt on any unity we think we believe in, and where '[n]othing can be counted on to stay in its proper place' (7). Koenig will become exasperated at Charade's jumping around among the segments of the story of her life, and later, in a sly dig on Hospital's part at the inability of the scientist to transfer the consequences of his speculations from the abstruse realms of theoretical work to the concrete practice of the narratives out of which we build our realities, he will say to Charade: 'Time curves, it can't be helped, but I don't see why plots should' (189–90). When his wife Rachel begins writing letters to dead people, the practical and theoretical ramifications of Koenig's beliefs about the curved nature of time collide and he is unable to cope with her insistence that her dead people are not gone (213).

Koenig means King in German (in an early version of the

book he was called 'King'), a language chosen perhaps because many of the most esteemed scientists in the heroic period of early twentieth-century physics were German or German-speaking (Koenig himself comes from Wisconsin Lutheran antecedents). The novel also explicitly echoes the story of Scheherazade, so that Koenig is a version of the ruler whom she keeps in thrall. This is made apparent in the dorm gossip that characterises his approach as '[a] good fuck, a quick parting kiss, and then off with my lady's head' (13). In line with this, the things Charade says unsettle his assurance and make him want to know more, to see her again; they exist as a test case of his propagation of such theories as Heisenberg's Uncertainty Theory 'about uncertainty as the essence of science, about the *necessity* of uncertainty' (15; Hospital's italics).[6] For despite articulating such theories, he is a controlling and controlled person, albeit unable to control Charade.[7] Charade became Koenig's lover only after being led to him by her Aunt Katherine's story of a night with him, and this positions Charade as the manipulator, the follower of leads, the stitcher together of stories. One of the consequences of this is that she stops Koenig's succession of seductions (like Scheherazade), and one of the ironies is that she turns an apparently random and completed encounter in his life – with Katherine – into something that generates more connection. Charade is not above using her sexuality to get what she wants from men, which is usually what she herself offers – stories. Later in the book, for example, she will have sex with the off-putting English cousin Sefton, in an attempt to get information from him about her father, Nicholas (278).

Charade attributes her sexual boldness to being brought up by a warmly unruly woman with no father present, which meant she 'escaped a lot of that caging, the bound feet business, the stuff that happens to girls everywhere, but especially in Australia'

(17). Hospital is fiercely devoted to her native land, but she is also fierce in her criticism of it. This throwaway comment here, however, is only part of a conversation in which Charade introduces the more significant theme of the search for the absent father in a tale involving an increasingly confusing number of people, a tale that is perplexing Koenig as much as the reader at this point.

Moreover, no-one in the tale corresponds exactly to the way they are labelled, and many characters are further nuanced by being paired with others. Sometimes these pairs represent contrasts, like Bea and Kay, and sometimes different versions of the same, as with Nicholas and Koenig, or Verity and Rachel. Even Koenig and Charade could be seen as a pair, representing different approaches to telling the stories of our reality. Indeed, the multiple various ways in which human beings are connected echo Koenig's ideas about the variable nature of the universe. Charade's 'mother' Bea turns out not to be her mother, and Bea's 'sister' Kay is a childhood friend, someone Bea has grown up with, not really Charade's aunt at all. Another woman, Verity Ashkenazy,[8] who is identified here only as 'the famous Other Woman in the piece' (18), turns out later to be Charade's birth mother. Finally Charade's father, who is a mystery to the extent that 'on even days he doesn't exist and never did' (18), gives the lie to his surname, Truman.[9]

Jennifer Strauss points out that 'the quest for the father' is 'an element that is highly problematic in feminism',[10] and the relation between Charade's desire for Koenig and her search for her father appears to operate in this problematic area. As Strauss goes on to mention, however, part of the feminist suspicion of this theme has to do with the ways in which searching for the father 'seems often to entail disowning the mother',[11] which is the opposite of what happens in *Charades*. Charade will come to realise as she tells the stories that bewitch Koenig that 'her' story is largely the story of her three 'mothers' – Bea, Kay and Verity – and that she has diverted energy into looking for her father when it is her lack of knowledge of her mothers that is more significant, leading to her physical return to her 'mother' Bea, to potential contact with her birth mother now that she has realised who she is, and immersion in the mothering space of the Tamborine Rainforest. Margaret Schramm points out that the quest for the missing father can be read as an allegory in which the protagonist, Charade, needs to integrate the sensual, intellectual and unconscious dimensions of herself in order to become whole. She achieves this through telling the story of the women, who represent three sides of herself – Bea the sensual, Kay the intellectual and Verity the unconscious.[12]

In some way, therefore, *Charades* is a critique of the quest for the father and an imaginative dismantling of his power, in particular the power to occupy the space of authority, to arbitrate on what is reality. Even the sex they soon begin having becomes an activity whereby Charade challenges Koenig's mindset and habits; where formerly Koenig had used women perfunctorily for his sexual release, he now finds that sex is something he cannot take for granted anymore, in terms of either when it will occur or where it will lead in their conversation.

Indeterminacy and origins

Charade is searching for something 'to hang onto' (25), as Koenig is searching for a theory to explain that second just after the Big Bang; and yet she is attracted by theories of indeterminacy and by Koenig's command of such theories as well as by his connection to her Aunt Kay. As an example of the determining effect of indeterminacy she cites Captain Cook's sailing around the Pacific and bumping into the east coast of Australia, without which she would not be here.[13] Once again, Hospital's interest in the butterfly effect is apparent,[14] and it is significant that she chooses an Australian example. On the one hand, it serves to mark the ignorance of Americans about large sections of the globe, and thus to dilute the authority of any American's pronouncements on reality (such as those by Koenig); but it is also an indication of the increasing role of Australia in Hospital's writing at this time.

Whereas in *The Tiger in the Tiger Pit* Australia is a place Emily passes through, and in *Borderline* Australia was a childhood memory for Felicity, in *Charades* it is the site of Charade's origins and thus the setting for much of the book, not just through her own memories but also through those of her 'aunt', Katherine, and later those of her 'mother', Bea. This displaces Charade even more from her 'own' story, and not for nothing does she characterise herself as belonging 'to loss and absence' (261). Moreover, linking Boston, Captain Cook and Australia as intertwined originators of Charade's identity both references the butterfly effect and brings together two of the places that mean the most to Hospital; bringing them together not arbitrarily but in terms that illustrate how locations almost on the opposite sides of the world are in fact inextricably connected. Hospital is a writer for whom apparently disparate realities insist on coming together, which is something that awes her and that she wants us to be awed by. Throughout her work, she returns wonderingly to the way phenomena converge, the way events have unforeseen consequences, and the ways in which human beings make connections that surprise and create new patterns ceaselessly. All the same, there remain realities that do not belong together: Beowulf is imagined sailing along the Great Barrier Reef, but the image breaks down, for there are events that after all 'can't be translated' (198), an important realisation on Katherine's part.

In creating patterns and establishing vectors of significance, people often tend to 'fasten on the trivial' (28), which Charade does not criticise. After all, reality is not made up only of all the connections that have been imagined but also of all the connections that have not yet been thought of, their number infinite: 'the conjectures not yet refuted, the hypotheses not yet dreamed up' (29).[15] No possibility can therefore be ignored, no union of unlikely items can be dismissed, lest it contain the key to a series of events whose consequences are of crucial significance. Here an anxiety about missed connections is blended with a creative playfulness with respect to the possibilities thrown up by the dizzying chains of cause and effect that can be traced from every event. In considering these things, Hospital is also attempting to juxtapose the contrasting ways science and literature deal with them. The basic starting point for this enquiry is the common perception that they consider reality very differently, a position put by Charade, who imagines that for Koenig 'I might as well be speaking Swahili' (39).

For Hospital, however, part of the point of the dialogue between science and literature is not to oppose them but to examine some of the confluences between scientific theorisation and literary experimentation. When Koenig points out that Charade's voice changes when she is telling a story, she counters that his voice changes when he is lecturing. Scientific theory and fiction are related along the axis of the human need for pattern and explanation, and come together in the modes of their telling. Moreover, whether dealing with the universe or with our own lives, as Charade points out, '[a]ny object looked at steadily and intently for too long begins to disintegrate before the eyes' (11), an indication that observation or closeness to something may not guarantee clarity, and that certainly includes observation of or closeness to our own life, supposedly the thing we are most familiar with. For Charade, for example, talking about her mother Bea would be difficult because '[i]t's hardest with someone who's too close' (262). Indeed, even before scientific observation may begin, the protocols or methodologies adopted have already introduced a structuring model for something that, in its interconnection with limitless other variables, is not contained within any structuring model until we devise one. The more we know about these variables and connections the less clear the object becomes; hence the scientific necessity to restrict one's focus, for as one cannot understand anything in all of its connections, one has to choose the boundaries within which one will look. Sometimes this choice takes the form of a wild leap, but such methods, as Koenig admits, 'throw up answers after all. And they reshape the questions too' (110). Even more than that, '[t]he observer, by imposing a particular set of questions, also predetermines the answers he will find' (249).

One way of questioning the realities that are important to us is to start at their beginning, and so we see that both Koenig and Charade focus persistently on origins, whether the origin of the universe or the origins of human lives. Accordingly, the book persistently asks questions about what a beginning might be in a world where everything is connected in as complex a fashion as a rainforest. Not for nothing is Koenig working on the moment at the beginning of time, and not for nothing is Charade obsessed with finding out about her father. For Scheherazade, keeping the beginnings of tales in the middle of her story-telling sessions repeatedly saved her life, and that of others as well, so we see that beginnings are something that we manipulate and that have strategic value depending on the uses they are put to, and the place where we put them, which can actually be in the middle. Charade is constantly going back to beginnings which slip and reshape themselves the more she looks at them. What is a beginning in a world where causes can be traced ever more backwards, ever more outwards, and may be ever more multiple? The beginning may even lie in a fantasy as much as in something that has verifiably happened, for a fantasy after all is something that has happened to the person who imagines it as soon as it is brought into thought. When thirteen-year-old Charade imagines meeting her father in Oxford, this fantasy may be seen as a beginning, the beginning of a quest and an alignment of her priorities, that has shaped her life from that point. While this is a fantasy from one angle, it is something that has had an effect on Charade, and therefore it has entered the real. This means that all stories are real, all fantasies, all projections and all versions of them. More, it means that there is nothing that is not real, there are only different ways of being real, the classification of which remains for us to decide. Yet while Charade says that history and literature are 'two sides of the same coin' (90), discriminating between different realities is nonetheless a constant responsibility, and the vigilance necessary in this enterprise parallels the vigilance necessary in reading God's will in the Evangelist tradition in which Charade's aunt Katherine has been brought up.

The event that Hospital has chosen to illustrate the seriousness of this responsibility, and the danger of accepting all realities as equally real, is that of the Holocaust. A crucial reference point in human destructiveness and brutality, proof that the much-vaunted European 'civilisation', progress and rationality could evaporate under the heat of essentialist classifications of groups of human beings, the Holocaust became for Europe the lesson it had not learnt from the carnage of World War I. To the horror of most people, a movement has developed claiming that the Holocaust never happened, that it was nothing but a Zionist hoax to gain sympathy and legitimation for a Jewish state.[16] Analogously, Charade claims that her parents 'both were and weren't' (45), and, as we later learn, her biological mother is Verity Ashkenazy, whose parents had probably been taken to Auschwitz in 1943, never to be seen again. The trouble with juxtaposing theoretical notions of the fluctuating nature of reality with the Holocaust thus becomes how to discriminate between ways of being and not being, ways of appearing in or disappearing from reality. To what extent do the variable positions in reality of whatever we start considering alter the nature of the ways we consider truth and responsibility? Physicists can treat elements of matter as consisting of waves or particles, depending on the hypothesis they want to test, and depending on whether they are more interested in the momentum or the position of what it is they are examining. Our view of human relations is similarly dependent on our starting point and whatever it is that we wish to find, except that in the latter case real human beings can suffer if we tell the story in a certain way.

One crucial test case for the nature of truth resides in the telling of the story of history, in which beginnings assume powerful symbolic resonance and influence the ways in which a culture views itself. For this reason, the novel touches more than once on the beginning of Australia's post-invasion history, in the shape of the voyages and choices of Captain Cook. Like so many things in this book, places and times are linked where we might not have expected. All Australians know about the importance of Captain Cook in the mapping and opening up of the country for British occupation; but Cook had many years of experience in Canadian waters as well, including sailing up the St Lawrence River with Thomas Wolfe in 1759, so that his history touches on the Queensland locations of the novel as well as the Canadian ones. When Charade talks of Cook to Koenig, she is led to say, 'I'm not making this up . . . This is history' (189). History is both a list of events *and* their significance for those who consider them. Koenig could not care less about Captain Cook, but Charade returns repeatedly to Cook, as a historical touchstone whose existence could not be firmer for the Australian reader, and as the locus of a series of events whose significance remains constantly available to be drawn and redrawn.[17]

The search for Charade's father relates to the same theme (her birth on Australia Day gesturing towards an ironic connection with the nation's Big Bang); despite the significance of her father and of his role in her personal beginning, she does not know where he is or what the nature of his relation to her origins is. In searching for him, she lights upon Koenig, a type of father-figure in a chain of such figures in Charade's life; he even resembles Nicholas Truman enough to have confounded Kay. To get back to her own beginning, Charade not only tells stories, she has had to listen to them, for our beginnings ironically occur at a time when we did not exist, so that the only way to have access to our origins is through the stories of others. Moreover, although we can only have access to our beginnings through stories, which may vary wildly, there does exist the solidity from our point of view that we did in fact begin. In the gap between this certainty and the versions by which it may be delivered to us by others lie the eternal mysteries of causality.

An interest in beginnings naturally leads to the consideration of childhood. Like the childhoods of central characters in Hospital's other books, Charade's childhood is a mixture of being marginalised or bullied because of her difference and of being compensated to some extent by acceptance on the part of someone wildly different – unbookish rebel Michael Donovan. In addition, her Aunt Kay's childhood was similar to that of Charade, yet another version in Hospital's work of her own childhood (when she was marginalised on account of her family's Pentecostalism), calling up the question: 'What was the secret of not minding? Of never being frightened? Of letting *Other*-ness slide off like rain from feathers?' (134; Hospital's italics). Suffering the agonies of feeling different from other children, Kay is intrigued both by an older girl called Verity, who appears dreamily unconcerned about being marked off from the others,[18] and by Bea, who is aggressively opposed to any form of conventional control by others. Our own beginning can only be explained by looking at the contexts in which we were made, which leads us to other people and in turn to their beginnings. We thus see Bea and Aunt Kay as children in Melbourne during World War II, already starkly differentiated into the no-nonsense and cheerfully transgressive Bea as opposed to the fearful and imaginative Kay. Childhood is also characterised here as a time of danger, when people and events can be opaque and threatening, like the American sailor who begins to molest the girls sexually. We see them later in Brisbane, where they continue to represent opposites, with Kay continuing to defer to Bea until the day she sees Nicholas Truman for the first time and fiercely wants him for herself.

Kay is a precursor of Charade, in her sense of difference, in her intensity, but also in her interests even as a child: 'an eighth-grade philosopher obsessed with the laws of causality' (149). As with all of Hospital's positive characters, '[c]lues are the stuff of Kay's daily life; gathering data; drawing conclusions' (150). With reality being the slippery realm that it is, we need to be constantly vigilant, and we need to be as self-consciously wary about the stories we are telling as of the stories we are hearing.

Women, men and rainforests

Faced with time curving and breaking into different pieces whenever she examines it, the solidity of place becomes Charade's touchstone, the place of the Queensland rainforest. *Charades* is Hospital's most developed paean to the power and beauty of the rainforest, a site that she has said has been more meaningful to her than any other, and one that reverberates throughout much of her work. The rainforest is central to her depiction of Australia, the occasion of some of her most intense writing, an intensity arising out of personal memory, to be sure, but also out of its capacity to embody many of Hospital's most privileged areas of concern. For her, landscape is above all an active place, an exemplum of the moral universe of the characters in the way it embodies unruly connectedness. At the same time, in writing of her preferred rainforest landscape, Hospital is often working within the rhetoric of displacement and loss, recurrent themes in her work. By representing the rainforest in this manner, Hospital is both recalling meaningful elements of what was for many years her lost homeland (an experience of loss assuaged, at least to some extent, by the frequent visits to Australia that Hospital's reputation as a writer has brought her since the 1980s), and, through returning in prose to the landscape that she finds most memorable, re-enacting that loss. The rainforest thus becomes a site of narrative and moral intensity in which both loss and gain, displacement and engagement, are referenced. In this way she avoids the exile's temptation to represent landscape simply in terms of nostalgia and uncomplicatedly accessible presence.

As a metaphor for human relations, the inclusive, warm,

enveloping rainforest also relates to a certain current in feminist thought which identifies these qualities as gendered, as feminine. If the rainforest, however, represents a denial of boundaries in general, then perhaps it also resists its use as a specifically and exclusive reference to the feminine. Hospital is as wary of rigidities of identification in this area as in any other. Nonetheless, it is generally women in Hospital's work who respond more readily to the energies of the rainforest, and women who feel more at home there. It could be that the rainforest, in its moist enveloping character, its rhythms of growth and renewal, is itself a feminine body, whose characteristics are transferred both to the metaphor of human relations and to textual structure. In this the rainforest might, in Pam Morris's words, accord 'with the inner specificity of the female body, figuring a mode of self-representation founded on the intimacy of touch'.[19] The rainforest, in its insistence on physical interference and plurality, thus becomes an implicit challenge to the unitary drive of the masculine to define itself and claim the defined certainties of power. Or is the rainforest yet one more construction of the feminine as Simone de Beauvoir's 'dark continent', beyond the pale and unknowable, and hence marginalised?

It might be more helpful to read the rainforest not so much as the warm, essentialised body of the woman, an assertion of a fixed and stable presence, but rather in terms of the body as an important site of woman's resistance to patriarchal authority: the body which women have used, consciously or not, in myriad ways, to present or imagine themselves in practices that deny or subvert their historically subordinate and objectified position within environments of asymmetric power relations. These practices, from celibacy through to self-mutilation, have been characterised by the male order as excess, as hysteria, as immoderation. If the rainforest exists as a metaphorical challenge to assertions of order, separation, boundaries, and to the irreponsibility of division, then it may be a body whose vigorous biological energy can be seen to function further as a profuseness that cannot be controlled by men.

The body that is the emblem of this link between the rainforest and procreation is that of Charade's 'mother' Bea, a name alluding to both the basic condition of existence (to be) and an insect associated with matriarchy. Given the appellation 'slut of the Tamborine rainforest' by the local population, Bea is enthusiastic about sex and procreation. Already as a child her friend Kay sees Bea as part organic, imagining that 'Bea's fingers and toes were sprouting little green pads, that her hair was green, that she was part of the plum tree and the buttercup patch' (126–7). A representative of an uncomplicated way of relating to life, Bea is a woman who lives connection; insisting on rigid boundaries seems out of place in the rainforest. With a large and friendly appetite for male attention, she proceeds to produce numerous children by different men, and even to adopt others. In this rainforest, men are surreptitious visitors, both ever-present and absent, their problematic relationship to the place perhaps suggested by the dead body Charade finds when she is a child, a man caught in the vines and clinging trails of creepers, unable to escape. This is a place in which a man can only be transient, for if he stays too long he will be trapped and killed. More, he will even be feminised himself, as the dead body swells up in a type of pregnancy,[20] giving birth in this instance to more nutrients for the rainforest, and thus replenishing it. In this rainforest, men retreat to the masculine certainties of the pub, the sphere of culture, surrendering that of nature to women. This is a conventional opposition, except that nature is not simply emblematised in the book as something womanly to be mastered by men. Here, nature is occupied by a woman, whose at-homeness in the forest reduces the local men and the zone of culture to something subservient to her power.

It could be said that the book asserts the rainforest as a site of woman's resistance, then, but at the same time it also appears to collude with another patriarchal construction of woman that sees them as destructive: the rainforest being a version of the enveloping and incorporating *vagina dentata*. Bea becomes a sort of witch who takes 'men's' children while denying them power in her world. The supposed enveloping destructiveness of women is a myth identified with atavistic male fears of women's procreative power, and Hospital is very aware of how men's fears of women and women's sexuality can turn to violence, as we have seen in *The Ivory Swing*, and will see in stories such as 'The Last of the Hapsburgs' or 'The Second Coming of Come-by-Chance', not to mention *A Very Proper Death* or *The Last Magician*. After the centrality of violence against women in *Borderline*, however, in *Charades* Hospital has moved to a world where women are more in control than men, where women feel more comfortable and where men feel somewhat disempowered by them. Rather than male discomfort with the book's main female characters developing into violence, though, it generally develops into becoming intrigued, or even into a sensation of resigned acceptance. The men who live around Bea are in awe of her, and she takes no nonsense from anyone. Koenig is so disturbed by Charade that he becomes dizzy when confronted by a hologram of her, an indication of the fact that he is unable to pin her down, but at no time does he wish to punish or belittle her. Bruce Merry points out that '[t]he males in the text all seem to have a flaw',[21] but one flaw they generally do not have is that of wanting to inflict harm on women.

Despite her loving handling of Queensland via the rainforest, Hospital is stern in her treatment of certain aspects of the history and myths of Australia as a whole. Several quotes from sources relating to the nation's early history reveal a foundation that was poisoned by hostility to the Indigenous inhabitants (albeit only touched on here), an excessive investment in punishment, and an extreme version of the centrality of men. In an invented originary folk tale, the King of England questions his two sons and a daughter, and prefers his daughter's answer to how to deal with the preponderance of males and maleness in the country's foundation: 'You must ensure that the men of that dreamplace continue to despise and ridicule and underestimate the women, she said. Then the women will learn laughter and independence and they will survive' (68).

The principal men associated with the Tamborine Rainforest are uneducated men such as Mick Donovan. Hospital has a special sympathy for the rough-and-tumble of demotic Australian society, which can perhaps be seen as a legacy of a general Australian valorisation of the common bloke or the no-nonsense woman. Charade's 'mother' Bea is a manifest example of the latter, bossing men around, not taking any nonsense, but not wasting much time worrying about their sexist banter or hopeful groping either. In this, however, she conforms to the only type of woman that men are happy to permit into the masculine space of the public bar, the barmaid who can give as good as she gets. Bea's experience as a barmaid has given her an insider's knowledge of men, and thus a type of power over them. Any woman who cannot put up with the rough and tumble of interaction with men, according to Bea, is 'High and Mighty' (62), maybe because they have read too many books. The men who hang around her are versions of a type of man who is warm-hearted but ignorant, albeit potentially dangerous depending on circumstances, with the tendency always to lapse into the snarling victimisation of difference, superbly delineated in *The Last Magician* and *Oyster*, and touched on in *Charades* when the rural pub crowd rounds on the delicate Verity (72–8). In another example, Michael Donovan's father speaks feelingly about the piglets who choke because people put paper and plastic in Food Only bins for material to be recycled as pigfood; he also likes to paint on the sides of old tea chests, but he beats Michael mercilessly when he feels inadequate and exposed. The tension between the demotic and the erudite provides one of the emotional stress-points of Hospital's work. University education and the discourses it generates are frequently criticised by positive characters, such as Bea, despite Hospital's obvious admiration for and spirited participation in such an environment. And in good two-things-contained-in-one fashion, Bea shortly after this criticism shows how much Nicholas Truman means to her, including his ostentatiously educated language, for she thinks of him as 'the golden talker with tales on his breath' (316), ever a positive reference for Hospital. In their relation to the demotic/erudite split, Bea and Kay are like two sides of Hospital's value-system, one more of the twinned pairs in her fiction.

Recording the plasticene past

When words are so ambiguous and multifarious in their meanings, another way of telling ourselves things about our history is through the supposed recording device of the camera. Hospital interrogates the nature of photographs in *Borderline*, *Charades*, *The Last Magician*, *Due Preparations for the Plague* and *Orpheus Lost*, as well as in short stories such as 'The Second Coming of Come-by-Chance', pointing out their artifice, their staged quality, even their lack of congruence with their subjects; after all, the way we often recoil in horror from photographs that supposedly register us should give us pause about the truth value of any photograph. At the same time, Hospital is fascinated by the effects that photographs can have on account of their claim to being a record, and our willingness to accept this. Like any other sign, however, they have to be read, to be decoded. All of our social interactions involve constant decoding of even the most apparently innocent and everyday actions, but we carry out this interpretation in physical contexts that are absent when we look at a photograph, which finishes at its borders and leaves us to imagine what it relates to beyond those limits. Looking at the same photograph of her 'mother' and father and Verity, for example, the young Charade finds a different history every day. The variety of the histories she finds attests to the mysteries that photographs conceal as well as their power to push us to story-making. Bea claims a photo 'is no more use than a snakeskin after the snake has crawled out' (86), which begs the question that occurs when one comes across a snakeskin: where is the snake? A photo directs us, it is true, but just as we do not know in which direction to look for the snake, neither do we know for certain in which direction to look with a photograph, as anyone who has participated in a 'Spot the Ball' competition can attest. We project, speculate, invent, imagine.

Photographs, indeed, encapsulate from one more angle the central conundrum of the book, one that is as invigorating as it is troubling: how can reality both be and not be at the same time?[22] For while photographs are invitations to extend and conjecture, they are also a reality that can help to keep the liars from winning, as demonstrated in the Zundel trial when Koenig's ex-wife, Rachel, identifies herself in a photograph of Holocaust prisoners

(224). How, then, can we construe Katherine's youthful defiance: 'I can do what I like with the past; it is easy as plasticene; it only exists now and then' (164)? It is no accident that within minutes Verity tells Katherine that that day is the anniversary of the last day she saw her parents, a day on which we gather her parents were transported to a concentration camp, while she was saved by a schoolteacher at the last minute. The past is in fact not easy at all, and we cannot do what we like with it, even if it does invite the active participation of human beings in representing it and in devising strategies to deal with its pains, pleasures or gaps. Verity has been unable to ward off the destruction of her security and references, and she remains an outsider in the present: she cannot do what she likes with the past.

The book reminds us that, just as science has to consider certain aspects of reality differently depending on the context, just as photographs may be both uncontrovertible and incomplete, so also the past is plasticene *at the same time as it is not*, depending on context. Contextualising thus becomes the central activity of our existence, with all that it demands of us as active readers and moral witnesses. The game 'Charades', after all, is one in which we have to interpret people's actions and translate them into more recognisable language. In the contextualising process, literature serves as a perpetual witness to and exemplar of our hermeneutic responsibility, but this interposes a further level of reality and responsibility, for the reader has to be vigilant against the author's manipulation (as we have seen in *Borderline*), whether playful, earnest, cynical or accidental. As Bea tells Kay: 'I could tell you anything, you were so stupid' (175). We tell and are told stories constantly, and while Kay's innocence is embarrassing at the time and in retrospect, it is also evidence that she does not accept the readings of most people around her, that she has her own frameworks. The trouble is, the same could be said of Zundel. Scientists challenge each other's versions of reality, while still accepting what is termed 'translational invariance', that is, that the laws of physics are the same everywhere, and the same now as they were at any time in the past or will be at any time in the future. In daily life, however, in challenging another's version, we may be challenging something central to their very identity, denying that they exist in the terms they propose. When a fellow student tells Kay that Verity is not tragically Jewish at all, Katherine sees this as a destructive impulse to demythologise, which, if not resisted at least partially, bleeds significance and care out of the world. This is an example of a type of version that must be resisted. Later in her life she shows she did not believe this account, associated as it is with a no-nonsense Australian view of reality that the book both validates – principally through Bea – and does not validate.

The narrative worlds of the present and the past in the book come together in Katherine's mistaken belief that she has spotted Nicholas in Toronto. Not only does 'Nicholas' turn out to be Koenig, but it appears to Katherine that Koenig's former wife, Rachel, had come from the same town as Verity in France. Ironically, however, Katherine has transformed her memory of the occasion to establish this link between them, since, as Charade finds out later, Rachel was not from Le Raincy at all. Even more significantly, Katherine remembers the occasion very differently from Koenig, who claims that they caught sight of each other in the gallery at the Zundel trial, the attraction being so intense that they left the chamber to find a hotel. Both Holocaust-deniers and Katherine have needs that lead them to alter history, so we are faced with the perpetual responsibility to arbitrate between histories and the uses to which they are put. Rachel, after all, is in

Toronto to bring charges against the Holocaust-deniers for anti-Semitism. From one angle, however, Holocaust-deniers are doing no more than everybody does as they intervene in history and make the connections that are important to them. Even if Koenig were the one altering the story of his encounter with Katherine, this would still prove the point. If everybody from Zundel to Katherine is doing no more than everybody else, how vulnerable does that leave us to having our stories altered, and what form can any appeal to historical truth take? How can our responsibility to others and to events be equated with the possibility that our words are so unstable? Is it true that, as Charade despairs, '[w]e all go round in circles, we're doomed' (261)?

Knowledge, accordingly, is looked at by the book from the differing angles associated with each of the principal characters. Charade explains to Koenig that she 'had to know everything' (263), and her desire to know, to make connections, is positioned positively, her constant telling of stories a version of this. In telling stories, we approach knowing. If we do not tell stories we cannot make connections, and without the connections we establish we are at the mercy of others' stories, not that Charade believes there is only one story, or that the connections between causes and events are linear. There are many ways in which connections operate, and one of Hospital's favourite areas of theoretical physics, chaos theory, tells us that they may operate in dizzyingly complex fashions, but that does not mean there are not connections or that we are subject to random meaninglessness. Charade may claim to be 'an editor of my own past' (263), and note the indefinite article here, but this is not so much to admit to tampering with the 'truth' as to show that she is self-conscious about what we all do whether we admit it or not. She realises that she intervenes actively in constructing reality, analogously to the theoretical physicist who knows that she or (more usually) he is involved not simply in discovering reality but in writing it in such a way that we can read it better. Importantly, to be able to read reality better often means that we need to be self-conscious about the fact that reality is always mediated and never comes to us directly or purely. Charade's realisation that you have to tell history from as many angles as you can to get at something of its truths is a realisation supported by the novel, despite Bea's assertion: 'who ever believed a word [Charade] said?' (287). Everybody in the book, however, is a storyteller, everybody occludes and disseminates just the version(s) that they want or that are strategically suitable for them, including bluff, honest Bea, who keeps from Charade the truth about her mother.

As is usual in Hospital's world, working on one's history involves exposure to mysteries, secrets, other versions and people who are trying to keep things from us. One of the principal sources of the destabilisation of history in Hospital's work is the family, as we have seen in *The Tiger in the Tiger Pit* and *Borderline*. Supposedly the places where people know each other best, or feel most secure, families are the location for the most strategic retellings of history, the most desperate need to persuade or hide or manipulate others. Sites of connection they may be, but they are also sites of separation, friction and anxiety, as outlined superbly by Freud in his classic essay called in English 'The Uncanny'.[23] It is not surprising that a pair of aunts refer to Nicholas as '[a] born storyteller . . . a compulsive liar' (273); in contrast, Charade says to Koenig, '[a] born storyteller, you're not' (240). This is refined in cousin Sefton's words to 'the same story over and over again, a thousand versions' (278). Ironically, the 'thousand' resonates with the book's references to the Thousand Nights, a positive reference for a novel in which the generation of stories is something that makes us most human and most alive, while if there is anyone who is a compulsive storyteller and who keeps retelling different versions of the same story, it is Charade. This same story is a story of family, that site in which our own 'big bang' occurs and our own universe is set in motion. Everyone is a family storyteller in this novel, in which Charade is led to believe so many accounts of her family history that she becomes confused about where exactly she did come from, thus paralleling the human condition with respect to our origins.

Not the thousand and first night

In the quest to uncover her origins, Charade is led back to another of Australia's own origins – England. Hyper-respectable English sisters Penelope and Alicia have taken on the responsibility of keeping up Charade's wider family tree, a type of story, of recording, that attempts to hold on to a version of order, of links, but which is constantly branching out in uncontrollable and unknowable directions. Charade embodies the unruly exuberance of family histories, coming as she does from the disreputable, out-of-wedlock side of the family. Humorous byplay is made of how one of the consequences of Empire – supposedly carrying the upright values of the British middle class – was the ungovernable breakdown of family patterns, leading to Anglo-Indian, South African and Canadian cousins, not to mention the 'provincial' Australians. Observing the maiden aunts, Hospital is indulging a pleasure in detailing minute textures that tell stories themselves – habits, gestures, intonations – a Jamesian lingering over surfaces which she scrutinises particularly when considering the upper middle-class. The English tend to be skewered in her fiction, exposed in a smarmy sense of superiority, so that the critique of recent Australian cinema by cousins Marlow and Sefton is rendered suspect by their depiction as hollow poseurs.

For Sue Gillett, Charade's 'comic encounter with her eccentric distant relations undermines the expectation of a complete and original presence'.[24] Helga Ramsey-Kurtz, in turn, sums up the failure of Nicholas or Koenig as ultimate reference points as nothing less than a discovery of 'the post-colonial "misalliances" Australia maintained with England and with America'.[25] In this reading, America and England are both found wanting as progenitors, self-absorbed and unable to connect their histories to that of Australia in any meaningful way, leaving it to Australians to write the stories of their own history, in the course of which Captain Cook is revealed as 'an individual as flawed as the two most important men in Charade's life, Nicholas Truman and Koenig'.[26]

The principal story Charade thinks she is telling is the story of her search for her father. In this story, Charade can never quite place where Verity fits in. Although Verity had a relationship with Nicholas, she remains elusive, as difficult to tie down in narrative as she was difficult to tie down in a conversation. Verity's special status is derived from her family's history (via her parents), linked as it is to the principal touchstone for our responsibility to history in the novel – the Holocaust. While details concerning Verity's past emerge slowly throughout the novel, it transpires that the main area of obscurity concerns her relation to family history (via her daughter Charade), echoing in some way her relation to world history. We learn eventually that the mysterious visits that Bea makes over a period of years to an institution in Goodna, west of Brisbane, are in fact visits to Verity. At first it appears we are visiting an old friend called Maeve, also known as 'Sleeping Beauty', adrift in her private memories.

The name 'Sleeping Beauty' alludes to the register of the tales told by Scheherazade, tales in which scarcely believable or frankly unbelievable characters and events abound, but which nevertheless speak to common human fears and desires (echoing the 'tales' told by theoretical physicists). In the case of Sleeping Beauty, the label is somewhat ironic and makes various suggestions at the same time. From one angle, Sleeping Beauty is a woman waiting for a man to wake her so that she can function, which in Maeve's case seems unlikely. From another, more general angle, Sleeping Beauty can be seen as a woman condemned to passivity or inaction by forces beyond her control. Widening the aperture further still, what is really 'asleep' is the meaning of this strange woman that Bea visits regularly, for no reason that the young Charade can discern.

The extraordinary nature of realities that are both ordered and beyond comprehension in terms of quite how or why the ordering works are referenced, yet again, in the epigrams from John Ashbery and from Neil McAleer's *The Mind-Boggling Universe* with which the novel's final section begins. The dream, with which the chapter proper starts, operates in a related way, bringing together references and apparently unconnected places and people. It may be that after all we should realise that reality has the order of dreams, that the multiple reference points and apparently absurd configurations of the dream correspond to how we should conceptualise reality, which is more dreamlike than we allow. In this type of reality, Australia and Cambridge, Massachusetts, are on the same loop and tunnels run from Sydney to Brisbane to Harvard Square, from where buses depart for Goodna. As if underlining the links between the logic of dreams and the nature of reality, in this dream the beginnings of an answer are afforded to Charade, for as the apparently absurd connections mount up within the dream they activate buried memories, and Charade remembers with a start that Sleeping Beauty must have been Verity. When she rings Bea for confirmation, Bea asks why '*knowing* is so great' (337; Hospital's italics), but of course the novel validates knowing always, even if knowing takes several forms. Charade has not found her father, but she has found her mother, who she was not looking for and did not know she did not know. In Bea's words, 'There's things that happen, and there's things that *matter*' (338; Hospital's italics). Hospital's work does not valorise not knowing, but at the same time it is aware that knowing is always already evaluating, judging, placing, and in this sense not simply acceding to truths but actively deciding what matters and how.

One way in which it does matter is that knowing who her mother is activates Charade's sense that she should be at home in Australia. The truth indicated by Verity's name has finally been revealed, and, indeed, Bea's and Kay's sexual connection with Nicholas makes both of them versions of Charade's 'mother' as well. Her travels in search of her father have apparently led her astray into the arms of Koenig, a university professor as Nicholas was, and also a man who has left the mother of his children as well as his children, as Nicholas did; but the knowledge she gathers from her repeated telling of stories during this relationship allows her unconscious to piece together the scraps into a knowledge that sutures after all.

The last short chapter contains Koenig speculating on the reality of reality and of the reality of Charade. In his analysis, her quest was asking 'unanswerable questions about the nature of psychic damage, about the role of victim, about blame and responsibility' (342), linked to the Zundel trial and the intertwining of history and accountability. Charade's father has abandoned his children and become a trace that she follows but can never catch, and perhaps analogously the book suggests that we can live in a world of an absent father, although we do need stories of him. In an interview, Hospital recognises the further reverberations of this: 'The sense of a deep desire to project some meaning and order onto all this flux, that's what religious literature is about – storytelling about an absence. I would say that's the genre in *Borderline* and *Charades* . . . storytelling about absences.'[27] Koenig's musing on Charade's father's name throws up the Christian appellations: 'Saint Nick? Old Nick' (342), intimating both good and evil in Hospital's repeated splitting or destabilisation of any name or term. In this view, the absent father has the potential to be anything, positive or negative, or perhaps both at the same time. Koenig has been the most visible father-figure throughout the novel, and he too has multiple significances, both stimulating and disappointing. Koenig becomes important to Charade as she works her way to her own theories of origins, as she charms the King in her role as Scheherazade; but at the end, unlike Scheherazade, she does not stay with him.

The American novelist Valerie Miner feels that the relationship between Charade and Koenig 'is left appropriately open. All you know is that they are both the better for their idiosyncratic affair.'[28] For Ramsey-Kurtz: 'Koenig . . . learns to accept at last that the ending of Scheherazade's story takes place outside the world he knows.'[29] In addition, Koenig has been unable to generate the grand unified theory he announced at the book's beginning, something that has seemed about to be reached several times over the last hundred years but which has continued to evade the confident predictions of physicists that they would 'solve' the description of reality for all time.[30] Charade's stories, however, have dissolved Koenig's certainties, as Scheherazade's dissolved those of King Shahryar. At one point in the novel, Koenig admits to having been thoroughly bamboozled by a performance of Christopher Fry's *The Lady's Not for Burning*, of which he could follow neither the plot nor the language: 'There are metaphors as convoluted as octopi, he can't make head or tail of it' (243). What he does realise is that he is overwhelmingly attracted to the actress playing the lady accused of being a witch, whom he later marries. This woman turns out to be a survivor of the Holocaust, who, like Verity, has been unable to overcome the trauma of the experience, and Koenig ends up not being able to make head or tail of her either. The two most important women in his life have thus been women he cannot read at all, women whose relation to their stories has exemplified the curvatures of time and doubleness of reality that he can theorise about but not live. In the book's final words, however, he is unable to call Charade, for he 'wishes to keep the ending open' (345), so that perhaps, at last, he is now living the consequences of his theorisation of the universe. Nevertheless, there is still something missing. In Margaret Schramm's summary: 'Unlike Koenig, Charade has conquered her past by accepting the uncertainty of it and by acting on her sense of responsibility for those she loves.'[31] Responsibility is as uncertain a concept as any, with no chance of ever being defined in a way that everyone can agree on, but if we make no effort to understand our origins, to tell and listen to stories endlessly, and to be open to the ways reality can be and not be at the same time,[32] we will have little chance of arriving at a dynamic and informed sense of what it might be.

CHAPTER 7

'All the signs on Four Mile Beach' *Isobars*

Human beings are the only creature to feel alone and the only one who exists as the search for the other.

Octavio Paz[1]

Where is the connection?

The success of Hospital's work in the 1980s brought many offers of positions as writer-in-residence or visiting professor, the most significant of which was that at MIT (1985–89). Among the offers were several from Australia, and in taking up some of them (Sydney 1989, La Trobe 1989–90, Melbourne 1990), Hospital was able to spend extended periods in the country of her birth for the first time since she had left in 1967. While Australia had figured increasingly in Hospital's work during the 1980s, the time now spent in the country led to an almost exclusive focus on Australian locations and issues in her next three books, including most of the material in *Isobars*.[2] The volume is a brilliant collection of stories that focus on multiple acts and varieties of violence and pain, along with how people deal with and represent them. From the chilling 'The Last of the Hapsburgs', which ends with a male assault on women's attempts to construct a zone of solidarity and non-competitive friendship, to the droll 'The Chameleon Condition', which imagines how it might be if a philandering professor involuntarily displayed his responses to the world through changes in skin colour, the volume ranges through anger to a wise appreciation of our efforts to erect bulwarks against the depradations of time and loss. Hospital's sharp and clever prose never meanders as it responds to what Bruce Bennett calls 'the challenge of mixed genres (essay/narrative, satire/romance, crime/religion)'.[3] Each story manages to surprise in its engagement with her basic themes, the most central of which could be summed up as our moral witness of others.

The first piece in the volume, 'Isobars: A Fugue on Memory', begins with a simple question with an apparently simple answer: 'Where does a circle start? Wherever one decides.'[4] The whole volume explores the ramifications of this question and answer in ways that underline the fact that this book is not so much a volume of separate stories as an isobar itself, a line connecting points of equal pressure, related to the manner in which *Dislocations* had also played variations on linked themes. The fact that it is an 'imaginary line' (1) licenses Hospital's subsequent exploration of the bends in space and time through which human beings make connections, or, according to Charlotte Clutterbuck, fail to connect.[5] Thus it is that the first piece in the volume centres on placing human beings, specifically women, in danger. Hospital admits that 'the damaged woman is a constant theme in my writing',[6] the damage arising principally from the violence of men, from fathers to lovers to authority figures. In this light, we are faced with the responsibility of observing well in this introductory piece, which is a critical meditation rather than a conventional story. Is that a woman laughing or is she being murdered? Is that man cleaning fish with a knife or is he stabbing the woman? Is that a representation of a knife against a real person's throat or is it the gratuitous bad taste of writing about violence? It is not just our perceptiveness that makes the connections, or misses them, but our ability to reach past what look like solid obstacles to possibilities of solidarity with others. *Isobars* thus becomes an appeal to our vigilance and to the ways in which we interpret and represent what we see, as Hospital's fiction moved in the direction of a darker vision of the tensions between the individual and social relations in which some form of violence seems inescapable.[7]

Throughout the book we have scenario after scenario in which characters need to interpret violent or distressful events, whether in the form of direct aggression, of oppressions occasioned by ethnicity, gender or class, or of the disruption brought about by anguishing loss or death. Monica, in the most gentle piece in the volume, 'Now I Lay Me Down to Sleep', thinks her way through her own impending death. As she and her brother Kevin stroll through Boston streets to the plot in the cemetery where she wishes to be buried, the vectors of family bonds, secrets and unfulfilments surface in her thoughts and their conversation. The mood is one of calmness, and life is characterised as a series of adjustments and resignations. The small triumph of Monica's brief affair with a bigamist without her mother's knowing makes her and her brother laugh uproariously as they lie on Monica's plot at the end. The minor scale of Monica's assertion of self against the pressures of Boston Irish Catholic family mores does not lead her to despair or remorse. Being able to lie on one's own plot in a graveyard and laugh is a form of triumph, for the imposition of blandness and respectability on a woman's life is, after all, one more of the many levels of violence visited upon women. Monica thus takes her place in Hospital's notable gallery of tough women who resist the varied affronts of their lives without whining or petulance.

'Now I Lay Me Down to Sleep' is unusual, for in general the stories show more conflict or troubling distance between human beings. Katharine, in 'To Be Discontinued', relates how an experiment showed men and women the same image of a couple on a bench, and while the women see love, more than twenty per cent of the men see 'homicide, suicide, jealousy, stabbing, kidnapping, rape' (123). How the distance between perception and meaning is traversed depends not just on how characters decode the signs but on how they are predisposed to demonstrate solidarity towards fellow human beings, something that is more easily managed in Hospital's world by women. In 'To Be Discontinued', a writer in the twilight of his career muses on 'the task of language, the task of narrative, to *connect* the random events' (120; Hospital's italics), but the experiment Katharine recalls shows that every perception is always already an exercise of decoding. As Katharine looks out of the window and observes people, she begins to interpret them and to connect them at the same time. Just as we are being engaged by the story she is constructing, we are placed on the other side of the events, only to find that the situation is ironically almost the reverse of what Katharine had imagined. Nonetheless, while Katharine may have constructed an erroneous narrative, the fact that she attempts to connect the people she observes indicates a necessary human response to others. The characters in the story slide incessantly between their memories and their relentless but speculative interpretation of what goes on around them, leaving the question supposedly asked by Einstein when he bumped into the then-young narrator at Princeton University in 1932 as an encapsulation of our discontinuous relation to wherever we are in space and time: 'can you tell me ver iss we are?' (128). The story's gentle humour confirms Einstein's own proof of the relativity of space and time not simply in the abstruse realms of theory or at the scale of unobservable atomic systems, but in the humble human here and now.

In dealing with the variability of reality, it is not simply a matter of reading the signs correctly, which would establish a hermeneutic of verifiable meaning – if only we learn to read the signs properly we will know what the truth is – as if only one meaning were the right one. And yet, the book points out, there are contexts in which it is crucial that one meaning prevail over others. After all, no matter how variegated reality may be, the policemen's raping of Adeline Crick and their framing of local Aborigines in 'The Second Coming of Come-by-Chance' is not merely one among a number of equally valid versions. Here Hospital faces up once more to one of the practical consequences of the contemporary idea that reality has no objective basis and is merely a collection of different stories told about it. If this is true, where does that leave the stories told by victims of violence? Where does that leave Adeline Crick's story of being raped by policemen? At the same time, Hospital is not a supporter or practitioner of a straightforward realism in which the version of a narrator can be trusted. In several stories we see that the version that is factually wrong cannot be simply rejected, for it might serve other purposes, purposes moreover that are positive in Hospital's moral universe. This dilemma is repeated throughout *Isobars* and her work in general: how to distinguish between representations when it is not just a matter of deciding whether such and such a version is correct but also what purpose it serves? In many cases, decoding 'incorrectly' is a more positive and useful activity than decoding more 'reasonably'. It is often rather a matter of reading the signs in such a way as to affirm the possibility of human solidarity and to make a connection with others against the depredations of violence. As five-year-old Emily asks in 'Isobars': 'Is anyone allowed to change places?' (8). And the implicit answer is that we are not; to be the male wielding the knife is not to be the woman under attack. It does matter where we are situated on the isobar, for where human lives are concerned there is no such thing as equal pressure points.

The language of micemutters

Two of the first stories are central in stating the issues at stake. 'The Last of the Hapsburgs', one of Hospital's most memorable, is a rich example of her compression of several story-lines into a few brief pages. The story shows from different angles how difficult it is to empower a space for oneself outside the imperatives of normalising conventions, here linked specifically with male priorities, in rural Australia. It begins as a depiction of a schoolteacher exulting in the north Queensland landscape while regretting the unintellectual customs of the area. Soon Lucia Davenport is hearing of an even more spectacularly displaced family – the last of the Hapsburgs in local slang. The next jump takes us to this family's house, a Black Forest farmhouse in the tropics, where mittel-European immigrants have retreated to enjoy a life of books and classical music, an existence inflected by loss and difference of an intensity unimaginable to Miss Davenport.[8]

Shortly after, Miss Davenport invites the family's daughter, Rebecca, and Hazel, an Aboriginal outsider, for an affirming swim in Mossman Gorge. Three boys appear, shout abuse, defecate in the water and steal their clothes. Her response is to think: 'The acts of men, even when they are boys . . . are shouts that rip open the signs that try to contain them. We have no access to a language of such noisiness. Our voices are micemutter, silly whispers' (27). The teacher is unable to explain the event to the girls, her authority negated by a few boys.

The story indicates one origin of the oppositions that generate the violence that courses through Hospital's work, that is, in childhood. Adult language and adult gestures are seen to arise out of, or to battle against, the establishment of deeply rooted power structures, so that by the time characters are adult what is left is often salvage, evasion or survival, whether they have fled from the other side of the world or have never left the district. This does not stop either Hospital or her characters from being angry, from speaking, but it does render that speaking as a problem. If men, from an early age, occupy noisiness, what language is available for women other than micemutter, even for the teacher who supposedly commands wisdom and language. More importantly, how can this be either resisted or used to subvert the structures of repression and silencing it embodies?[9]

In many ways, 'The Second Coming of Come-by-Chance' deals with similar material to 'The Last of the Hapsburgs'. In both stories we have female schoolteachers who are outsiders in rural Queensland communities, and who attempt to connect with other local outsiders, including Aborigines. Their reward for this transgression is to be defiled by local males. In 'The Second Coming of Come-by-Chance' Adeline is raped by two local policemen, who subsequently frame the Aborigines Adeline has been visiting, more than one of whom are later hanged. This means that not only does Adeline feel tainted but she also feels responsible for the death of the Aborigines: 'I have the blood of innocent men on my hands' (50). There is a puzzle, however; indeed, there are several puzzles in this dense short story. Why is this tale of corruption and violence contained within a story describing the re-appearance of a town from the receding waters of the Burdekin Dam, and the apocalyptic responses this emergence stimulates? An answer appears to lie in the problems of representation cited above.

After its biblical opening lines, 'The Second Coming of Come-by-Chance' begins to explore the problem that any unusual event throws up: the wildly different analyses of its significance. A young lad had fallen into the water and found himself face to face with a church, and then we read how the Bishop of Queensland interprets the incident, as well as the version of the local pastor. Newspaper reports follow, but are tainted by what was once the lofty southern dismissal of anything that happened in Queensland, and we are positioned by narratorial sarcasm to feel that there is something inadequate about all of the accounts. In the competing versions of the second coming of Come-by-Chance, moreover, the realistic fabric of the tale is rent by one strange detail – although everybody present at the site can see the town re-emerging from the waters, 'no trace of it showed up in photographs' (42). With the photographs of the occurrence absent here, it is left to words to mediate the event. If both newspapers and local observers are not to be trusted, how can we deal with events that are so surprising that we do not have easy explanations of them or verifiable representations of any sort?

We are in this unstable position when Adeline enters the story, after the quotation from the Banjo Paterson poem which made the place-name famous.[10] We have suddenly moved from the collective energies of versions that are all untrustworthy for different reasons (and the fabrication of Paterson's poem could be said to belong in related territory), as well as from mockery to fierce concern. Whatever people wish to make of a town reappearing from the depths, there are things that emerge from the depths that should not be scoffed out of existence or left to the hurly-burly of competing interpretations, yet at no time is Adeline's story of rape by men entrusted with society's authority permitted to gain credence. What seems to unite the two types of evidence is that they all emanate from men. No matter how far-fetched or biased, men's interpretations constitute the majority of public discourse. As in 'The Last of the Hapsburgs', men largely own language in rural areas, and women's versions are reduced to 'micemutters'.

By going out to visit the Aborigines, Adeline had doubled the desire of the policemen to punish her, both as a woman and as sullied by contact with Aborigines, the two categories seen by the policemen as submissive objects to be dominated and oppressed. When Adeline refuses to be cowed and says she is going to tell, her version simply evaporates before the power of official renditions, leading to what Selina Samuels sums up as 'her terrifying insight into the arbitrary nature of truth and of experience'.[11] Adeline in fact suffers from two opposed scenarios. In the first, when the event happens, only the official stories possess power and hers is ignored. In the second, many years later, when stories multiply in all directions, the result is just as harmful, for stories of extreme experience that deviate from the customary narratives consume each other, leaving all of them vulnerable to manipulation and rejection. When all stories are debased by this proliferation, then not even the stories that should be told are believed.

'The Second Coming of Come-by-Chance' brilliantly sets up the dilemma: which stories to validate? How can we make our way through the competing uses to which stories are put? Is there a limit to the number of versions we can tolerate? What happens to the extraordinary story when all stories are extraordinary? Is there any way to determine where our ethical responsibility to truth lies among such hermeneutic conundra? Logically, there is not, and the story remains troubling for not delivering tidy answers or neat justice. Types of answer, however, are provided by other stories in the book, particularly by the possibility that one may attempt to resist the ethical anomie that one is cast into through solidarity with the suffering of others.

Decoding bodies

The story 'Dear Amnesty' focuses in puzzling fashion on the complications brought about by empathy as Sarah becomes so absorbed in her letter-writing activities on behalf of prisoners taken up by Amnesty that she begins to bear the physical marks suffered by Rosita, one of the prisoners, on her own body. These connections cause her pain, but also a measure of satisfaction in that she feels linked to someone after her husband of many years, yet another injuring male, has left her. Her past is not a location she can comfortably occupy, so her reaching out to Rosita also becomes a way of coping with her displacement from her own history. As she experiences the pain of Rosita she believes, in the words of the doctor (another voice of conventional reason, like the doctor in 'The Chameleon Condition' and the newspapers in 'The Second Coming of Come-by-Chance'), that she is 'draining off some of her pain into [her] own body', in what the doctor terms 'sympathetic magic' (101). Despite the doctor's kindly attempts to get her to let go of this attachment, her neighbour, Mrs Donovan, has quite another interpretation, blithely denying any possibility other than 'women's problems. What do doctors know?' (102). Mrs Donovan has read Sarah according to her own experience. Sarah is not having a miscarriage or suffering 'women's' problems, but Mrs Donovan has nonetheless established a link with Sarah that is ultimately a more correct witness to what Sarah is experiencing than the doctor's observations. From one angle, Sarah's experience of her connection with

Rosita is impossible, delusory; but from another angle she has done what is so important to Hospital – kept alive the witness of violence committed on the powerless, especially on women, and ironically this necessity is a type of 'women's' problem after all. In the words of Joseph Slaughter and Jennifer Wenzel, 'Instead of locating politics solely in the public realm, Sarah recognizes the ubiquity and correspondence of inner and outer politics'.[12] Without this witness, the suggestion seems to be, we have no way of confronting the violence. And if that requires aberrant extremities of reading practices, then that must be faced up to.

The interdependence of experience and body reaches extreme proportions in 'The Chameleon Condition', a fantastic tale in which the need to be read by others becomes eroded. Far from constituting anything positive or useful, however, this actually leaves the character to whom it occurs highly vulnerable and exposed. Removing the need to be decoded actually removes our basic right to represent ourselves. In this story the body becomes its own site of witness to emotional responses; that is, the protagonist's body literally changes colour according to his emotions, so that he is always already decoded, and he can harbour no secrets of his response to his world. This does not make his life easier or help those around him. On the contrary, it ruins his life, for he has no zone where he can represent himself, where he can act (and the term is deliberate) as his own witness. His body gives him away.

When his skin changes colour for the first time, he is having sex with his lover, called, teasingly, Eve, as he is Adam, 'a type of the weak first man', in Bruce Bennett's words.[13] The vivid blue of gratification disappears before she notices, but from then on Adam's body is constantly changing colour and showing people what he is feeling, once they realise what is happening. The condition is diagnosed by a doctor as occurring 'when the subject has no – ah – appreciable sense of self. When he measures himself by reflected opinion . . . subjects are afraid to speak in their own voice' (90).

Adam is here becoming that impossibility, the always already decoded body, presenting the opposite problem to that of the greater or smaller degree of personal priorities that determine how others read us. Being openly readable is a condition in which reflection rather than projection becomes the body's mode of display. Furthermore, this is closely related to Adam's philandering, his inability to make decisions, to be interested. Unable to commit himself to his wife, he is equally unable to commit himself to any intellectual conviction, unable to situate himself anywhere, with the result that he ends up having the nightmare dream wherein his first wife, his second wife and his ex-lover Eve are playing cards together and cannot see him when he taps on the window. He has become invisible, through being too visible. To be a person after all is in part to resist others, to assert one's beliefs and to conceal one's secrets, to be a text that others have to work to make sense of. Under normal human conditions, interpreting others interestedly becomes not only normal but necessary for individual health and interpersonal relations.

Revenants connect

The ordinarily reasonable is consistently subjected to enquiry in *Isobars*, and whereas in her novels Hospital includes dream sequences or unexplainable coincidences, in her stories she frequently makes the inexplicable the entire fabric of the tale. In 'Eggshell Expressway', for example, prostitute and drug-addict Lisa's regular client appears to be the shade of someone who has been dead for a couple of years, and the events of the story are a rerun of the underground sex that led to his suicide in the first place. Perhaps more significantly, in this tale written specifically for the anthology *Expressway*, edited by Helen Daniel,[14] Hospital produces her first vision of the Sydney underworld that would be expanded into the Quarry of *The Last Magician*. In both worlds there is a connection with the judiciary; in 'Eggshell Expressway' the judge is undone by his taste for sex with underage prostitutes in a fleapit, committing suicide when blackmailed, but in *The Last Magician* the connection becomes more sinister. There, Judge Robinson is in collusion with the very underworld he claims to oppose, while at the same time he enforces the social triage, or selection, that keeps an underclass in the Quarry. Hospital's sympathy is clearly with the manipulated women at the bottom of the hierarchy of power, as well as with the worldly-wise toughness they demonstrate even when looking into an abyss of human iniquity that might very well bring about their own death. Death shadows such women and their world, and in this story the revenant of the dead judge also serves as a premonitory beckoning to Lisa, who overdoses at the end.

It is common throughout the volume that whenever people try to make sense of things they come up against bends in the fabric of time, secrets and danger. In 'A Little Night Music' the protagonist finds she has been sitting next to, has even kissed and had her breast kneaded by, the spirit of the man who had suicidally blown up the flight Lucy had been supposed to be on the previous day. This gives her, among other things (his hands are deathly cold), a sense of connection with the alternative fate she almost had, one of those 'moments of crisis and illumination that blur the distinction between past and present' of which Selina Samuels speaks.[15]

The intensities of family history in Hospital's work provide especially haunting experiences of the unstable nature of time, and of the connections between the living and the dead. In 'Uncle Seaborn' there is a link between a child who dies on a nineteenth-century voyage to Australia and his brother who is born a week later. The brother, Seaborn because he was born at sea, constantly feels the sea and the shade of his brother calling to him. Despite being drawn to water and becoming a gifted swimmer, he dies in a rip tide. His nephew Clem also feels the call of the ocean, sensing the presence now of two beings calling to him. At the end Clem runs happily into the waves, swimming towards two shapes in the water. In this mysterious tale the past and the present speak to each other in ways that cannot be realistically accounted for. Moreover, this is all the more necessary in the case of Australia where family histories often speak of rupture, of a break between one part of the world and another. In 'Uncle Seaborn' Clem searches back through family papers and mementoes, feeling to some extent the melancholy of his forebears, who were uprooted from much of what they knew and had to live through the death of a child as well. Intuiting the pain of colonial separation, and absent in a Canada to which he has come to examine family papers, Clem urges himself to '*[c]onnect, connect*' (29; Hospital's italics) with his own family. The pain of the past will have been worth it if connections are kept up and bonds strengthened, yet at the end the power of the pain the family has had to go through is too strong: it calls him to unite himself with the element that separates the twinned inheritance of family history, this side of the world and that. It is a joyous union for Clem, but it is shadowed by what it will add to the family history of untimely death. It is not easy to transplant human beings from one side of the world to the other, and members of the family get caught in between, the estranging sea their deepest home.

Iconic beaches and their signs

The beach is supposedly an emblem of the hedonistic enjoyment of the Australian outdoor lifestyle, but in Hospital's story 'Bondi' it is a place where the inequalities and hierarchies of Australian life are seen to be violently present. It begins, however, as a piece of domestic life, two female cousins on the beach tossing up their options for the day and for their lives. Leigh muses over her badgirl role, and the complementary role she plays to her friend, Cass, conventionally married and secure. Being a rebel, nonetheless, brings its own security, habits and conventions that can be as comforting as any other role, to the extent that in this zone Leigh feels 'safe' (68). It often seems in Hospital's work that she values those characters who defy the safe options, who step into the path of danger, who put their bodies at risk. Thus, Leigh is celebrated as a harum-scarum, colourful enjoyer of life, while Cass has timidly stepped back from the raggedness of risk. At the same time, we see that Leigh in fact needs Cass to exist as an image and symbol of safety, and indeed that both of their options are revealed as bourgeois possibilities in an Australia where for some marginal groups this choice does not exist.

This safety is, however, immediately called into question when the beach around them erupts into a brawl. Described at first with the detachment of an observer – 'this is some fight, some thrill' (75) – it suddenly takes on a nastier side: the fight has racial causes it seems, xenophobic white Aussie blokes making sure the 'wogs' (75) do not take over the beach. Still, the observer insists on a detached parodic tone even as she realises that 'it's getting ugly' (75). When the lifesavers wade in, they are cast in the role of knights coming to the rescue, while the police are Keystone Cops. The 'wogs' (Palestinians) hare off in a comically excessive (and eerily prescient, in the light of racially motivated beach violence in late 2005) escape route to Cronulla (some miles from Bondi). At this point the story has cast the brutish aggression, including the use of broken beer bottles, as a piece of colourful male display, a contemporary site for the demonstration of male valour and strength. The disembodied observer here occupies a typically Hospital narrative space – a space where the implied narrator shades into the most relevant character at that point in the story, so that the reader is unsure whether the point of view originates in that character, which it had done in the story up to this point, or in some implied authorial presence. The comic register seems inconsistent with Cass's concerned character until that point. This has the effect of opening up a gap in which the reader is unsettled, although not completely destabilised. Hospital likes to make the reader wonder, but does not like to disintegrate the point of view so radically that the narrative questions become disassociated from the moral ones.

When Cass arrives home, having lost touch with Leigh, we are clearly back with her as narrator. She finds that Leigh is there with one of the Palestinians, injured in the head by a symbol of the Australian summer, a cricket bat, and the visual and emotional responses are Cass's. Moreover, they are back to those of the concerned, hesitant Cass we had known earlier in the story, and not the amused and removed chronicler of the violence. Cass has been troubled throughout the story – by Leigh's edge-dwelling irresponsibility, by the hedonism on the beach and her own response to it, followed by the violence and by the male needs it represents. Home brings no refuge, however, as she is confronted by the evidence of that violence in her house, and by her inability to deal with a feeling of complicity when it comes to the position in Australia of ethnic groups identified by the majority as other. Finally, the next morning, she goes down to the beach alone and treads with her naked foot on a hypodermic needle.

This brief story packs a dazzling array of concerns into its few pages. It unmasks the hypocrisy in Australian catchphrases like 'it's a free country' or 'fair go'. It indicates the violence that lurks just under the surface of the outwardly relaxed Australian lifestyle, and it identifies it as predominantly white male in origin. As a consequence, safety is an illusion, whether we are bourgeois or rebellious. The cheery hedonism of Bondi leaves behind an ugly detritus of syringes and condoms, Sydney often serving in Hospital's work as an 'image of the polluted paradise'.[16] Leigh might do drugs, deal and rip off dealers, blow thousands of dollars on parties, thrash her body and get beaten up, but Cass is no safer after all than Leigh is.

At the beginning of the story the woman on the edge feels too safe, while at the end the middle-class housewife feels too threatened. Another of Hospital's pairs of characters, they exist to reveal safety as a membrane that can be easily ruptured. The character living dangerously helps someone else to escape damage and disappears 'safely' back into her turbulent lifestyle, while the character living cautiously suffers what may be deadly damage through the hypodermic needle on the beach. In this case, the safe lifestyle of Cass parallels in some way the safe lifestyle of the nation: both are an illusion, both may be punctured in the very midst of their iconic sites and activities.

The beach features centrally in two more of the book's stories. In 'The Loss of Faith' it once again serves as a site of male display (with another emblematic Adam), although here it is women, not ethnic others, who are the victims. This Adam is related to the Adam of 'The Chameleon Condition' in that he has difficulty relating responsibly to women, and he is also a university professor. Yet somehow, through his reading of New York, where he thinks he sees his ex-wife Faith on the subway, and later learns that this was the day she died in Australia, he makes emotional as well as verbal contact with his family, his country and his past. In the dream of his taking a perfect mark on Cronulla beach, he establishes this nostalgic contact. It is a contact, however, that possesses more than a little ambiguity, for it envisages Adam's repeating something that in the past was the occasion for Faith's disillusionment with him. In Adam's recollection he has omitted the fact that catching a football was an exhibitionist act that brought him into admiring contact with young women on the beach, and made his wife tense with foreboding. The pieces of one's memories may never be able to be put back together exactly, and yet this remembering of himself as a Max Dupain beach hero suggests that whatever the guilt, whatever the desire to reassemble, Adam can only ever reimagine himself in this role in which his principal connection is with the narcissistic image of himself. The Adam in 'The Chameleon Condition' displays himself without wanting to, while this Adam can only imagine himself as display. In his reading of himself and what connection with his family might mean, he does not make the positive step of sympathy towards others which is associated with many of the women in this volume. Contact with others for Adam resolves itself into sex, and, in Charlotte Clutterbuck's observation, '[f]or Turner Hospital's men, sex is a way of disconnecting them from life, isolating them as affair after affair detaches them from first wife and children, second wife and children'.[17]

'I Saw Three Ships' depicts a man who makes wildly fanciful conclusions about a woman that do not read her as a sex object, and yet his assumptions establish positive connections in a way that more 'correct' suppositions would not. The man,

Gabe, observes, then talks to, a young woman he sees regularly on Collaroy Beach in Sydney. In a world where he has been traumatised by loss and the violence of war (World War II), the girl provides him with a regular pattern, along with something he can build into a vision of positivity and suture; it is no accident that her name is Angela.

The girl is also lost and feeling sullied by life's contracts, and has noticed Gabe sitting fishing, marvelling at what she sees as his 'patience . . . tranquillity' (55). This erroneous reading of his character does not just surprise him but opens up a perceptual gap in which he has to admit to himself that he is in fact the 'original cantankerous, irritable husband, father, grandfather' (56). This leads him to read events and signs around him in the context of his loneliness, along with those of his broken body and spirit, to the extent that 'he had decided she could save him' (59). In this nimbus of hope he associates her with light, with nuns, with purity, with a sort of holy craziness in her presence at the water's edge and her desire to go underwater diving: 'he thought of novices in a cloister . . . But she is more remote than that, he thought; she puts up a higher wall' (62).

Just when it seems that Gabe and Angela are getting close enough to help each other with their different pain and sense of futility, Angela comes to suspect that Gabe wants to have more contact with her because he has realised that she is a prostitute. Gabe, however, is imagining a very different type of contact with her, the mere opportunity to see her, to be near her, to bask in her pure radiance. Angela leaves the beach wearily, without ever realising how Gabe has really perceived her. Until the moment when she thinks Gabe is seeing her as a Kings Cross hooker, which would be to see an empirical truth about her, Angela has also been nourished by the contact between them. Both of them had thus read each other wrongly, but the one who walks away from the encounter having gained something is Gabe. The old man's imaginative reading validates the girl in a way the apparent truth might not have, while at the same time he gains help with his own emotional distress. His reading was unreasonable perhaps, but it was creative rather than destructive, and it was useful to both of them – at least until Angela supposes he has worked out the truth about her occupation. For our emotional health, and for that of others, the interpretation that works may be the one that establishes solidarity rather than the one that sees plain fact.

The isobars of fate

'Queen of Pentacles, Nine of Swords' has interpretation at its centre in the form of a fortune teller, a reader of cards. It also has one of those disjunctive pairs that Hospital uses to frame the issues that absorb her: Sita, a young woman from India in Canada, and a Euro-Canadian fortune-teller. Added to this cultural pair, the story quickly throws in paired time periods – the past and the present, eighteen years after the encounter on the first page of the story when Sita walks into the woman's apartment and surprises everyone by starting to crochet. Hospital's use of past and present is marked in her novels, where there is more space to manipulate the developments and ruptures that the passage of time brings about, but she is also able to cut back and forward between past and present deftly in her short stories. As Selina Samuels points out, 'for many of Hospital's characters, memory appears to transform time utterly, telescoping the past into the present and removing all sense of linearity'.[18] So it is that as the fortune teller gets into her car to go to the police station to see what has happened to Sita, she looks in the back seat to check that their two sons are strapped in, something she must have done many years previously, but not recently – an action that speaks of the bond that developed out of that first, estranging meeting.

At that encounter, the fortune teller had interpreted the cultural disjunction as an obstacle to reading the cards, for Sita came from a culture where reading the future is widely accepted and believed, unlike European Canada, where it is considered a nostrum for the lost, the lonely and the bewildered, carried out by charlatans. Straightaway, the woman admits she is a fraud. Sita's response is to wave the objection aside; it is not the mediator who is significant but the signs themselves. And sure enough, the cards confirm other readings of other types she has had before in India – disaster is awaiting her and the baby she is carrying will die.

The baby does die, but the story rushes past this, for it is not the disruption it is interested in, which is rather a confirmation of Sita's understanding of her life as interpreted for her ever since her 'inauspicious time of birth' (156). The next scene sees the women looking through second-hand clothing when Sita informs the woman that her (arranged) husband is leaving her and claiming the children, because of her affair with a professor (another of Hospital's alarmingly large gallery of predatory educationalists, as was the school history teacher with whom Sita became pregnant in the first place). Like everything else, this is not a disaster for Sita, for it is part of the pattern of her life. Foretold and expected to follow a pattern, her life forgoes the possibility of remorse or regret but also of engagement to some extent, of tragedy even, since Sita faces the slings and arrows jauntily. She may have turned her life into a self-fulfilling prophecy, but Hospital is attracted to such devil-may-care characters who treat life's knocks with cavalier insouciance.

By finishing the volume with 'Here and Now' Hospital can be presumed to have felt that the story took its place in the meaningful pattern suggested by the title of the whole collection. If 'Isobars: A Fugue on Memory' is a positioning text for our reading of the stories to follow, one warning us that the violence committed by men upon women might deflate the confidence with which we postmodernistically assert the equality of the stories we tell, the versions of history we generate, what concluding function might 'Here and Now' be performing here?

The story centres once again on a wrenching from daily routine caused by the violence of loss, in this case the natural death of the protagonist's mother, communicated by telephone from Australia to Canada, which brings the two 'heres' into alignment. And quickly, as in 'Isobars', events begin to come together, like the ice crystals and the ice patterns on Alison and around her. In this case the points on the isobar within the story suggest once again that it does matter where you cut the circle. Alison's retired colleague Walter's pain over his son's accidental death in Australia in the past clearly relates to Alison's sorrow, and yet at the same time this connection does not mean that his point on the isobar is the same as Alison's, just as his here and now are different from hers. Walter's touching of his personal isobar, in which his admiration for Australians' saving stranded whales led to his sending his son to the country to straighten him out, where the son died on a road that encodes the country's tropical beauty, as far from Canada as could be imagined, cannot connect Alison's own patterns. Indeed, so out of the surrounding frame is she that her mother has died tomorrow; that is, she has received the news on Sunday that her mother has died on Monday, given the time difference between the two countries' respective time zones.

The circular pattern to both the story and the volume thus

establishes itself in Alison's conclusion: 'Tomorrow, Alison thinks, I will fly all the way back to the beginning' (177). At the same time it denies itself, in that the connections that spread through the short story never make for closure or completion; the circle or isobar may exist but the characters exist at different points on it. The beginning has constantly to be gone back to, Walter's reading of the cracks is not hers, she has to read her own. Nonetheless, there is contact here. Walter cannot inhabit Alison's meanings, and Alison slithers uncertainly along on the surface of Walter's meanings, but they *are* attempting to testify to each other's grief and loneliness, and, as is frequent in Hospital's fiction, it is an old or elderly man who is able to relate to women in ways that are not threatening or insulting. It is true that the contact established between Walter and Alison cannot heal their pain, for ultimately violence and loss cannot be negated by empathy. Nevertheless, blundering in on others' signs is at least to bear witness to them, and without this witness we are simply murdered by time and men, something that will become spectacularly apparent in Hospital's next novel, *The Last Magician*, in which the desperate decoding of the sources of violence becomes a matter of life or death for the book's protagonists.

CHAPTER 8

There is no straight way *The Last Magician*

What returns to haunt the victim . . . is not only the reality of the violent event but also the reality of the way that its violence has not yet been fully known.

Cathy Caruth[1]

Displacing reality

Hospital's increasing focus on her native land reaches its climax in her next two books, both of which are set almost entirely in Australia. In terms of narrative strategies and thematic concerns, nevertheless, there is clear continuity between her previous two novels and *The Last Magician*. *Borderline* and *The Last Magician* are linked through the spotlight they direct at disjunctions between the ordered façade of Western society and the vicious forms of social control that lie behind the order, while *Charades* and *The Last Magician* share an interest in the playing out in adulthood of the stresses and strains of an Australian childhood. All three books vigorously challenge the reader to follow complex works in which the ways we represent reality and arrive at truth are questioned. *The Last Magician* begins, accordingly, with a narrator feeling lost, in terms of how to connect up elements of her life and how to talk about them: 'Everything I say is provisional', the narrator, Lucy, will often remind us.[2] This represents the reader's position as well, as we are faced with two principal mysteries – what happened to Cat, who has not been seen for a long time, and what to make of the turbulent collage of reflection, intertextual allusion and teasing, double meanings, realist narrative, time shifts and moral outrage that the novel displays.

On the first page we are told of bones stuffed under boulders, pushed down 'with the blunt end of something far more complex and disturbing than hate' (3), in a typical Hospital conjunction of the concrete ('blunt end') and the abstract ('something far more complex and disturbing than hate'). By establishing violence and death in the form of someone's bones as references at the beginning, Hospital casts a shadow over the narrative and introduces a mystery. Not for nothing is the dark wood at the beginning of Dante's *Inferno* alluded to in the novel's first line. But just as Dante had a guide through the Inferno, so we will have a guide through the novel, although in Hospital's moral universe no-one is as removed and out of the fray as Dante's guide Virgil. Our narrator guide is called Lucy, and who better than one whose name is derived from the Latin for 'light' to lead us through? Moreover, St Lucy is not only the patron saint of people with weak sight but is also invoked in Canto II of the *Inferno*, still in the Dark Wood, as having intervened to encourage the faint-hearted Dante not to give up. Light, what is more, is a quality that in itself cannot be seen but which renders the outlines and colours of whatever it touches, so that in this sense Lucy reveals things, but it is the reader who must look and decide what has been revealed.

The reader is asked to work hard in this novel, particularly at the start. Not for nothing are hidden bones dragged into sight near the beginning, for this represents what must be done repeatedly throughout the book, both by Lucy and her allies and by the reader: that is, to try to drag into view things that sinister forces in Australian society would like to keep out of sight. This is the book of Hospital's in which the reader most loses his or her orientation at first,[3] our position being analogous to that of the man on the Manly ferry near the beginning who tries to chat up Lucy only to receive such a barrage of references and allusions that he backs off, overwhelmed and repelled, as her urgent flow of associations moves towards the dirt and the despair of the lost and marginalised. If we persist through the swirl of information the beginning of the book throws at us, we will be rewarded with an intense vision of the darkness of human beings combined with the compromised possibilities of art to deal with it, to help us through the dark perhaps but never to reduce it to order. This disorientation is necessary so that the reader may also feel as lost as the narrator, because part of the point of the book is that we realise how much reality is an effect of language and discourse.[4] It is also why Dante as an intertext for Hospital is more relevant visually and emotionally than intellectually, and why the *Inferno* and not the rest of the *Divine Comedy* is summoned in this book. The world of the novel does not cohere as did Dante's, and it lacks an ultimate authority binding all elements of reality. Nor is there a goal that can be achieved which can be said to be our salvation. However, the complexity of Dante's vision of the interlocking circles of existence, the arduous and baffled movement through these circles, the restless moral questioning and concerned observation that the character Dante undertakes, and the sense of the layers upon layers of the lost, all provide resonant models for how Hospital's principal characters relate to the world.[5]

Accordingly, Lucy has to be jolted out of the comfort zone of her present reality at the beginning of the book and sent off on the quest the rest of the book encompasses. This jolt occurs when Lucy is watching an avant-garde film in London (here doing duty as a zone of diasporic Australian absence, in which national problems can be evaded) and sees herself amidst a collage of images and allusions to the characters who will feature at the centre of the book: Charlie Chang, the filmmaker; Robinson Gray, judge and representative of authority; his son Gabriel; Cat, whose bones we have encountered; and Catherine Reed, a colleague of Lucy's in the documentary film business and a childhood friend of Charlie, Cat and Robinson Gray. Lucy needs to know how she got into a film she has no awareness of, she needs 'like any archivist or reader of entrails, to salvage the future or predict the changeable past' (69). Her response is to return to Sydney and begin trying to unravel the mystery.

Mysteries lie at the heart of this novel, as of all Hospital's novels with the exception of *The Ivory Swing*. The surface mystery of this novel involves Lucy, Charlie, Gabriel and Catherine's trying to determine what happened to Cat, who has not been seen for a long time. To find this out becomes a process that spirals into an investigation into the nature of inequality in Australian society, into the ways class and race injuries harden into position in childhood, and into how to present the results of this investigation. Wanting to discover what happened to Cat is one more of the patterns in Hospital's moral universe in which, in Margaret Schramm's words, 'major characters feel deeply responsible for women who exist on the margins of society and are victims of violence',[6] making Cat a sort of twentieth-century Beatrice towards which the novel strives, albeit not as a vision of purity but as a version of the turbulent independence Hospital values.

Given her constant awareness of the responsibility to unveil the operations of violence, an intensely postmodern writer like

Hospital is faced with a serious interpretative problem – how to point an accusing finger when you believe that truth is variegated and shifting. The fact that this hermeneutic problem recurs in all of her books does not obviate the need to return to the difficulties, given that they lie at the heart of what it means to write or to create both for her and for her narrators.[7] The reader's desire to solve the mystery will accordingly be constantly diverted and displaced by Lucy's commentary on the slippery nature of recounting, on the multiple nature of identity, on the complex nature of everything from time and space to loyalty and truth. In her excellent article on this aspect of the novel, Sue Lovell indicates how orphan Lucy's lack of an identifiable origin 'makes it even more necessary for her to become a narrating protagonist strenuously involved in the process of textualising her own posthumanist subjectivity and desire'.[8] Lovell goes on to outline how it is necessary that we recognise how implicated we are in constructing the reality we are both inhabiting and shaping at the same time, because recognising this creates a space in which we can more actively reflect upon and attempt to enact our own desires. We can become less passive. This is not, however, to say that we can mould reality to suit our desires, for clearly we will run into others' desires which may be opposed to our own, and we are all subject to the unexpected consequences of the butterfly effect in any event.

Becoming less passive before the bullying operations of power that menace us is crucial in Hospital's world, although her work does not show the ultimate victory of good over evil. As in her earlier books, there are victims, people who are killed, like Cat and probably Charlie and Gabriel as well by the end of this novel; but it is imperative for her that we do not abandon the desire to make the connections that will expose how such things have happened, or even how they might have happened. Following on from the concerns of *Borderline* and *Charades*, *The Last Magician* is mesmerised by the bizarre chains of cause and effect that fissiparate off in all directions ('a goanna moving its tail on a rock near Perth, by a long and escalating chain of air displacements, can unleash flooding in Queensland' [82; on p. 338 it is a butterfly]), by the seemingly insurmountable presence of violence both personal and systemic in our lives, and also by the desperate ingenuity with which we try to bear witness to these things.

Hospital returns to one of her favoured metaphors for the entanglement of cause, effect and human beings on the first page of *The Last Magician* – the Queensland rainforest. While the rainforest echoes the Dantesque 'dark wood' mentioned in the first line, to a certain extent it replaces or extends it, as if a dark wood may be a useful metaphor, but in a Queensland or Australian context a rainforest is even better. Carrying this metaphorical resonance, the abundance of the rainforest, as we have seen in *Charades*, continues to be a sign of Hospital's many-threaded narrative strategies. Everything signifies in Hospital's fiction; everything is implicated in everything else in some way, everything leaks into everything else, nothing is ever really separate, including words and people's names that are often used punningly or ironically to multiply their referents. The image of a vast, muddy goldmine in Brazil can merge into that of a rock face in Sydney, and where we are can suddenly seem less solid than we thought.

The intensity and dangerous growth of the rainforest in *The Last Magician* are echoed in the central metaphor of the novel, that of the quarry, the many-levelled underworld which props up and defines respectable activity and power in Sydney, Australia and even the world. Inspired by Sebastião Salgado's famous photograph of the Serra Pelada mine in Brazil,[9] the quarry is a labyrinth, like the rainforest, and the novel is full of images and metaphors of entwining, interference and layering. In many sections the book itself seems like a collage, a rainforest of references, allusions and hints. The quarry is a place we may or may not visit directly, but it visits us in any case, and its existence is something against which the city above, the life of the nation, defines itself. Not just a dark underside of supposedly normal life, Hospital's quarry is also a physical location of tunnels and holes under the ground Sydney is built on, a warren inhabited by an underclass who serve the priorities and appetites of those in control.[10] As Lucy says, 'there has always been another world, a nether world, invisible, nestled inside the cracks of the official world' (19).

The quarry is an underground of violence and desperation related to that world in *Borderline* which comfortable people in the Western world do not see or cannot imagine: the dark corners and edges of the city where others despair, are thrust and crushed by those in power, or even continue the job and destroy themselves. The world that pretends there is order, indeed the sector of that world that imposes it, is represented in *The Last Magician* by those figures who administer it, particularly Judge Robinson Gray, who tells Gabriel that '[w]hat the law decides *is* truth' (199). Gray is a crucial figure in this arrangement, for he is not only aware of the existence of the quarry but also involved in maintaining it. An important aspect of keeping the quarry in its place occurs when the majority of Gray's class enjoy their class privileges by denying the quarry's very existence, not only relegating the quarry's inhabitants to a twilight underclass but writing them out of society altogether. Thus it is that at one point we get a vignette of quarry-denying at an upscale party in Point Piper in Hospital's best abrasive register.

At the same time, it is not only those in power who stigmatise the quarry, and Hospital links the rhetoric of the governing class to that of the 'common man' through the taxi driver who says '[t]hey should drop a bomb on it, blow the whole quarry to kingdom come' (330). The sense that this man is a class traitor is hinted at in his name, Joe Blake, colloquial rhyming slang for a snake. However, when Lucy rushes back to Sydney to try to put some order into her experience of the film she has just seen in London, she is told by one of Hospital's numerous heart-of-gold, unintellectual and pragmatic workers, the barmaid Sheba, that 'the problem with people like you and Gabriel [is that] you just won't admit the way the world works' (8; also 200). To a certain extent the book goes on to test the tension between accepting how the world supposedly 'works' and interrogating the order that the forces of authority would like us to accept as this 'working'. Yet although Hospital's writing generally respects the worldly wisdom of the unintellectual, Sheba's position is uncomfortably close to the position of Robinson Gray, the chief representative and architect of the maintenance of social hierarchy in the book. Later he will talk of his rebellious son Gabriel to Lucy, criticising 'the overly pure in heart . . . fanatic reformers' (262), claiming that his own efforts on behalf of social hierarchies and controlling exclusions are an act of resistance against fundamentalism and puritans of all sorts. For Gray this translates into the need to control anyone who criticises the status quo and who cannot accept the abuse of power wielded by people such as himself: those who cannot accept, indeed, the way the world works.

In order to oppose this vision of regulated order controlled by a moneyed, white elite, we need to be led to an understanding of the first epigraph to the book, James Gleick's '[t]he first message is that there is disorder' (1). 'Disorder' and 'chaos' tend to be positive terms in Hospital's fiction, signifying not simply meaningless disarray but the interplay of bewilderingly complex patterns and connections. Committed seekers of truth, like Dante, will not be put off by the fact that the world is 'thick with messages' (8), as Lucy says, and they will enter the dark wood in search of what those messages might mean, even though, unlike Dante, they doubt whether they will all be pieced together in the end.

Entering the quarry

Lucy has knowledge of the quarry through working as a prostitute, and sometimes the tunnels of the quarry she makes contact with exist in the present, as when a twelve-year-old boy cries after having been sodomised for a packet of cigarettes (not even the food he wanted); but at other times the quarry is revealed in the tunnels of the past and the flickering phantoms of memory that she, Charlie, Gabriel and Catherine investigate. In terms of the physical quarry, however, she enters it first in the novel when she meets the film's director, Charlie Chang, who runs a bar in Sydney that he calls, in Hospital's occasionally overdetermined fashion, The Inferno.

Watching Charlie's film, Lucy had felt herself entering the eighth circle of hell (64), which, in Dante's *Inferno* is divided into ten rings. The eighth circle of Dante's hell is also the level of 'those who committed Malicious Frauds upon mankind in general',[11] and it is an extremely full level of miscreants, occupying far more of the *Inferno* than any other level. Charlie's bar itself is called the first circle of the quarry, a realm of hedonistic appetite, of blotting out the daylight world, and of violence. The quarry is a zone where the victims and underclasses are pushed by those in power, but it is also a zone where the latter cruise, amusing themselves with those who are condemned to the dark desperation of its spaces, so you have to look to see who is who. There is a certain ambiguity about this quarry, for while Hospital is ablaze with indignation about the way society relegates human beings to its underside, she also perceives intensity and integrity in the quarry. Many inhabitants, particularly women – towards the end of the chain of power – demonstrate a moral honesty, an absence of the hypocrisy that characterises the world above.

This ambiguity is not really resolved, unless in the implication that it is best to be someone like Charlie or Lucy, people who visit the quarry for its honesty and energy but who can rejoin the daylight world when they choose. They are observers, even sympathetic participant-observers, versions of the artist perhaps, but they still suggest a type of slumming, using the inhabitants of the quarry in the service of their personal quests. Lucy is an inhabitant by virtue of being a prostitute, but she also admits that she is '[a]n explorer. These places interest me, but I can leave' (34–5). That Hospital is aware of the danger is evident in Lucy's referring to herself as a 'tourist' (276), and in the many quarry-dwellers who become hostile to Charlie or Lucy as they move through the tunnels, like the woman who, when asked a question by Charlie, replies, 'Fuck you, darling' and 'She spits in his face, then she withdraws behind the wall' (88).

Moving into the streets and alleys beyond the bar, or the tunnels and rock faces, Charlie thinks he might find Cat – who he has not seen for over twenty-five years – because more than anyone else he knew she represented self-possession and defiance of the system. When reading about the quarry we enter some of Hospital's most hallucinatory writing, for in the world of the novel the quarry is represented literally as a vast network of tunnels and levels reaching out under Sydney, which Aamer Hussein sees more generally 'as a Third World located not far away in the South but in the urban and mental landscapes of the supposedly developed world'.[12] Indeed, Hospital's attention to the quarry is resonant with her having being mugged in Boston by four youths at knifepoint in 1987, an experience which, for a long time afterward, left her with a 'personal inner sense of the pit opening beneath me'.[13]

Despite Hospital's nightmarish vision of the urban underworld, for many readers the most incandescent writing in the novel and the most stark representation of social exclusion are to be found in the more straightforward Book II. As English novelist Jonathan Coe sums up: 'few novelists have written with such authority about childish passions and the influence they carry over into what passes for adulthood'.[14] Canadian novelist Aritha van Herk sees in Book II's clash of personalities and different social trajectories a drama that does not require the allusiveness and narrative questioning of the rest of the book. Her perception of *The Last Magician* as centrally 'bounded by class concerns' situates it as a historical enquiry into the operations of power in Australia,[15] to the extent that she is impatient with the strand in the novel that concentrates on kinks in the nature of reality. One explanation for the harrowing power of Book II lies in the fact that it returns to locations and times intimately familiar to Hospital, the childhood of Robbie, Charlie, Cat and Catherine in Brisbane in the 1950s, the aetiology of their relation to each other, and their positioning with respect to the quarry.

Memory and history

Book II begins with Gabriel's anguished memory of his father, Robinson Gray, engaged in inserting himself into history and public event. Memory is related to history and to narrative, but memory has something added, the intensity of loss. If memory references painful experiences then naturally pain comes with the memories. However, even if memory references pleasure then pain is still a component of the experience because it is pleasure that is experienced as absence. In Lucy's words, 'the past has heft and jagged edges' (23). And it cannot be controlled, or can only partly be controlled, for it rushes at us and clutches at the present; it is part of the present even if we try to deny it.

Gabriel's father, later Judge Robinson Gray, has observed a neighbour's getting into the paper on the occasion of the phasing out of Brisbane's trams. Intensely jealous, he deliberately stages an appearance on a tram to build up his public profile, and, as he practises on his son the day before uttering it (supposedly off the cuff) to a reporter, he claims that '[t]he present crosses the Great Divide and descends into history' (149). Wanting to be a part of history, of public event, he damns himself in the present of his son's perception of his father's inauthentic nature. This episode indicates Hospital's insistent attacks on the appropriation of the public sphere for the aggrandisements of personal power. History may be dynamic, like personal memory, but whatever our difficulties in representing it, our responsibility to history remains firmly delineated in her fiction. The public sphere must not be allowed to be appropriated by liars or cheats using it for their own benefit. Neither must any of these be permitted to oppress others' stories. History in her work is made up of the circulation of different interpretations, different memories, not of their suppression in the name of some unitary version, or the version that suits those in power.

We have already seen an extended unpicking of family dynamics in *The Tiger in the Tiger Pit*, but relatively little space was dedicated to childhood. Here we have a prolonged and merciless depiction of the way triage and separation already start operating in our schooldays, a bitterly dystopic view of Australian childhood before the 1970s that goes against the nostalgic patina that Australian culture gives to the middle past. The levelling environment provided by school entails a vicious policing of difference, from which Charlie had most to lose because he is of Chinese extraction although born in Australia. As the novel proceeds, it validates this divergence from the norm through the fact that, in Sue Lovell's words, 'being forced to live through difference produces an ability to step back from each context and take note by applying a critical, interpretive eye'.[16] While this is a position Charlie can occupy as an adult, there is no escape into the role of the outsider as a child, so he has to deny his Australianness in order to stop the bullying. The anonymous boys who hang around menacingly after school represent an Australia that 'hated Grammar School types, but not as much as they despised girls and wogs' (209). In Catherine's eyes, 'schooling in Queensland in the fifties and sixties was still as bad as anything in Dickens. It scarred all of us' (204).

Cat is also introduced into the scene on the tram, apparently as the polar opposite of the respectability and decorum of Robinson Gray. The novel characterises this as the 'discrepancy between Cat's power and other kinds of power' (202), polarities that, when they meet, react in extreme fashion. Gabriel is aware that his father has been shaken by the strange woman on the tram, and later that his mother has had to pay for this unsettling with facial bruising and a black eye. In fact, this event is the catalyst for Gabriel's being taken away from his mother and Brisbane to live in Sydney, with the usual disorienting lack of proper parental explanation, indeed the Great Divide of Gabriel's history. Since that moment Cat has been the source of a riddle in Gabriel's life, a riddle that requires investigating, and a piecing together of the past in a wholly different fashion from the version imposed on him by his father, so that finally we have come to one explanation of the quest for Cat. We still, however, need to know why Charlie is searching for her.

Cat represents the disorderly, the colourful, the individual in a land that does its best to crush difference. For this reason she befriends Charlie, an outsider like herself, when they are children. Cat is very much an active principle, impulsive, optimistic, but uninterested in attainment – unlike Charlie who is being groomed by his family for scholarly endeavour. One sign of her impulsiveness is that she touches Charlie, kisses him in fact, thus crossing a boundary. The crossing of boundaries, limits, borders is crucial to breaking down the power of hierarchies and purities in Hospital's world, metaphorised here by the overgrown riot of Cat's family's property, a profuse abandon of rainforest and weeds, a tableau of interpenetration, a denial of separation. It is also metonymically related to Hospital's prose itself, both in its verbal plenitude[17] and in its interest in areas of existence that some types of literature tend to avoid in their drive for what the narrator belligerently terms a 'literature that is unassertive, limpid, economical, and lean' (258). Hospital's belligerence when goading literary critics veers towards caricature – her critics are always genteel and refined, sherry sippers and asparagus eaters (301), a reductiveness that grates, but one that indicates her feisty willingness to stand up to all and sundry, including those arbitrators of value in one of the worlds to which she belongs.[18] Like Cat, Hospital's work is unruly and aggressive, refusing to be dictated to by either commercial or fashionably artistic considerations. The principal rebuke to critics concerns their supposed preference for the indirect, what for her is the toned down, 'the soft way the light falls on rape' (301) as Lucy characterises a critic's admiration for Yeats's poem 'Leda and the Swan'. Cat's headstrong nature is, however, also physically dangerous, for pushing against everyday constraints includes pushing up against peril, represented on the one hand by her game of lying on the railway tracks until the last moment and on the other by the even more dangerous strategy of defying those who have the power to harm her.

In the struggle between Cat and Robbie's types of power, the novel is clearly on the side of the rebellious expression of difference that Cat represents, as do Charlie, Catherine, Lucy and Gabriel in varying ways. However, as Charlie can see, '[t]he trouble with Cat's kind of power . . . is that there are people who develop a passion to break it' (211). Those who simply represent official power, such as Miss Oswell, the schoolteacher, are unable to break Cat's power, since all they have to oppose it is the repeated insistence on their own values, allied with somewhat crude forms of punishment. In order to break the power of someone who denies your frames of reference, you need to discover what their frames of reference are and use these against them. The boys who act as an anonymous but destructive and vicious teenage version of society-in-general discover Cat's vulnerability when they realise how much she cares for her brother Willy, who is intellectually handicapped and has little 'will' of his own at all. The boys make Willy lie on the railway tracks in the game of chicken that Cat, Charlie and Catherine have been playing, but he does not realise that he has to get up before the train gets there and is killed.

In the assumption of guilt it is noticeable that Charlie and the girls feel that Willy's death is in some way something they are responsible for, while Robinson and the boys do not feel responsible at all. Feeling connected to others is something that both conservative tradition and feminist consciousness-raising ascribe to women, and, generally speaking, Hospital's work articulates a view of solidarity and responsibility as being largely gendered. Robbie's use of the word 'responsible' at the trial is cynically cognisant of the social value of the term but hollow of real responsibility (in an earlier draft, Robbie had been labelled 'the Hollow Man').[19] Part of the reason Charlie is later tormented by the past is derived from the imbalance between what they all paid for that past, events that had been 'costly, very costly, for Catherine and himself, and infinitely more so for Cat', while 'these same events had cost Robinson Gray nothing at all, or *almost* nothing' (279). This is immediately apparent in the visit after the trial by Robbie and the other Grammar School boys to Cat's house to punish her, Charlie and Catherine, but especially Cat. She had lost her brother, been sentenced to be taken away from her beloved father, while they have got off scot-free, yet they still want to teach Cat a lesson. In Charlie's view they hated her 'for being articulate' (223), and they wanted to defile and shame her, for to shame someone not only enacts revenge but goes a long way to ensuring that the victim will not talk, that Cat's opposition to their values will be silenced. By pissing and shitting on the representatives of social marginality, the Grammar School boys guaranteed their silence, a silence which the present time of the book breaks as Lucy, Charlie, Gabriel and, to a lesser extent, Catherine attempt to bring the truth back from beyond the Great Dividing Range of lost histories. The period they need to go back to in Book II is often considered a golden age in the timeline of the nation's history and identity-formation, and Hospital does not entirely deny it. She catches the carefree abandon of childhood at this time superbly via the children's epiphanic experience of the rainforest and the pool at Cedar Creek Falls, below Mt Glorious to the north-west of Brisbane.[20] Significantly, it is in this pool that Cat's bones are later discovered, sullying the one location of freedom and solidarity the children (including Robbie) had enjoyed, leading Belinda Mackay to point out that '[t]his paradise, when lost, is seen always to have contained the seeds of its own destruction, and becomes a metaphor for Queensland itself'.[21]

Difference and shapeshifting

One of the central themes in *The Last Magician* is that of difference, particularly the violence that difference calls down upon itself in an Australia that in no way provides the fair go beloved of its conservative mythmakers. In the novel, characters are constantly having to face up to difference of one sort or another – either the difference *of* others or the fact that they are different *to* others. At the same time, the principal characters find that in certain ways and under certain circumstances they become that difference, they become absorbed by and infused with that difference. This can be seen in various guises. Lucy, for example, calls it 'shapeshifting',[22] a type of magic as well as an embodiment of the situation of the writer. It occurs first when Lucy is a girl observing an extreme example of class difference, an unkempt, derelict women exposing herself. Not knowing where to look, she is suddenly inside the woman, looking out at the shocked mob. From that moment she is unable to inhabit the social space marked out for her by her background. When she has this experience she sees 'that there were parallel worlds, that you could cross a line' (37). We get several variations on this entry of people into one another throughout the novel, although none so radical as Lucy's. What it eventually establishes for her is that interrogating the whole construction of society on the basis of hierarchies of power 'seemed to me the only question worth asking' (91).

Related to this, Charlie, Cat, Catherine and Robinson Gray are all part of each other in some sense, which at first is hinted at but obscure. When asked about Cat, Charlie replies enigmatically, 'She's part of me' (163), and when he meets up with Catherine after a long absence later in the book, he thinks: 'My twin . . . *Myself*' (284; Hospital's italics). When Catherine, Charlie and Cat are together '[t]hey are whole again' (287). Robinson Gray will come to represent the world that keeps the quarry in place, but he is not simply a cipher for the law of authority. Aritha van Herk observes that this novel dares 'to engage with violence as an intimate act only too closely affiliated with love',[23] and Robinson Gray's relation to the others is taut with the desire to be included, albeit along the axis of his leadership and independence. When he is a boy, for example, he does not reject Charlie as other boys do, and Charlie is deeply grateful. Robbie is also related to Cat in that he has the authority to decide on his own rules to some extent, to step outside the conventions of boys his age, even if he steps outside them in the direction of control and hierarchy rather than unruliness and defiance, like Cat. His independence does, however, lead him to the conclusion that the law is there to be manipulated in the interests of those in power, a hubris whose object is the aggrandisement of himself and his social class.

Catherine Reed, aligned with the outsiders Charlie and Cat in childhood, comes from the same solid, educated class as Robinson Gray, but is aligned athwart his priorities. At the same level of intellectual attainment as Charlie (they are the cleverest girl and boy in their class), she is not as clearly a representative character as the others, and her presence in the book grows more gradually. Catherine exists to tell us that class and privilege may encourage a certain relation to wielding power, but that it is possible to question privilege from within, thus avoiding a simplistic division of the characters into symbols of class. It is Catherine who reveals that Gabriel is Robbie's son, splintering the solidity of the elegant Point Piper dinner party, upsetting Robinson Gray's hold over the direction of conversation. As self-controlled as Robbie, she is, however, not controlling, nor is she able to be controlled by him, providing at points throughout the book a commentary on Robbie's self-regard and manipulativeness as well as softening, albeit not by much, the level of the book's vituperative commentary on the socially privileged.

In her work as a documentary-maker, Catherine is moreover another type of recording device, like Charlie and Lucy, one who gives the spokespeople for varying worthy causes an opportunity to speak on television. Yet even though she allows others to speak, and she 'practically never talks' (120), there is always selection in that she has to decide who to make a program about. The idea that one could be simply a ventriloquist for others is questioned throughout the book, in which all forms of representation come to us mediated by the priorities of the tellers. Even a recording device such as a camera is used by its wielder for a purpose, something which Charlie's collage work demonstrates. The problem is, however, that this leaves the creative splitting and reassembly of truths that is art constantly under pressure from Robinson Gray's assertion that '*[w]hat the law decides* is *truth*' (266; Hospital's italics).

Magic and art

The selection of data and the processing of clues lie at the heart of the story, both as a world in which the characters operate and as an experience for the reader. Paraphrasing Eliot's 'Burnt Norton', the novel tells us that '[h]umankind cannot bear very much lack of meaning' (300),[24] a central claim in Hospital's work: that whatever the apparent confusion and breakdown, human beings want and will attempt to construct meaning. Hence the importance of James Gleick's *Chaos*, a book that confirmed to Hospital that even the most apparently random behaviour of the objects around us may have a complex type of patterning after all, suggesting, in Gleick's words, that '[i]n nonlinearity and feedback lay all the necessary tools for encoding and then unfolding structures as rich as the human brain'.[25] But one should not forget that the second epigraph to the book comes from Woody Allen: 'There is no question that there is an unseen world. The problem is how far is it from midtown and how late is it open?' (1). The levity of this citation may seem unrelated to the seriousness of the themes of violence, inequality and difference, but the unfolding of the structures of Lucy's thought at times enacts a type of knowing humour that echoes Woody Allen's bathetic deflation of the portentous. To some extent the tension between the demotic and the erudite that courses through much of Hospital's work is picked up in the alert playfulness with which Lucy intertextualises and interrogates her experience.

The hermeneutic problem embodied in Lucy's and the novel's multi-angled approach to representation has been mentioned already, but a hermeneutic problem for a writer is also an artistic problem, and the novel contains a rich examination of the nature of various creative strategies for dealing with this problem. The basic assertion behind the need for these strategies is that we do not simply find or live reality in unmediated fashion. Hence Lucy's intertextual use of Dante at the beginning of the novel, as also her immediate denial of the terms she first offers, and her version of two lines in Canto I of the *Inferno*: '*Ah, how hard a thing it is to tell of that wood*' (3; Hospital's italics). The difficulty of the artist's contract is not something new, of course, but the verve and cunning with which Lucy/Hospital deal with it comprise either a large part of the book's excitement or a large part of the book's difficulties.

The title provides an initial clue to the nature of the task, but, like every other clue in the book, it is hardly straightforward: who is the Last Magician and why is this the title? For most of the novel the principal candidate is Charlie, and Charlie's 'magic' is centred on his creativity. Charlie's art can be said to set the book in motion by unsettling Lucy and inducing in her a desire to piece together the apparently disjointed elements of the film she sees in London. When Charlie explains what he is trying to do with his films or collages he talks of how he can only know what he has seen by processing it, whether through more expected processes like creating photographs or artworks, or unexpected ones such as buying old photos, '[s]o that I will see what I've seen' (95). These activities are versions of the surrealist aleatory practices designed to circumvent the controlling mind, in turn derived from their understanding of the work of Freud, in which the unconscious has a rich, symbolic life that we suppress, displace and otherwise evade in the interests of identity constraints of one sort or another. Charlie's claim that we never know what we have seen until we have processed it places great responsibility on this processing, and indeed knowing *becomes* processing, echoing Susan Sontag's assertion that '[t]here can be no evidence, photographic or otherwise, of an event until the event itself has been named and characterized'.[26] Looking closely might not be enough, so we need 'to set everything down, to record the minutiae, to add to the documentation on premonition and coincidence and chance' (95–6). Our memories are selective, whether through inattention or repression, and must be jogged in order to get us past their control mechanisms. Our past is therefore continually shifting as we edge past this control, read a clue differently, find a missing link, to the point where, in Lucy's gloss, 'the past lies in wait, just ahead, around every corner' (106). Linear time is thus an illusion created by an inferior mode of history-telling, a mode that Hospital's books contest and play with constantly.

The significance of this theme may be seen in the privileging of representation, and the nature of Charlie's film, at the very beginning of the novel; but at other significant moments throughout the book the narrative drive is often interrupted to direct us back to metatextual considerations of representation. After Book II finishes with the emotionally charged account of Robbie and his thuggish mates defiling Cat, Catherine and Charlie, after having brought about Willy's death, Book III begins with an apparent digression about Munch's painting *The Scream*, which morphs into a commentary on Charlie's photographs and the collages using photographs that Charlie creates. The apparent digression is crucial for, as Julian Cowley points out, it indicates Lucy and Hospital's belief 'that art has the capacity to make audible the otherwise silent scream; her evidence is Munch's woodcut, *The Scream*', silent but unforgettable.[27] In addition, the painting embodies the antagonism between the worlds of the screamer and the worlds of authority moving along the bridge towards the screamer, 'straight as the law, relentless as death or the black fact of power' (227). From this opposition, Cowley continues, 'Lucy perceives that art may make an intervention, but it is art that departs from the strictures of Aristotelian tradition that are here identified with the vengeful imperatives of the Law'.[28] So the denial of linear narrative and the apparent discursiveness of the prose are not only a hermeneutic of interpretation but also an ethics of witness, in fact the most responsible manner in which 'the horror' (300) can be faced in art.

Thus it is that Charlie is not an artist who is simply trying to express himself but rather one who is trying to find something via his photographs, which encompasses involving the readers of these photographs in the quest as well. Photographs participate in a circulation of codes in ways that other, more apparently personalised modes of creation do not, due to their belonging to an economy of images that we all feel we have access to via the fact that we could potentially have seen the images depicted. This feeling is summed up by Susan Sontag as 'the most grandiose result of the photographic enterprise . . . the sense that we can hold the whole world in our heads'.[29]

The point about photographs, according to Charlie, is that '[p]hotographs *beckon* . . . Photographs seduce' (229; the latter phrase is repeated on 322). What is in the frame plays a part in their seduction, but what is not there, what is left out or obscured, also plays a part. To try to look around the corners in photographs, to really study them, is 'a passionate act of transgression' (243). Moreover, photos are not simply detached images but are inserted into histories. To prove what he means, Charlie tells two stories. The first is about a photo that when taken freezes a moment of the happiness of a family holiday, but when it is developed and seen it reveals the secret behind the shattering burglary of their apartment. The second concerns photographs that Charlie believed expressed something general, but which seemed to a friend to be a specific accusation of pedophilia, leading to his suicide. These anecdotes lead to Charlie's being termed 'the last magician' (234) by a detective, a label referring to the power of his images to reveal truth by means whose operation remains mysterious. The suggestion that, in Sontag's words, '[p]hotographs furnish evidence',[30] spurs Charlie's memories, and opens the possibility that he might be able, via his art, to return to the memories and events from twenty-five years before, leading him to return to Australia after living in the United States.

In this project he feels that the photos that precipitated his return will also hold the key to making sense of the past. Silvia Albertazzi points to one type of evidence provided by photographs as showing 'people, things and landscapes as they are no more, testifying to their having been real and alive at a certain time in the past . . . a kind of magic'.[31] Yet single images are not enough; they need to be worked upon, as in the lengthy annotated catalogue of Charlie's photographs. Somewhere in the intersections of the truths offered by this catalogue, Charlie senses a fuller truth, but the more extensive his explanations of each photo become, the more details are added, the more elusive this unifying truth becomes. For indeed, as is probably the case for most modern readers of Dante's *Inferno*, the truth lies not so much in any overarching theology as in the energy of the details of human variety and excess, fragility and nastiness, along with the efforts of the seeker to take it all in and yet still feel there is something positive to be walked towards. What Dante has done has been to *narrativise* his representation of human sinfulness, and, in related vein, a photograph, in Cowley's words, 'needs the dynamic of narrative to flow through it'[32] in order to enter history. Charlie intensifies the photograph's call for the viewer to insert it into a story by decomposing the image and combining it with others in collages that destabilise the image as unitary, and present it in juxtaposition with others, calling forth from the viewer an attempt to establish connections, to write our own narratives.

One ostensibly 'true' type of narrative is that of the police report, the apparently bare listing of events in historical sequence. When the police attempt to pin Lucy down as to the exact order and nature of events, it becomes evident how difficult it is, how we are unable to observe all sides of what happens around us at all times, and so therefore how we rely on other people's narratives of their actions in order to build up our own story. When faced with the police attempt to get her to lay events out clearly, Lucy's version seems to be muddled, half speculative, riddled with holes. On the other hand, the police version seems shallow and lacking in contextualisation, and moreover just as partial as any other version. Instead of relating an objective sequence of events, the police are revealed as storytellers whose interest in telling things a certain way follows their own agenda, generally sinister, in the service of authority. While their question-and-answer method is hypothetically interested in arriving at truth dialectically, it masks a desire to reconstruct a previously decided narrative.

The last magician may be Charlie, but it is also revealed in an epigraph to Book IV to have been the label applied by John Maynard Keynes to Sir Isaac Newton. Representing the Enlightenment, Newton is an unlikely and paradoxical candidate as a magician, but when Robinson Gray repeats Keynes's epithet, we learn that Newton's 'main interest was deciphering the secret codes of the universe' (336), linking him to the novel's other decipherers. Alistair Stead suggests that, '[i]f the investigative Charlie is comparable to Newton, it may be because, like the discoverer of the laws of motion who was also an alchemist, "He looked both ways"'.[33] Charlie claims that '[i]t's nothing to do with magic . . . We know the answers to the burning questions but we are afraid of them, and so we need a screen. We need to project explanations and read them back' (14). Claiming that the answers are already known seems inconsistent with the book's uncertainty about what happened to Cat, and the numerous conundra that are thrown up in the course of the characters' investigation into her fate. On the other hand, it can be said that the answer to the 'question' concerning the nature of power and its priorities *is* already known, and the book constitutes a projection of some responses to this knowledge. For knowing the answer in general terms is one thing, but seeing it from as many angles as possible is another. Thus it is that, in Lucy's words, Charlie 'used to juggle coincidence, he used to shuffle incongruities and hold them up to the light and show that their contours matched' (56). In this approach, there are no incongruities, the apparently jagged edges of reality do fit together, although it takes a magician to show the ways in which it might be done, and what we are shown in the novel is a type of reality whose order is mysterious, the fractal geometry of chaos. Charlie's video art makes Lucy lose her sense of balance, and this is one effect Hospital is aiming at with her assemblage of mystery, coincidence, bizarre cause and effect, slippery representations of narrative voices whose status is always uncertain, along with shocking events that are designed not to allow us the easy denial of the Point Piper dinner guests. If we do not lose our sense of balance, we will never 'believe any plughole drops straight into hell, any railway line will grow moss and will harbour a fallen body' (64). We will allow reality to be manipulated by those who want us to keep quiet and stay in our places. Readers need to be pushed off-balance to get us out of any comfortable illusions of coherent sense that we might have about the world. We need to be made dizzy like Lucy so that we can share the experience of trying to discover how the pieces fit together, what the pieces are, and how many different ways they can be rearranged. We need to respond to the beckoning of the pieces and rush from our own mental Londons to Sydney ourselves, a magical transfer from book to our own lives that

Hospital the artist aims for, desiring our participation in the battle against control and violence.

In this process, Charlie's collages recall nothing so much as surrealism, which tried to establish an escape from mimesis as the organising principle of the art work via practices that circumvented the controlling consciousness and that set up surprising juxtapositions which would reverberate beyond the consciousness of the viewer as well. These collages are echoed in Hospital's intertextual references and allusions, punning and playing with meaning generally, as in her disrupted and reassembled time schemes in which past and present do not follow each other in linear fashion. Moreover, in the best summary of this practice, Elza Adamowicz's *Surrealist Collage in Text and Image*, we read that '[i]n the context of the Surrealist political agenda, collage, disrupting social order, is a powerful instrument for a critique of doxa'.[34] Not simply because it reorders material but because, anchored in the real of its found materials – and the apparently random nature of Charlie's accumulation of images is central to his project – it proceeds to 'unmask, critique and renew the perception of utilitarian reality and modes of representation and expression'.[35] Related to this, when Charlie had sent out his film as a speculative message, hoping to jump-start a reaction somewhere that could play a part in the quest for Cat, he is enacting a surrealist belief in the significance of the chance encounter. Sending out such a message might seem absurd, but Charlie knows that finding where 'interlocking circles begin' leads to the conclusion 'at arbitrary points' (72). And in a novel that validates the mysteries of causality and connection, Charlie's faith is not misplaced.

The last and shortest book in the novel tests what Lucy has gained from her experience after she and Catherine have fled back to London in despair over Charlie and Gabriel's disappearance and probable death at the hands of the forces of control centred on Robbie. This last book also tests our negotiation of the reading protocols the novel has enacted, beginning with a deliberate reprisal of its very first line, with the difference that, where Lucy was once 'lost' (3), now she is 'wholly lost and gone' (319). The spotted leopard and the grey wolf that visit her dreams are animals that threaten Dante in Canto I of the *Inferno*, representing different types of sins, while the winged cat echoes both Cat and the third threatening animal in Canto I, a lion (except that Cat can hardly be equated with the sin of bestiality represented by the lion). Once again, the intertextual reverberations interrupt our tendency to make simple transfers between source and contemporary text, existing more as a collage than a map, leaving us with meaning gaps that we have to fill in ourselves. In Adamowicz's words, 'Grounded in eccentricity and excess, collage is fundamentally transgressive, exploiting categories that question or collapse boundaries, by working at the edges or margins of linguistic, literary or art-historical codes'.[36] Via the collage of her prose, in which the collage-process of Charlie the last magician enacts related strategies, Hospital takes us to some of these edges, edges where she hopes the magic of ethical response will take place.

When Lucy thinks near the end that 'the truth is, we don't know anything, and even less do we want to know' (347), this is denied by a novel in which she and other people do desperately want to know. In Charlie and Gabriel's desperation to find Cat there is nevertheless something they do not want to know: they do not want to know she has been killed, for not only would she be gone but they would also have confirmed aspects of Australia and of Gabriel's father that they both do and do not want confirmed – that difference will not be tolerated, that there are powerful elements in Australian life that will punish and destroy whatever defies them, that we cannot relax, that we have to oppose somehow. Lucy in turn does not want to know that Charlie and Gabriel died in a bar-room brawl occasioned by Charlie's taking photographs in places where drug deals were being negotiated. And once again, as happened with Jean-Marc and Felicity in *Borderline*, the narrator, and possibly the reader as well, if the magic of empathy has happened, do not want to believe it.

Despite all of the book's strategies to throw the reader off balance, 'things that passionately wish to connect do connect' (179), as Gabriel's mother, Constance, who has found peace and constructed a framework for understanding and forgiving, asserts. The trouble is, connection may take many forms, not all of them constructive, just as, according to Lucy, magicians do not just do wondrous things, they 'tamper with things' and 'they don't consider the consequences carefully enough' (324). At the end of the novel Lucy makes her way back to Gabriel's mother's home in the Queensland rainforest, a Paradiso as it is also an Inferno, a sign of dynamic fruitfulness but also of a raw organic survival of the fittest. The butterfly effect is literally referenced in Cat's butterfly clip in Sheba's hair in a photo of Sheba taken by Robinson Gray, but then again perhaps it is simply one like it, for they can be bought in Woolworths after all; the same occurs with the earrings hanging round Sheba's neck, which could have been Cat's or merely ones like them. Earlier, Constance had pointed out that '[b]ehind every lie . . . there is a wound. One should be gentle with the bloody gashes in other people's lives' (180). At the end she reveals that the night when Robbie met Cat on the tram he had gone out and come back covered in blood. The novel wants us to be able to discriminate the gashes that we should not be gentle with, for the violence committed by the strong against the weak is always one of Hospital's targets.

What we know, Lucy decides, is that Cat was killed, but nonetheless that love exists. The trouble is, love is so multiform and so shot through with contradictions that all we know is, as she says, 'the fact of love' (348), that is, that love exists, but we do not know what love *is*. Like everything else that is important in Hospital's world, love is not so much an identifiable location as a flow of meanings, and flows, in their movements, leave things behind, so that to know that love exists is also to know 'the fact of absences' (349). Cat's physical absence sears and obsesses her childhood friends, while the absence of justice in her fate gnaws at and obsesses Lucy and Gabriel as well. This desire for justice sees Lucy and Catherine clinging on to the hope that Charlie and Gabriel are still alive, that they have escaped and opted for silence in order to ensure their safety. And so the narrative makes yet another circle, for just as Charlie became involved in an obsessive search for the dead Cat, refusing to believe she was dead, even constructing evidence that she was not, now Lucy and Catherine make plans to begin searching for Gabriel and Charlie. People have died, their fates are mysterious and there are aspects of that fate we do not want to find out, but hope, however banal it sounds, is a fierce imperative in Hospital's world. Dante had it, and Dante found his way out of the wood, although he needed guidance and encouragement, even protection, at many points. Giving up may tempt characters in Hospital's world, but ultimately to stop searching for answers is to surrender to the forces that want to control us. Meaning needs to be worked for, and in this quest the magic of the connections with which art beckons to us is one of our most potent resources: 'the artist . . . is a preserver and recorder, and also, a transformer, an alchemist, a magician. Every artist is that', claims Hospital.[37]

But this brings us to a final question: why the *last* magician? From one angle the last magician is the one who acts last, and in terms of this novel that is the reader. Lucy refers to the viewer of photographs, or the reader, as 'a magician of sorts' (243), as we make our own connections, write our own narratives out of the mixed and discontinuous evidence. It is also true that apocalyptic references run throughout Hospital's work, urgent with the sense that we too are all on the edge of the pit, that we need to act *now* to oppose the forces of violence and unfeeling. The deaths of figures in the novel who oppose authority indicate the danger, and although the book ends with Catherine and Lucy expressing their solidarity in the fight, the absence of loved ones shadows their resolution. The final words of Elza Adamowicz's book on surrealist collage speak to the end of this one, for Hospital would indeed remain hopeful that her textual collage continued to be uncomfortable: 'the dragon's tail in the bourgeois salon, the rococo ornament in the Bauhaus, the white-haired revolver – remain irretrievable objects which will continue to howl long after the critic has fallen silent'.[38]

CHAPTER 9

'What branches grow out of this stony rubbish?' *Oyster*

. . . one tragic irony of the frontier dream is that its proponents can never cease to feel surrounded. For, however far back the frontier is pushed, there is always something threatening on the other side.

Paul Carter[1]

Off the map

Oyster concludes a triptych of Hospital's novels focused on Australia, taking in the rainforest (*Charades*), the country's largest and oldest city (*The Last Magician*), and here the mythically testing environment of the outback. *Oyster* is set so far out it is on the edge of the desert, not far from that site of fabled promise and epic disaster, Cooper's Creek (Cooper Creek on maps).[2] This setting in far-west Queensland appears as a zone of foreboding,[3] in which the longest drought of the century figures as an absence of spiritual sustenance like that in T. S. Eliot's *The Waste Land*.[4] Accordingly, at the beginning of the novel there hangs over the town of Outer Maroo not just drought but a 'moral decay' overlaid with 'the simple stink of fear' (4)[5] and materialised in the stench of rotting sheep and dead cattle. The dry outback landscape reprises here its function in Australian culture as a place where individuals are stretched and tested, where the physical challenges appear to raise the issue of one's spiritual health, and, by extension, where questions are asked of Australian society as a whole.[6] As in *The Last Magician*, the answers to those questions in *Oyster* are not particularly encouraging.[7]

Outer Maroo is where the lost come to remain lost, beyond the reaches of officials as well as of the complexities of personal lives that have become too painful or tangled to bear. Although the townspeople assess themselves as sturdily independent – according to frontier value systems traceable back to the colonisation of North America – their insularity ironically leads to individuality being viciously subjugated, to the point where Outer Maroo has become a place where the individual has to conform or suffer the violent consequences. To that end the town has developed protocols that keep the outside at bay: telephones only work locally, Telecom vans blow up, the school board tries to control all learning, any letter posted is stamped and processed but never despatched, no information is provided for people passing through, and nosy outsiders disappear. Local grazier Andrew Godwin sounds the note of hysterical rural paranoia when he tells his wife that '[t]he greenies, the Abos, the unions, all these communists, they've got the government over a barrel' (243). In this vision, the government is not simply an irritating enforcer of taxes and rules but has to be resisted because it is 'coming to take our land' (243).

At the beginning of the book the sense of apocalyptic foreboding prepares us for the entrance of something or someone around which meaning will accrete, when Oyster finally walks in from the portentous desert side of the town in Book II and promises meaning (albeit a meaning denied by his enigmatic name).[8] By then, however, we have discovered from Book I (which relates events that occurred after Oyster's arrival) that he went on to establish an ostensibly idealistic spiritual commune which in fact controls its members ruthlessly, and is involved in the mining and distribution of opals via illegal international channels. Eventually, Oyster's control breaks down, the commune is destroyed by explosives and the town is consumed by fire, leaving the few survivors to tell the story.

Through Oyster, the book taps into the end-of-the-millennium disposition to perceive heightened significance in events, and although Hospital's work is fascinated by the state of mind that reads portentous meanings everywhere, she is wary of the judgemental neatness and finality promised by the voices of apocalypse. The apocalypse promised by Oyster turns out thus to be merely local, destroying himself and those who have believed in him or profited from him, and moreover does not happen in the year 2000 at all. As far as Oyster is concerned, Hospital relates how she initially imagined she would be dealing with a fallen hero figure, but the more she investigated such cult leaders the more she found 'that these people were mostly psychopaths from the start. All they had was a will to power and they intuitively knew that this was a good field in which to operate'.[9] In any event, the dream of, and the desire for, a purifying apocalypse is an attempt to deny history, the cycles and sequences of which are confusing, their meanings contextual and multivalent. The explanations promised by those who in 'The Second Coming of Come-by-Chance' are termed 'the signs-and-portents groupies' are too orderly,[10] and it is one of Hospital's prime assertions that 'time does not run in a straight line, and never has' (42).

Thus it is that the narrative announces that it will be tangled, will present mirages, will be as bent as the air above the desert, in its effort to be true to the complexity of the events it will tell us about. We are frequently reminded that time and space are shifting, entangled entities on the remote fringes of habitation. As one of the narrators, Jess, tells us: 'It seems to me, out here, that time and space and sound are merely functions of one another and that they are related as solid and liquid and gas are related. They sneak across their own boundary lines' (136). One of the consequences of the bends that time takes is that telling a story is not straightforward either, for both lived events and their telling take place in time. How to tell a story becomes an exercise in managing time and structuring the teller's priorities, so that, unsurprisingly, *Oyster* does not relate events in a straight line. The first thing that must be decided is where a narrative begins, for there may be many beginnings. The initial narrator, Jess, decides in the Prologue that the day when Oyster arrived, four years ago, must be considered the temporal beginning of the tale she wants to tell.[11] And yet the story proper starts in Book I with the events of last week. The beginning of a story in clock time may not be the best place to start after all, for a story does not exist as a naturally occurring object, but rather as a decision on the part of its teller to bring together certain elements and to erect a particular structure according to the journey the teller wishes the hearer to make. The journey Jess wishes us to make is one in which we arrive in Outer Maroo as outsiders, who experience the disorienting premonitions of disaster and the claustrophobic repression of opposition that have built up in the town since Oyster's arrival. As the novel progresses, more and more signs of this violence are suggested or presented, and increasingly Outer Maroo comes into focus as a nightmare realm of fear and oppression, a contemporary re-enactment of its originary apocalypse – that visited upon its original Murri inhabitants – and an ironic Australia in little, metonymic of the nation's self-congratulatory insularity, lack of wider references, and suspicion of difference and learning – 'in

Australia . . . tolerance for different norms is not high' (103) – all allied to the dominance of unreconstructed male power. In order to see this, we are taken on a roundabout route through the events of the last four years, and introduced to many of the town's characters before we are introduced to Oyster directly on page 273.

Arriving but never leaving

After the haze of innuendo and danger that hangs over the descriptions of the town, and the thoughts of its inhabitants, in the initial pages, things are brought into focus by the arrival of a truck from that regrettable connection to the outside world that is Quilpie. This allows the narrator to detail how suspicion of others has become so acute that any who arrive are not permitted to leave. In the truck are two strangers, whose fates will demonstrate how far Outer Maroo has travelled in its determination to shut itself off from the outside world – Sarah, an American searching for her stepdaughter Amy, and the Greek-Australian Nick from Noosa, also looking for his lost child, Angelo, both members of Oyster's commune.

The first chapter is narrated by Mercy Given, a sixteen-year-old girl from a strict, biblically oriented family, who feels trapped in Outer Maroo and threatened by the town's enforcement of obedience. Unlike most of the others, she craves contact with the outside world, which she reaches out to in her reading and in her thoughts as a form of defence against the violence and incomprehensibility of the town. Mercy echoes Hospital herself in her small size and in her family's insistence that she not read anything except the Bible, let alone watch TV or listen to the radio, 'so she is positively ravenous for anything in print' (53). As a consequence of her upbringing, Mercy 'constantly expects retribution of a fearful but unspecified sort' (53), a sensation that reverberates throughout Hospital's work, ensuring that her main protagonists are attentive, questioning, sign-reading, and looking over their shoulders. Yet where Lucy in *The Last Magician* had been worldly-wise and well-read, in *Oyster*, as Anne Steacy points out, 'It is the naïve, fertile mind of Mercy Given that is charged with deciphering the abundance of clues and passing on the story'.[12] Mercy's value is indicated also by her having escaped from Oyster's commune at one point, the only one to do so and live. This is later rendered as an escape through a tunnel that defies normal spatial laws, an event that is also rendered as a hallucination, echoing that tumble down a hole that defies the rules of nature experienced by Alice in *Alice in Wonderland*.[13] The fact that she had been clearly tricked with the promise of seeing her brother Brian, as opposed to the initially willed presence at the commune of the others, and that her violation had been particularly brutal, had lead Angelo, Nick's son, to smuggle her out in Donny Becker's delivery truck.

For Mercy, the example of disobedience to the diktats of the town has been best epitomised by the teacher Miss Susannah Rover, the only person, apparently, who had been able to leave. Mercy repeatedly recalls Miss Rover's acute analyses of the rotten state of affairs in Outer Maroo in her own mental journey away from Oyster and the town's control. As Anja Müller says, 'In describing language both as structuring and unnerving, the teacher formulates a personal politics of transgression which is not one of defiance but involvement'.[14] Mercy becomes responsible not simply for remembering Miss Rover's words but for acting on them, a transfer of meaning and responsibility from one dissenting woman to another couched in biblical language, echoing the biblical discourse that is so important in the book.[15] Hospital is attracted to the heightened resonance of this discourse at the same time as she is horrified by the certainty that takes hold of many people who wield it against the world and against others.[16] Oyster is never more repellent than when he is pouring forth torrents of apocalyptically biblical oratory, one more confirmation of Eugen Weber's study of apocalyptic and millenarian beliefs, in which he states: 'Rampant hate becomes more baleful when Biblical authority stands behind it.'[17] Nonetheless, in considering her situation, Mercy takes sustenance from the language of the Bible, for the novel both ironises the portentous orotundity of the scriptures and acknowledges their consoling substance (as well as impishly naming Mercy's family's dogs Exodus and Leviticus).

Mercy evinces her real difference from the town in that she is excited 'to find that there are vantage points from which she, Mercy, is *foreign*' (117; Hospital's italics), an openness that is the novel's best route to moral health. Yet it also brings the burden of excessive information, for the more open she is the more she arrives at a point where '[e]verywhere Mercy directs her eye or her ear there are contradictions so great she cannot understand how the fabric of the world contains them' (122). She is accordingly a character who feels empathy with outsiders, and who is constantly reaching out in her language for the press and colour of both the people and the objects around her, partly out of curiosity and partly as a form of defence: 'She can feel the pressure of words rising in Sarah, can see them pushing against Sarah's throat. Then she can see Sarah's thoughts on a screen inside her own head' (132). This appreciation of the other is subversive in Outer Maroo, and constitutes yet more evidence of Mercy's position as the threatening and threatened agent of change.

Mercy's very determination to remember Miss Rover, and to try to connect the tribulations of the present to the events of the past, positions her in opposition to the historical imperatives of the town. For one of the town's contradictions is that memory operates in reverse here, as the requirement to forget. In the past of Outer Maroo the obligation has been for individuals to forget the lives they led before they arrived there, to forget the rest of the world. Later it became the need for the town to forget the events that the book will narrate, events that the former introverted imperative has enabled. The principal event is Oyster's founding of a commune in the area, called Oyster's Reef, a twinned reference to the sea that once flowed over inland Australia but has dried up – a drying that resonates as a spiritual punishment – and to a vein of opals, the traffic of which Oyster wishes to control. At the same time, he appears initially to be in earnest with his apocalyptic warnings, and his gathering to him of people wishing to prepare themselves for the cataclysms promised by the new millennium, mostly young people who arrive in the town from all points of the globe, but who never depart and are rarely seen outside Oyster's compound. As one of them, Amy, says when she comes, terrified, into town to speak to Mercy, people cannot use their original names out there, and many simply disappear. When Amy's stepmother Sarah arrives looking for her, Mercy will try fruitlessly to get Sarah to leave on the truck she came on. Unable to convince Sarah of the danger, Mercy crazily defies the town's iron customs and takes the outsider home. Sarah is not simply an outsider, but an American Jew in a place that references Jews constantly through the use of the Bible, and yet whose relation to the modern world, or any profound knowledge of religion, is revealed in Mercy's admission: '"I didn't know there were still Jews", Mercy said in amazement' (99).[18] From this act of defiance the final unravelling of Outer Maroo's vicious tyranny, and the destruction of the town, begins.

The menace that pervades the narrative exists as threats aimed at Miss Rover and at blow-ins such as Nick and Sarah. It hangs in the air, behind the characters' words, in the centripetal pull of the town that does not allow anyone to leave.[19] We later find that Miss Rover's 'leaving' was in fact being kicked to death and her body being fed to a feral pig in a mineshaft, and the violence returns when two of the town's youths, Donny and Tim, kill the Given family's dogs (ironically offending against the scriptures) and set a car to blow up against their house as punishment for the family's harbouring Sarah Cohen. Mercy prevents the explosion and causes the car to crash out on the road instead. One of the two youths who die in the crash is Donny, the boy she had fantasised about sexually and who had helped to save her from the clutches of Oyster. By trying to blow up the Givens' house, Donny is acting against his better judgement, indicating the hold the town's orthodoxies have on him. This is a world that makes Mercy dizzy: its lines of causality appear bent and excessive, for it has forced her to be the cause of the death of the only boy she cared for.

Leaving but returning

While outsiders arrive and never leave, there are people who have left but who will return – although from another angle they have never left – the local Aborigines. There is a more significant presence of Aborigines in this book than in any other of Hospital's works. As Indigenous issues became more important in the country's moral and emotional economy, Hospital also became increasingly sensitised to the material and symbolic position of Australia's original inhabitants.[20] Without wanting to tell Aborigines' stories for them, she has nonetheless borne witness to their presence in the country, as well as to some of the violent contexts of that presence. The invisibility of Aborigines in many of the stories told in Australia is a type of aggression, which means that non-Aboriginal Australian writers now need to consider thoughtfully how best to reference Indigenous stories without appropriating their voices.[21]

Significantly, it had been the young Murris, those not yet beaten into resignation by a system in which they are the ultimate outsiders, 'who led the insurrection at the Reef' (309), thus starting the unwinding that would bring down Oyster's commune and the tyranny he had established. This indicates the Murris' agency, along with their moral claims on the land, and at the same time establishes a symbolic rendering of accounts with the general tyranny of Australian history. The fact that Hospital keeps the Murris mostly offstage, however, is an attempt not to appropriate to herself their voice, to try to tell Murri stories for them. After all, as Miss Rover tells Mercy: 'the Murris know how the miners and the cattle cockies think, don't they? But not vice versa' (353).

The Murri character Ethel is introduced early enough in the book to show that Australia cannot be told without reference to Aboriginal realities, particularly in a zone such as Outer Maroo which was founded by the people who massacred the local Murris in the 1870s, the latter's bones still being evident to the searcher. Despite the destruction visited upon Aboriginal lives and sites by white people, 'Whitefella Maroo been and gone once, and been and gone twice, and we're still here, my mob and me' (40), Ethel observes, although she alone is kept on at a station 'when the rest of the Murris pulled up stakes and moved off to Bourke' (55). Her dispossessed status is further signalled by her being a sexual object for her grazier employer, Andrew Godwin, and the attitude of white people towards Murris ranges from dismissive to hostile. One of Andrew Godwin's sons, Junior, respects Aboriginal traditions of land conservation, which leads his father to call him, bitterly, 'a communist' (246). Nonetheless, Ethel exists as a marker of the fact that from the Indigenous angle everyone else in Outer Maroo is an outsider, and she is able to predict, and then observe, the destruction of the town from her more realistic understanding of history and apocalypse. At least one Murri thus remains when the invaders have been destroyed, referencing the endurance and ultimate victory of Aboriginal people. Finally, when the town has been laid waste by fires both deliberate and accidental, Ethel predicts that now that the evil has been extirpated the rest of the local Murris will return, reoccupying finally the land that had been theirs. This is an ambiguous outcome for Fiona Coyle, portraying 'a more violent future characterized by intolerance, as one society obliterates another in waves of respective chaos and the re-establishment of an alternative order'.[22] In this vision, Outer Maroo's fate shows a world where Murri and white realities cannot fuse into any hypothetical 'third space', but one where Aborigines can only live happily in the absence of white people.

Pointedly, one white character who does respect something of both Murri history and their approach to the land is Bugger Harvey. Harvey condemns himself in the eyes of the locals by appreciating Murri company, not because he wants to abrogate to himself their moral authority, but to get drunk and to forget, for if anyone had a justification for wanting to blot out elements of the past, it would be Murris. Oyster also hangs out with the local Murris when he first arrives, despite local white people's suspicion, and many Murris join his commune; but his motives are self-interested, using Murri knowledge of opal deposits for himself, and acting on tips provided by Bugger Harvey, who he murdered after falling in with him on the remote Innamincka track. Harvey had come by Aboriginal knowledge of the landscape through his contact with local Murri people, and he tells Major Miner that he does not need to use gelignite to find opals, for 'the earth is our mother, like the Murris say . . . you don't *need* to tear her up . . . because she's generous' (310; Hospital's italics), a generosity that sees Harvey strike the rare black opal. Harvey identifies increasingly with the Murris, and is accordingly even more of an outsider in a town that sees itself as rebellious and marginal, but which reproduces traditional conservative positions with respect to the basic opposition on which Australian history is built. That Oyster's arrival is predicated upon Harvey's disappearance and probable death figures a replacement of the beginning of a flawed but hopeful and respectful Murri–white relationship (one imagines Harvey sharing wealth with the Murri people who are his community) with a relationship based on exploitation and paternalism, of which they have had more than enough already. The conflation of this history with recent events in the area is made via the desecration of sacred bora-bora rings by sinking opal shafts next to them (61), reprising the original nineteenth-century sinking of shafts 'inside a bora ring' (69), which was also followed by a purifying burning of the town. The present echo of events in the nineteenth century serves to indicate how incapable local people have been of learning from their history, thus dooming themselves to repeat its materialistic and murderous patterns.

At the latest point the novel has arrived at there are only three of the original townspeople left in Outer Maroo. Like Ethel, Jess and Major Miner are spared for reasons of moral justice (although sacrifices have been made, principally that of Miss Rover). Jess is known as Old Silence because she does not speak, a role she has willed for herself like Ada in *The Piano*, one of the results of which is that she is told secrets both knowingly and unknowingly. Her narration of her childhood, another of Hospital's visions of childhood as a time of almost unbearable intensity and manipulation by forces over which one has no or little control, is a story of family breakdown that leaves Jess with irreconcilable views of the world. One view comes from her warm, nomadic railway ganging family, the other from the ordered conviction of the Sisters of Mercy who take her in from age seven. These two incompatible references arouse in her 'the lure of *nowhere*' (148; Hospital's italics), a lure provided by Outer Maroo, which harboured her after she had stabbed a would-be rapist and fled. Almost all scenes of childhood in the book indicate pain and loss, although this may be partly explained by the town's function as a retreat for damaged people. Yet even Dorothy Godwin, of wealthy grazier stock, reads the fortunes of her life, along with those of the region, as a tale of loss: of traditional (white) livelihoods, of elegance, of security, of selling out to American corporations as well as to the grubby occupation of mining.

Not for nothing was Jess a surveyor and cartographer in her former life. Hospital has great respect for Paul Carter, whose work on the subjective, cultural aspects of maps and spaces ties in with her own perceptions of the fluid boundaries between frameworks of order and conscious or unconscious individual priorities. Indeed, she admits that:

> the idea of *Oyster* was born out of discussions with Paul Carter [who] introduced the possibility that a map could be used to conceal as much as to reveal. My memory is that we each dared the other to write something to prove that a map could hide a location: hence Outer Maroo.[23]

The willed relation of Outer Maroo to official maps thus reminds us of the social contexts that surround our charts: 'a desire to impose order on the ungovernable, signifying an undying and touching faith in magical thinking, which is what mapmaking is' (140). Moreover, as Miss Rover says, '[w]ords are maps' (63), for maps are not simply representations of space but also concepts, and vice versa. Our concepts are part of maps, are maps themselves, directions, organisations of space, signposts, and they chart nothing less than:

> Random violence, galaxies, deserts, city states, continental plates run aground, world wars, childhood, droughts, nebulae exploding, cups of tea, parents, teachers, surveying instruments and charts, flags, nations evolving and devolving, ancient hatreds, ancient fears, ancient passions ceaselessly renewed, apocalyptic fantasies, millennial dreads, city by-laws, earthquakes, inundations. (140)

Jess's lover is Major Miner, an explosives expert and opal hunter, whose name is 'adapted from Joseph Heller's Major Major (in *Catch-22*)'.[24] Sensitive to the noises within rock, the sounds that come from the supposedly silent spaces around us, Major Miner, who survived prison camp after the fall of Singapore in 1942, and who prefers to avoid the mess of talk, is another loner, attracted to Jess's silence. When Jess does begin to speak, she and Major Miner are revealed as agents of opposition to the tyranny that has perverted the town's isolation and independence to serve the ends of those with power. Once again, the arrival of Nick and Sarah is the catalyst, for Jess and Major Miner are galvanised in their desire to aid Nick and Sarah. Nick has stolen a four-wheel-drive and could flee the town, but will not leave until he can solve the mystery of what has happened to his son. This leads Jess and the Major to resolve that the only way to get them to leave is to show them the Reef, which both they and the reader have only the vaguest of ideas about despite the advanced stage of the novel we have reached.

The language of certainty

The events that Sarah and Nick precipitate lead to fires and explosions that get out of hand. The conflagration ironically reinforces the apocalyptic insistence by the novel's most repressive characters that the Lord's chastising fire is nigh. The fires become 'the Day of Wrath' (41) foretold in the warnings from Leviticus about devouring fires by the fundamentalist Afrikaner station-owner nicknamed Mr Prophet (199).[25] These fires, however, have actually come to devour the town itself and not its enemies. Indeed, Major Miner reads the destructive opal craze reignited by Oyster in terms of the spread of a bushfire (306).

Biblical rhetoric is applied by various voices in the book, often ironically but also as oppositional discourse to that of Oyster and individuals such as Prophet (really Dukke vanKerk, 'kerk' the Afrikaans word for 'church'), one of the owners of the school, for whom 'everything we need to know is in the Bible' (69), and who is a supporter of strict creationism, and hostile to any form of enquiry that challenges his interpretation of the biblical Word. It is not the language that is at fault, however, but the selective and violent uses it is put to, for while Prophet is seen as fierce and punitive, Mercy's also firmly religious parents are rendered as possessing a 'vast and frightening innocence' (126) in their belief in 'original goodness' (192), in standing by the Bible and in rejecting any wider form of enquiry or knowledge.

When Mercy's father talks of the attempts on their life by conservative forces in the town – for he is one person who has not been swayed by Oyster – he is calm in the conviction that whatever happens is God's will. Mercy is irritated by his refusal to face up to individual human responsibility or to intervene (191).[26] At the same time, he serves to indicate that evangelical Christians need not be simplistically vengeful. Appealing to the Bible as a set of stable guidelines, however, is to appeal to a notoriously multivalent and contradictory text, described by Miss Rover as nothing less than 'fabulous' (200), one more irony surrounding the desperate attempts to derive certainty from a book that, like all books but more than most, is a kaleidoscope of shimmering angles, a document of human variation, dreams, hates and speculation. Miss Rover teaches about reality through *Alice in Wonderland* instead, where 'suspensions of normal logic hold sway' (345), a book which understands human unreason and the tortuous paths by which we understand or justify anything, but which is not interested in punishing or prescribing. To be properly responsive to the world is to be able to move within the multifariousness, to be less certain, to be aware of the corners, the variations, the quiddity of things, like Mercy 'who knows too many languages, but is at ease in none of them' (210) and who 'finds knowledge itself to be inexhaustible and exhausting' (258). The forces surrounding Oyster despise and reject books – 'the vain pride of human learning and books' (330), as Prophet says when shouting down Charles Given, a brave voice claiming for God a gentler presence than the punitive figure of power preached by Oyster. The inflamed congregation ransacks Given's study and burns his books, even beating Major Miner unconscious when he tries to rescue some of them.

Hospital's prose is itself evocative of the resounding portentousness of biblical language, albeit in the service not of certainty but of variety, individual perception and rapidly shifting perspectives. The novel is constantly bringing the focus back to details, to objects, expressions and fleeting emotional states, preferring the shifting nature of details over the harshness of certainty and hierarchies. As Sarah Cohen says in a poignant passage of empathy between her and Mercy's mother, Vi: 'They're overwhelming, aren't they, the memories of little things? . . . Details that get stuck in the mind, they're so potent, they're like concentrated essence of the past' (130–1). In this sense, details can serve to deny the broad and rigid truths touted by evangelical enthusiasts; indeed, 'it is even said to be the mark of true saints that the tiniest details can distract them' (258).

The desert prophet

As the novel develops, Oyster's presence is veiled from us in the elliptical comments of others: the character after whom the book is named seems eternally delayed, a process metonymic of the operation of the promises such a figure represents. When Oyster does arrive, his difference is marked by arriving from the west, from the side of the desert, and not from the side of outsiders and the government, and also by his absorbing beauty, a sign of the extraordinary individual in Hospital's work, but not an indication of moral value, whether positive or negative. His mysterious arrival and magnetic presence have an unexpected effect on the hard-boiled locals from the start, transfixing them. We are introduced to his confident oratorial sanctimoniousness when he begins to speak in orotund biblical fashion on the pub verandah, giving a lecture on how oysters are seeded in Broome as if he were giving a sermon. The outback pub, with its darkened interior, is suggestive of the comforting community of a church, as also of the darkened interiors of the minds of many of those who inhabit it, notwithstanding their laconic humour. The pub crowd gives him credit for having appeared from nowhere, for the masculine heroism of apparently being wounded in his leg, and for having a rifle. Possessing three magnificent opals also claims their attention, for opals command respect in opal country, especially an opal country that appears to be running out of opals.

It is somewhat of a mystery how Oyster comes to break into such a suspicious and generally hard-bitten community, especially as his cult draws waves of outsiders to his opal-mining commune out at Oyster's Reef. The town already harbours the fundamentalist congregation of the Living Word, however, and Hospital suggests that there exists an accommodation between the pub community and fundamentalist congregations in the outback, largely on account of their shared suspicion of government and their ethic of self-reliance. Even the most suspicious characters such as Jess and Major Miner (but not, apparently, Susannah Rover) repeatedly refer to how surprised they were that Oyster managed to communicate with them, with the town at large, to make them feel included. One of the ironies of the self-excluding community is that its inhabitants want above all to feel included. Unable to achieve this uncomplicatedly in the wider, more complex and fragmented society, they reject that and retreat to a zone where they hope the boundaries they set up will keep out the multifariousness of outside society and produce the confirming explanatory grids they hunger after. Oyster has the gift of making the lost and searching feel included, and Major Miner's memories record Oyster's early days in Outer Maroo as hopeful, and the energy from the commune as positive.

It is also a mystery how Oyster seems to know about the opals on Andrew Godwin's property, how he knows local gossip and vectors of power. Only at the end do Major Miner and Jess put two and two together, for the Major had seen Bugger Harvey set off with the same opals down the back way to Lightning Ridge, the same direction that Oyster had appeared from, already knowing a great deal about Outer Maroo. Jess had seen that the blood on Oyster's leg was not his own when he exposed himself to her the first night, hoping unsuccessfully that she would have sex with him, an early sign of his less than holy intentions.

The confidence with which Oyster takes off his clothes and presents his naked body to Jess speaks of being so convinced of his rightness and power that Jess is led to comment: 'There is something about hubris . . . that does inspire genuine awe' (327). Accordingly, extremist communities, such as David Koresh's Branch-Davidian sect near Waco, Texas, or that of the frightening Canadian cult leader Rock Theriault, fascinate Hospital,[27] and the novel is partly an attempt to account for the mechanisms and consequences of the appearance of a self-proclaimed leader. Bronwyn Davies points out that the book 'shows how submitting to domination may seem easier than resistance but constitutes such submission as deadly'.[28] The series of letters written by his followers at one point tries to present in its many-sidedness some of the reasons why people move into the orbit of someone like Oyster, from blissful abnegation of the self into the hands of a controlling figure, to opportunistic experiment, to aimless drifting, followed by inertia or even inability to leave on account of coercion and the centripetal force of Oyster's commune. Amy's letters chart a progression from belief and optimism to tiredness and loss of faith as the chilling realities of the violent, authoritarian regime become clearer. The careless allowing of babies to die, the renaming of people, the refusal to allow men and women to form relationships, the denial of permission to leave the group once entered, all paint a frightening picture of the power of the messianic figure to dominate and crush the will of others.

We get a sight of Oyster's meretricious hypocrisy when he induces Mercy to go to the Reef. There she sees a dusty hive of activity recalling aspects of the Sebastião Salgado photograph of Brazilian quarry-workers that is referenced several times in *The Last Magician*, the workers appearing like 'the living dead' (357). Oyster launches into a rhetoric of baptism, purity and salvation, in ways that do not impress Mercy, for whom his use of the Bible is repulsive; but she has decided she will do anything to make contact with her brother Brian, who has been swallowed by Oyster's world. Family is one of the first things to be denied the acolyte in such sects, for it is one of the things that might have the emotional power to counteract the brainwashing carried out by the leader figure.[29] Mercy has also been told by Donny Becker that Brian will not last long, that he will be consumed by Oyster's rapacious sexual appetite for both boys and girls, though Mercy does not at this time understand what Donny is telling her. She will, however, when Oyster takes her into the depths of his underground complex and forces her into an act of fellatio with him, all the while uttering a speech of sententiously biblical references to her eating 'the fruit of the Tree of Knowledge' and promising that 'it shall all be revealed' (365), which is only too disgustingly apparent to Mercy. After passing out, she wakes up to find she has been raped as well, and is now forbidden to leave the compound.

Blessed is he that readeth[30]

Mercy, one of the supposedly least powerful people in Outer Maroo, is nevertheless instrumental in Oyster's downfall. In Miss Rover's words: '*[a] belief in powerlessness is seductive, Mercy, and so is belief in a Higher Power. They both let one off the hook too easily*' (116; Hospital's italics). Mercy had objected to her father's acceptance of the will of God as constituting an endorsement through inaction of Oyster's power, and she has been proven right. Tyrants need to be opposed, and even the meekest possess the potential to bring down the mighty and proud, for once one diverges from what is expected, fissures and cracks open up in the structures of repression with unpredictable results. When Mercy takes Sarah Cohen to her home it seems like a small enough act of defiance, but it sets in motion a chain of events that ends with the destruction of Oyster and of Andrew Godwin's power.

There are 'so many different ways of being certain you are right' (203), as Mercy sees, and the trouble is that the more people believe they are right the more other people appear to need controlling. Thus it is that the two parents who come to Outer Maroo to try to find their lost children (whom they will find to be dead) belong, in the case of Sarah, to a group that represents the horrors of exclusion on a global scale (she is Jewish), and in the case of Nick, to a group that represents the pain of, and need for defensiveness against, exclusion on a local scale (he is an Australian and Greek as well). Nick knows all about the need to fit in, 'to swim unseen behind words the way Australians do' (104–5), so that the way in which the slightest social interaction becomes a test of one's conformity in Outer Maroo is merely a more policed version of what he has experienced all his life. Both are represented as acutely sensitive to the fierce separatism of classification and fundamentalism, for, as Sarah realises, 'being secular offers no protection from the true believers, or from the irrational, or from extremes' (385).

Living in the world means that the beliefs of others are a part of our lives whether we like it or not, and one of the consequences in Hospital's vision is that secular unbelievers need to think more about extremes of religious belief and behaviour, as has certainly been proven true in the years since she wrote the book. The final vision of Oyster's domain is of Sarah and Nick hiding in the now empty tunnels of the Reef, having cleaned a small area of the wall, embracing and staring into the dark. They have lost their children, but they have survived the anger and violence of the town, and there is a plan to save them, along with Mercy, Jess, Major Miner and Ethel. Jess and Major Miner decide to stay off the map. They are the true eccentric outsiders, distinct from those only too willing to devise other hierarchies, other forms of control, to replace those they claim to reject. Ethel represents a balancing of accounts that sees the land back with the Murri, partly through their own endurance and resistance, partly through the self-destructive strains in European-Australian culture.

The novel allows us to imagine Mercy driving Sarah and Nick away from the explosions that are ripping the area apart. Mercy drives towards Brisbane, a city of a hope so intense that she starts to reference it in her imagination in the biblical language she knows, ironically citing the Book of Revelation, the book whose language has been implicated in the novel in so much exclusion and destruction. Hopes for revelation, for the wonder of certainty and calm, do not just belong to those who would oppress in the name of what are claimed to be the truths of scripture. Mercy, Sarah and Nick move towards the golden city, damaged but hopeful, supporting Russell West's claim that 'the quest which drives the plots of Turner Hospital's fictions . . . is a search for a single, stable place'.[31]

The languages of ends and explanations may result in the destroying fire for some, albeit not necessarily those for whom it was foretold; but Hospital's non-linear book is an implicit refutation of the narrow linearity through which the claimants of truth bully those who do not agree with them, as well as an implicit endorsement of the power of stories that escape rigid boundaries to enable spaces in which we can refuse to be bullied. For Donald

Greiner, the novel is 'primarily . . . about the nature of narrative itself',[32] for it is in our relation to stories and explanations that our social politics are revealed: 'Storytellers are threats to people who fear the complexity of language because meaningful tales do not observe the kinds of boundaries found on standard maps.'[33] Like readers who want neatly-packaged narratives, millennial thinking is attracted by ends, and cannot deal with the messy, fractal flows that characterise existence, the multiplicity of connections that every event or person has, the apparently shapeless fuzz of life and lives. Not for nothing does Sarah say she is 'frightened of endings' (167) shortly after referring to the chaos theory her husband was working on, an approach to reality that sees significance and beauty in the complexity of many of the supposedly most shapeless aspects of existence, from clouds to the behaviour of liquids. Despite the survival of most of the town's morally just inhabitants, however, and the punishment of the tyrannical, we do not know whether the closure of Oyster's death occurred. The manipulative destructiveness he represents, however, definitely did not perish. Hospital was accordingly not finished with the broad areas dealt with in the book, returning to them in her next novel, albeit in very different settings.

CHAPTER 10

A moment out of place
North of Nowhere, South of Loss

Time in the everyday lifeworld is not undifferentiated and unhierarchical – it is textual, lending itself to the formation of boundaries and to a process of interpretation delimited by our experience with those boundaries.

Susan Stewart[1]

The ache of memory

After the University of Queensland Press published her *Collected Stories: 1970–1995* (1995), containing all of the stories from *Dislocations* and *Isobars*, as well as seven new stories grouped together under the heading 'North of Nowhere', Hospital published a new volume of short stories in 2003, containing these seven stories plus seven more, under the title *North of Nowhere, South of Loss*. The title gestures enigmatically to her intense feeling for Queensland ('North'), allied to the strength of her attachment to her home in recent years, the American state of South Carolina. The northern Australian state and the southern US state seem related to her: in their climate; in the way more powerful states have looked down on them as backward; and in their histories of oppression of Aborigines and Torres Strait and Pacific Islanders and African-Americans respectively. Moreover, both states have felt misunderstood and overlooked by the centres of power, and are accordingly determined to preserve their distinctiveness in the face of homogenising pressures.

In terms of the collection's thematic range, the despondent reverberations of the title reference Hospital's continued sense of the ambiguous operations of memory, in which the stronger the presentness of memories the more the ache of their pastness is enhanced. The way the title slides from a geographical relation, albeit a paradoxical one, to a metaphorical or emotional relation reverberates with the ontological vertigo present in all of the stories, arising from the unrepresentability of time, memory and motive. The relation between representation and recall thus provides an issue around which much of the book is organised, and it is significant that at the end of 'Frames and Wonders', in which two characters debate versions of their common past, the central character announces that she can only be considered in a certain way 'in French'.[2] The languages we use to present our stories are determining, but, the book asks, does this end up straitjacketing us within frames, or does it instead ensure the wonders of difference and the richness of stories? This question is dramatised in repeated perspectives on the ways the connections operate between human beings who share a past or a situation that they see differently, an experience that provides, in Jill Bennett's words on the impact of surprising works of art, 'a jolt that does not so much *reveal* truth as thrust us involuntarily into a mode of critical inquiry'.[3]

'Frames and Wonders' is especially symptomatic of Hospital's dramatisation of the emotional investments we make in our narrations of the past. In *S/Z*, that prolonged enquiry into the nature of realism, Roland Barthes talks of 'an initial rite [by which the writer] first transforms the "real" into a depicted (framed) object; having done this, he can take down this object, *remove* it from his picture: in short, de-pict it'.[4] Hospital's story echoes this observation, not only through the word 'frames' but via the several pointed allusions to paintings and books that keep returning the reader to the way in which we tell our stories within networks of references that have accreted around us in the language(s) we speak, the history we studied, and the cultural baggage we carry. We tell stories to each other within these frames, which means that the same story of the past can never be told by two people, given that no two frames are ever identical.

The central literary intertext to 'Frames and Wonders' is Proust, whose work constitutes a detailed examination and exemplar of the processing of time by the imagination, both consciously and unconsciously. Proust is transparently indicated by the use of names of two of the principal characters from *In Search of Lost Time* – Odette and Swann. Swann calls the woman Odette because he thinks of Proust's character as a coquette who is finally won by Swann in the novel, figuring what he presumes his role will be with respect to the woman in the story. The names, however, resonate not only with the passion Swann feels for Odette throughout lengthy earlier portions of Proust's work, but with Swann's anguished feelings of jealousy and suspicion, and the sensation of failure when they finally do get married. For both Swann and the reader of Proust, his relationship with Odette is most luminous and thrilling when they are not tied to one another, and when Swann has not become so proprietorial.

In Hospital's story Swann is proprietorial about how he would like their experience to be recorded, rejecting the images of a street photographer, despite Odette's hunger for images of them together. He claims true knowledge about their past, averring to an experience that Odette denies, despite the fact that Swann claims to have photographic proof. His explanation of her denial refers to another of the frames within which we process reality, that of her Anglo-Saxon origins, which he claims have led her to repress her relation to passion; in this case, to deny history. The fact that she doubts the very existence of the village in which the photographs were taken – La Forêt le Roi – despite the fact that the village can be found in any detailed atlas of France, suggests, as so often in Hospital's work, that the truths of history are not necessarily those established by supposedly objective evidence. Swann's interest in photography is seen by Odette as an interest in a process that fixes reality in a way that end-stops debate, and the presence in the story of deer and birds resonates with her feeling that she is being controlled, trapped, watched and even hunted. His desire to map the grid of their passion over that of the Sun King, Louis XIV, and his mistress Louise de la Vallière appears to be a disguised attempt to secure the narrative of their relationship according to references that are significant for him, ignoring any frames within which she might want to see their story. The second section of the story accordingly announces 'This is not a sign', alluding to the text written within Magritte's painting *La Trahison des Images* (1929), an image which alerts us to the fact that even a soberly realistic painting of a pipe is not the same thing as a pipe, that it partakes of another order of reality.

In the third section, 'Afternoon of a faun', also alluding to a work of art in another medium, Debussy's *L'après-midi d'un Faune* (1894), they see a doe, and Odette is reminded of a line in an Old English ballad, 'The Three Ravens'.[5] This ballad tells of a dead knight and the death from grief of a woman, symbolised as a pregnant doe, compressing a tale of illicit love, ensuing pregnancy and an honour killing into its few lines. Swann mentions a case recently of a priest and a pregnant woman, both of whom were found naked and dead in the forest. For the Frenchman the forest is an erotic space in its darkness and secrets, while talk of such things frightens Odette; the iconography of naked women in the landscape relates to a whole cultural tradition of the ownership and use of women by men, as one more object in nature to be dominated, to which Swann's rough taking of Odette from behind as they observe a stag is related. Naked women in the landscape are pointedly evoked in the section 'Le déjeuner sur l'herbe', named after Manet's famous painting of a nude woman in the company of two dressed men (considered scandalous in 1863), a depiction of the rights of male power over women, captive to the male gaze within the painting as well as to the history of representing women for males to view. When Odette asks Swann for a photograph of them having a picnic, he is more interested in his framing of her in his network of historically referenced photographs, at which point she snaps and implies that he is in denial about the fact that she cannot stay with him, that their relationship cannot be more than an interlude in their lives.

At the beginning and the end of the story the characters muse in the present over the impossibility of their (presumably illicit) relationship by way of the metaphor of the impossibility of the existence of the village. At the end, nonetheless, it is Odette who claims she has the photographs, that she does remember them after all, so that while talking over the past has reanimated his controlling fantasies in her memory, for her they now operate differently; the frames have altered from being his photography to her narrative structure. The names of some of the story's sections may be considered her riposte to his wanting photographs of her framed in terms of mythological and historical associations. Now her memory of that day is not that of the controlling framework but a memory of the sign of history and the passing of time, in which stories mutate incessantly. One of the wonders that has ensued is that, when she was experiencing the day, it seemed like a place and a time that he was inhabiting and that she was outside of, manipulated by his knowledge of the location and by his metaphors. Now, as it is recalled, it has become more hers, and her recreation redraws the framework of what Swann had once presumed the right to establish. Memories bind these lovers of long date together, but also separate them. Given that this phenomenon is common knowledge, and even, as Suzanne Nalbantian points out, that neuroscience now considers confabulation 'to designate a normal element of healthy autobiographical memory',[6] Hospital's story is not so much a stating of a problem as a worldly-wise enjoyment of the fissures that two people's intimate memories open up. Thus it finishes with both characters referring to photographs of each other that they love. After all the quarrelling over their versions of the past, they agree to validate images that each holds of the other.

A photograph is also central to 'Flight', in which Cecily receives a postcard sent from Australia of a picture taken at the Château Chambord in France in which her face figures (echoing the mystifying international transport of images in *The Last Magician*). This brings back a memory of being closely scrutinised by a man at the Château Chambord, leading to a search for the company that produced the postcard, and eventually the anticipation of sex with the same man, who turns out to be the photographer of the image that has been transformed into the arty postcard. The astounding collocation of differing planes of existence has led to this moment that offers a healing sense of connection, offsetting a different set of coincidences back in Australia that had led to someone's death in a car accident, which Cecily blames herself for.

The story's title is alluded to constantly, beginning with a sequence of birds threatening to fly into a window in the nightmare that opens the story. The intertwined nature of aspects of what we call reality, and what we think of as realms outside logic or explanation, is summoned up by this opening sequence, for the story slips in and out of the here and now as it goes in search of connections in dreams, old manuscripts, personal memories and unexplained coincidences. The birds are accordingly woven together into a network of references: the birds swarming in the dream, the bird in the dream that crashes into the window, the bird in the Venerable Bede's parable about our lives being like 'the flight of a sparrow through a lighted hall' (132), and the bird that is inside the Château Chambord when Cecily is visiting. Birds conventionally signify freedom, but here this is set against their fragility, allegorising the supposed freedom of human beings at the same time as our vulnerability to time and chance.[7]

Cecily's story enters familiar territory in Hospital's fiction, wherein '[i]t is possible, for example, that random arrangements of certain objects constitute some kind of magnetic field' (135). It is common in her writing that a series of baffling events is narrated while a character puzzles over them, generally coming to the conclusion that they are not meaningless at all, that their conjunction contains a meaning or meanings if only one can trace back the forces that have brought them together. A hunger for design permeates Hospital's work, so that a figure such as Leonardo da Vinci, who devised the spiralling staircase in the Château Chambord, is considered positively inasmuch as he believed in the value of 'potent alignments and perfect symmetries' (135). Nevertheless, while things may be brought together or into alignment, they might just as inscrutably fail to connect meaningfully, instead touching and then moving apart again, like sections of the stairway. The mere desire for meaning is thus no guarantee, for it is another given in Hospital's fiction that the fit between cause and effect is impossible to predict or to enforce. Criss-crossing events, others' desires, and unexpected effects create such a rich swirl of potential directions or conjunctions that we need to be able to change direction quickly or we will be hermeneutically and ontologically submerged.

In 'Flight' the strange coincidences begin to accrete around the possibility of healing for Cecily, but they can lead in quite other directions as well. That apparent chains of causes and effects can lead in unexpected directions, and have the capacity to rewrite the plots of our lives, is nowhere more chillingly revealed than in 'For Mr Voss or Occupant', a dark tale that entangles canonical Australian literary and cultural references with the false leads of the Hitchcockian murder tale. The title is inevitably shadowed by Patrick White's iconic novel *Voss* (1957), summoning up the novel's eponymous protagonist, a defier of the country's landscape who ends up being defeated by it. The reference is intensified by the central character in the story being called Laura White, Laura being the name of the woman to whom Voss writes to propose marriage in the novel, albeit only after he has left to pursue meaning in the landscape. The Voss in Hospital's story is called Laurence Voss, Laurence and Laura echoing each other, while Laura's surname mischievously stitches White himself into the story.

The confusions hinted at by these criss-crossing names begin when Laura uses one of the junk-mail garden catalogues that come for the former owner of her house, Mr Voss, to order something for herself. As the address is the same, she does not bother to cross out Voss's name but enters her credit card details and sends it off, feeling indeed that 'they were kindred spirits' (53), imagining a link in a way that will come back to destroy her life.[8] Be suspicious of presumed links, the story hints, or we may enact our own identity theft. Mr Voss's whereabouts are in fact a mystery; no-one knows where he went after the bank foreclosed on the house. For a time, he had been suspected of murder after the disappearance of his daughter and his estranged wife, and there is a bad feeling about the house in the neighbourhood. A local policeman calms Laura by telling her that the real murderer had been caught but that Voss had been so disturbed by events that he ended up in a psychiatric institution.

Things are brought to a head when Laura's daughter Jilly goes off on the bus from Brisbane to Sydney, supposedly to pick up a ticket to join her father in New York. Events revolve around Laura and Jilly being out of touch during the bus trip, along with the unlikely proposition that a wealthy father would oblige his thirteen-year-old daughter to go to Sydney by bus to get a ticket to New York, when it would be easy to travel via a connecting flight from Brisbane to Sydney. Jilly disappears, police information suggests that Laura is using Voss's name as an alias, while it transpires that Mr Voss has had a relapse and thinks he was the killer of his daughter and ex-wife, and that he had been hovering around the house all the time.

Voss fulfils his false memory of himself by murdering Jilly and shooting himself, and the tale ends with Laura predictably shattered, her happy homecoming to Brisbane having ended in tragedy. Ironies abound in the tale, a macabre vision of the inoperability of either sympathy (Laura was highly sympathetic to what she knew of Voss's story, and sensitive to her having usurped his house) or suspicion (she and Jilly had notified the police of the man in the red Toyota who drove past and looked at Jilly). In the end Laura is faced with 'the grimmest joke in horror's bag: that the innocent and the damaged were capable of fearful crimes' (74).

The tragedy that had happened to Voss has now been re-enacted by him; history is a chain in which we enter other people's stories without realising it and without being able to step out of them when we wish. Voss committed suicide, an avatar of White's self-punishing Voss, and the scale of his actions ensures that he will haunt Laura's story forever, as White's Voss haunts his Laura. A form of haunting lies at the centre of history, as expanded upon in the work of psychoanalysts Nicolas Abraham and Maria Torok, who suggest that 'what haunts are not the dead, but the gaps left within us by the secrets of others'.[9] Like the wild, overgrown Queensland garden of Voss's house – providing a contrast to the deserts of White's Voss's fate – history delights and shelters, but also hides and menaces. History's claim to order the world is constantly diluted by the intersection of histories, and we relax at our peril our vigilance over what is never completely our story.

Beyond nowhere

In the story that provides part of the volume's title, 'North of Nowhere', the protagonist's impulse is definitely to step out of the story that has been scripted for her. Bethesda has come to Cairns to escape the memories of her dysfunctional family in the small town of Mossman, her mother dead, her father in and out of prison in Brisbane, and her brother a drug addict whom she has not seen for two years. Evading the past completely, however, is impossible; our control over the past is always incomplete, and Beth's brother finds her at a bus-stop and ends up stealing her pay. Moreover, the past also visits us in our dreams, where it assails us in a swirl of images, displacements and connections, meaning that even our beds at night are no refuge.

In opposition to the predation of the past, Bethesda offers the biblical resonances of her name (a pool in Jerusalem with healing properties; John 5); that is, her own ability to heal others. If we have limited defences against our own memories, especially given their avenue into us through dreams, other people with their different stories become especially important in the possibility of healing, even if temporary, and this is what we see at the end of the story. Bethesda is living at a hostel for girls, but all the hostel has to offer those it assumes responsibility for is a regimented vision of order, from a starting point of scorn for its charges. The girls, in turn, intensify the oppressive regime at the hostel by picking on anyone they perceive as weak. When another girl cries in her sleep, Beth climbs into bed with her to hold her, and this calms the girl. This girl, from Cooktown in the far north, had been described by the district nurse as coming from '[n]orth of nowhere, believe me. In every sense' (29). While this is precisely the sort of person the hostel has a special responsibility to care for, and the other girls to feel solidarity with, everybody's response is to reject and victimise her. Living up to her name, Bethesda is the only one who tries to comfort Sue, and to some extent this removes her from the attacks of her own dreams. In this, she and the story gloss Todorov's argument in *Life in Common*, where he points out that '[i]n the Warsaw ghetto . . . the surest way to survive was to devote oneself to another'.[10]

In Australian history in general, the most significant Other has been the land's original inhabitants, a kind of colonial 'limit case' in Bob Hodge and Vijay Mishra's summation, in that they 'posed the minimal material threat and the maximal threat to legitimacy', as indicated by 'the tacit recognition of an absolute legitimacy which is inscribed in the name that the colonisers gave to these people: Aborigines'.[11] 'Our Own Little Kakadu' approaches this troubled area in Australian culture through the appropriately tormented character of Jug, who is going through mental anguish as various planes of his reality clash and disturb the foundations on which he has lived his life. Memories of his childhood and violent father come back to torment him, a metaphor perhaps of the nation's violent past and growing-up phases, at the same time as recent interaction with local Aborigines has intensified Jug's sense of the power of what is not physically apprehendable, a sense that had initially been established by a relatively recent conversion experience in a local church.

What is real in Hospital's fictional world is not simply what is most apparent or obvious, and this is soon brought home when Jug's son's girlfriend, Liz, an Aborigine, says that what's wrong with Jug this time is that '[h]e's been sung' (106). Hospital is committed to the world's being a more mysterious place than either the conventions of realism or common-sense would have us believe, so anyone prepared to affirm realms other than the palpable has her respect. People breaking down, or on the edge, also have her sympathy, so Jug's situation serves as a double challenge to everyday realities. Jug had been sung because of his work on a mining company road through Kakadu that has traversed sacred sites. Just when it seemed he might not carry out the company's wishes, he changes his mind when Liz tells him that she is carrying his grandchild and that Jug is destroying the child's birthright. The appeal to his sense of family and futurity infuriates him, in a conflation of his famously short temper and his barely suppressed hostility to Aborigines, and the potential bringing together of two tensely positioned peoples through the symbol of birth is broken.

Jug's subsequent mental torment places him outside all consoling structures, as he feels the accusatory presence of past generations of Aborigines and then realises that 'nothing fits' (113). Arriving at this realisation he has stepped out of the everyday world, which 'is full of fucking people who don't know what's real and what's not' (105). Whether one believes that this is the result of being sung or the result of a synapse between Jug's Christianity and the awareness of the severe disjunctions between his life as a road-builder and his values, the story comes down on the side of the reality of Jug's vision of a continuity between the dead and the living. As a consequence, Jug evolves into what Donna Davis calls 'a devoted servant of the all-powerful living earth'.[12] The rest of his family cannot understand why he lets everything grow wild and will not fence in or control either wild or domestic animals, but Davis's reading of Jug's realisation that 'what one does to the land one does to all human beings, past and present, because all coexist' is convincing.[13] Hospital's determination to depict a born-again Christian road-building contractor coming up against Aboriginal sacramental values indicates her willingness to take on challenging and sensitive issues, and it is noticeable that, although Aboriginal perspectives are invoked in the story, the principal points of view are those of white people who, because of their tropical location, are forced to respond to the perspectives of Indigenous people in ways that most non-Aboriginal Australians are not. The story does not presume to speak for Aboriginal spirituality so much as for a view of the world, wherever it comes from, that sees time as a continuum, with all of its implications for our responsibility towards the land and others.[14]

Destabilising the certainties of place further informs 'Litany for the Homeland', in which the feeling of home paradoxically begins with its absence, for leaving a home behind forces us to compare it with a state of being not at home. One may see shapes on the moon from Brisbane through a telescope, but not the faces of one's beloved grandparents left behind in Melbourne. Looking through a telescope into space leads to the realisation that we live in 'the outer bush-league suburbs of the cosmos' (257), from where we may further conclude that '[i]n margins and in longings: this is where all homelands begin' (257). Australians whose origins were elsewhere are said to be 'visitors' (258), a contemporary awareness of the temporal priority and moral high ground occupied by the nation's Indigenous inhabitants, even if most non-Aboriginal Australians are not visitors at all, given that they will never go 'home', and the home that speaks to them may be felt as deeply as it is by Indigenous Australians, albeit differently. Thus it is that the last passage of this general rumination upon place and belonging mixes the material experiences common to all groups, such as bushfires, with differing cultural explanations, such as the Second Coming or the Dreaming, in a sentence in which all Australians are joined together.

This general section gives way to narrative memories, when the girl, who hides her name from us as she is experiencing identity rearrangement after having moved from Melbourne to Brisbane, recalls Paddy McGee, a 'wild boy' (259) who beckoned to her to cross the line of the fence and play with him. This boy has surfaced before in Hospital's prose, the rascal with the heart of gold, a permanent indictment of the system that establishes respectability as the sign of value. The girl who crosses the fence to play in the trees with the half-wild boy steps into the territory that all of Hospital's heroines occupy: beyond the conventional but aware of the transgression, occupying it mentally in a way Paddy does not, analogously to the way we might feel a place more acutely after leaving it.

Paddy disappears, but there are Paddys everywhere in the girl's life from then on, and now grown up she talks of Franklin, another outcast at MIT where she is teaching, his assignments full of violence. His outsider status reverberates within two framing references – growing up in Harlem and being a Marine – both experiences that have left him full of raw and intense images and experiences that he cannot banish, that have become his homeland. Franklin wishes he could process these experiences in some useful way, and the stories he writes are a step towards that, towards getting back in a way to another land.

The final home portrayed in the story is that of a Cree in mid-winter northern Manitoba who is transformed by being able to show the narrator where he was born, a location in existence for only part of the year, for he was born on a frozen lake while his mother was ice-fishing. He touches home more feelingly by being able to show it to someone else, partly echoing Hospital's practice, as she restlessly shows us where she came from over and over in her work. Wherever she is, Hospital is touching Queensland, a homeland whose margins are everywhere: when the Cree shows the narrator his birthplace, she says: 'I swear I smelled the frangipani tree and Breakfast Creek' (271).

The end of the story returns thus to a meditation on the nature of home, in which the home of Queensland is both central and yet experienced in terms of edges, outside the centres of power in all cases: 'The world spins in the margins of space, Australians float in the edges of the world, Queenslanders live in the rind of Australia, I have always drawn breath in the cracks of Queensland' (271). For this reason, home can be touched when one touches other margins, other people who are outsiders for different reasons, people whose home is in some way athwart the comfortable sense of home that exists as the notional place that more securely anchored people are imagined to inhabit. The perspectives provided by looking through different viewing mechanisms reveal, however, that we are all marginal in some sense, all temporary occupants of a homeland that can melt, be taken away from us by traumatic experience, be taken over by others, or that we can never process comfortably. At the end of the story the 'visitors' have now become 'the latecomers' (272), and ownership has become something that survives in terms of our emotions and connections more than anything else.

In some sense, 'Litany for the Homeland' attempts to respect the priority and connections of 'the first ones' (272), but also to claim that Australia, or Queensland in this case, can be home just as much to 'the latecomers'. While this has been argued forcefully across the Tasman by New Zealand historian Michael King in his influential *Being Pakeha*, many Australian cultural commentators find it difficult to occupy this position, one which is increasingly associated, moreover, with reactionary forces.[15] Hospital's litany for her homeland runs throughout most of her work, opposing a simplistic notion of belonging to one that is able to question nostalgia, straightforward identification, and certainly the ways in which we represent places and homes, but one that is still able to affirm strength of attachment. Indeed, the attachment to home is intensified when we are forced to look at it through a metaphorical telescope from other places, and in this Hospital's work belongs squarely within that current of contemporary writing that has given us increasingly nuanced perspectives on absent homes and their interfaces with adopted homes.

Philippa and Brian

Underscoring the book's pungent investment in scenarios of home as both always already present and absent at the same time, this volume is unusual in having a series of stories featuring the same Brisbane characters: Philippa and Brian. Philippa and Brian's connection is fraught with a closeness that is abrasive and competitive at its centre, and, as Philippa is associated with the Humanities and Brian with Physics, the relationship provides Hospital with opportunities to articulate some of the competitiveness through competing modes of explaining or studying reality.

In 'Unperformed Experiments Have No Results', for example, causality, coincidence and pattern are mysteriously diluted. Observing a canoeist on the St Lawrence River, Philippa is reminded of Brian, with whom she had gone to school in Brisbane. The title refers to physicist Brian's assertion that only by framing hypotheses and following them will you find something out that is worth knowing. Whatever happens, there will always be results from an experiment, whether to confirm or to dash one's theories. It transpires that Brian has disappeared, and the canoeist has also disappeared. Philippa connects the dots, despite Brian's being last seen in Melbourne or Tokyo, seeing in the narratives of the astounding travails of the Jesuits in seventeenth-century Canada a type of connection with the mysterious canoeist and Brian. The experiment that she is performing is conceptual, but only by travelling up the river of her imaginative connections will she approach some sort of meaning of the events she wishes to understand. As for the canoeist, paddling upriver is difficult work and may lead to the destruction of his basic equipment (a birch-bark canoe/his mind), but the canoeist and Brian serve as related examples of the driven scientist for whom trying something out is always better than sitting on one's hands. This provides a link between the outer reaches of the artistic imagination and the restless imaginativeness of the scientist, a division that is typically bridged in Hospital's work in mysterious fashion through a conflation of kinks in time, dreams and the psychic connections between characters: 'There's a name for it: *sympathetic magic*' (94; Hospital's italics).[16]

Brian and Philippa's differing relation to the evidence of memory and history had been examined in the volume's opening story, 'The Ocean of Brisbane'. This piece concerns their return to Brisbane, a city towards which they have opposed, but also related, responses. They both feel the place acutely, but where for Philippa the vertigo that ensues when she is back in the city is something that only reinforces her love of the place, for Brian the power of the past depresses him and he is unable even to spend time with his mother, fleeing the day after the guest lecture he has given at the university. Philippa cannot offer anything to take the pain away, given that what she wants is precisely to experience the intensity of the past, because, whatever her experience of absence and loss, the things that are absent and lost would be even more so if they were suppressed. These two different experiences of memory are not resolved but exist aslant each other, partly touching, partly repelling each other, and in the final analysis, as Philippa muses in her confrontation with the theme, 'I computed the odds against solving the structure of memory which dissolves and devolves and solves nothing' (4). The odds are stacked against any form of enquiry, but the type of enquiry provided by the creative imagination is as necessary to the human encounter with the past as the scientific model. Indeed, that model has proven unable to resolve crucial issues in Brian's relation to his memories, and he recurs throughout the stories as troubled and unable to exist within everyday protocols of human interaction.

Philippa and Brian return in 'Cape Tribulation', the title referencing a location in Queensland as well as the mental state of the relationship between the characters. The story connects the characters' reading of Captain Cook's journals and Brian's present emotional turbulence, paralleling the problems Cook had negotiating the Great Barrier Reef. Brian is disturbed and slips in and out of the present, Cook's log and communicating with Philippa. His mind goes under, and what brings him back to the surface is returning to memories concerning himself and Philippa, and to Cook's journals. When he meets up with Philippa, however, she remembers things quite differently from him, even denying his memories. Suture for Brian has been made by way of elements that we suspect exist in such a conjunction only within his imagination, and yet this may be what we need to resist the depradations of time and history. The story ends with Brian grief-stricken over the loss that the past represents, the personal and Captain Cook twinned once again in the consideration of how much was lost from the *Endeavour* when the sailors had to throw weight overboard in order to get through a shallow part of the reef. Just as we have no way of knowing what was lost from Cook's ship, we have no way of knowing what has been lost from our memories as we proceed through life, or what was lost from Brian's mind under medication. In answer to Philippa's optimistic words, '[i]t might all be found again. One day. You never know' (127), Brian agrees that one does never know; for Brian, the past principally offers the inevitability of loss and the sundering of connection between histories, a connection that had sustained him in his voyage out of madness, but which he now realises may have been an illusion. In the end, the two perspectives cannot be reconciled, and sit alongside each other as equally possible responses, neither prevailing over the other.

In 'Night Train' Philippa is present again, yet another alter ego for Hospital herself on her way to her first teaching position, in far north Queensland. Brian is going in the opposite direction, desperate to get away from Brisbane. Even at this time Philippa wishes time would go backwards, and aches for the pleasures and certainties and rhythms of childhood. Perhaps there is more than the eternal *ubi sunt* theme here, as the story enunciates the historical poignancy of a childhood when white Australia itself had yet to grow up, and still lived the innocence of certainty, largely untroubled by its history of dispossession and violence, unconcerned about environmental or geopolitical complications, when employment was easy to achieve and the future appeared to promise simply progress and wealth. This feeling is increased as the story occurs at the time President Kennedy was shot, often imagined as the loss of American innocence, and by extension global innocence, the beginning of the end of a period of rhetoric centred on progress and the joys of increased consumerism.

The interchange between Philippa and Brian occurs in a dream-like fusion of memory and allusion, the two of them together on the night train, followed by a jump to Philippa's waking up when Brian calls to tell her Kennedy has been shot. Whenever he rings, Philippa is yanked back into the past, which is like being in the tunnel on the night train: time and memory have the force of the wind effect created by moving through a tunnel, the darkness of a space that affects our perception, and the hemmed-in inevitability of one's direction. Brian keeps returning to the theme of a boy who was run over by a truck, for he feels that the boy has not been adequately mourned, like his own father. This creates 'an event horizon' (252), something that sucks other events into it, or distorts them around it. When Brian's speeded-up life goes off the rails, he enters a coma and dies, leaving Philippa to mourn him. The story becomes this mourning, commemorating him and the intellectual sparks they generated together, but when is the mourning chain ever satisfactory? Gaps always remain, events have a force and a velocity like the night train, we are being taken to an estranging destination which is in our home state. The intensities of childhood, furthermore, can never be adequately mourned. Brian represents a double loss: the loss of childhood and the loss of the attempt to hold onto its icons, so that the story becomes an event horizon itself, a desperate attempt to be at the end of the phone when our past calls, aching with the pain of lost time and the effort to make connections that will do justice to the richness of those people who have meant something to us. Bronwyn Rivers sums up this aspect: 'The sense of disorientation felt by these characters is powerfully reproduced in the format of a narrative fragmented into separate short stories.'[17] To have written a unifying or coherent explanation would not have done justice to either the complexity of the relationship or the depth of the struggle necessary to represent it in writing.

Southern losses

The principal loss associated with the Southern states of America is the defeat in the Civil War (1861–65), and, as felt by Southern whites at least, the still keenly felt loss of a way of life rooted in a sense of belonging that could never be the same. Hospital's trio of stories set in the South deals with issues of belonging and race from angles in which everyone is perceived as sharing experiences of loss and disconnection that are partly attendant upon history but ultimately derived from the human condition, in which absence, damage and difficulties of connection assail us all.

'Nativity', for example, suggests Christmas and a new start, but the story largely focuses on the disruptions of a family's history, shadowed by the varied legacies of the family history of North and South. A father enters a hospital parking lot, concerned over his daughter who is having birth complications, anxiously desiring to bridge the distance that has grown up between him and his daughter, not to mention his ex-wife, as well as worried about being a university Classics professor (representing the erudite in a demotic world, and representing the distant past in a world that values the present and the future). The picture is complicated by the fact that Jonathan is white and his adopted daughter Stacey is black, destabilising the easy assumptions about identity that animate inter-ethnic interaction everywhere.

In the hospital, Jonathan meets Stag, whose real name is Virgil. The survival of Classical names among Southern African-Americans is a form of continuity of that which Jonathan fears lost or irrelevant, but one laden with irony, given that the tradition such names represent is that in which slave-owners gave slaves names derived from their own Classical educations. Continuities never exactly run along the lines we expect or approve of, for such names are inflected by the arrogant power of people who not only presumed to name others but to name them in such a way that the named become perpetual evidence of the fissure between their powerless status and the historical grandeur of their names. Bearing names whose significance was formerly known only to their namers, slaves unwittingly provided a lesson in the unreliability of labels; a lesson, nevertheless, lost on those who presumed to categorise and market human beings according to imagined hierarchies of absolute value and identity.

After special medical attention, the baby emerges, and there are tears and togetherness all round, including with Jonathan's ex-wife. His daughter's partner's mother, Callisto, who handles snakes on Sundays in her church, had glossed this activity for Jonathan as '[a]ll things are possible to them that believe' (179).[18] Pointedly, however, belief is not Jonathan's strong point. Every social interaction for him is heavy with doubt and the need to conceal evidence about himself and his function in the world.

At the end Jonathan feels he can get cigars and balloons, which re-establishes the connection with the insurance salesman he had met in the carpark, the representative of the demotic from whom he had initially recoiled. While the story's ending may be one of Hospital's most conventional, in which the miracle of birth really does bring together families, insurance salesmen, Black American wide boys and Classics professors, in fact many of her stories finish on an upbeat note of connection. Indeed, the miracle of human connection, despite difference and doubts, is a theme she returns to incessantly, and in this the different chromatic identities of parents and daughter are significant, for what value can we place on connection if the only people we can connect with are just like us and believe the same things we do?

'Credit Repair', set in a housing project in Atlanta, subjects the interface between white and black to more severe scrutiny. The white narrator lives in the project and helps people with their credit, while the other main characters are Carol, a white social worker, Solana, a black Legal Aid worker, and Tirana, who they are helping when the fire trucks arrive to douse a blaze set off by an illegal barbecue. A little boy gets badly burnt, and the rest of the story consists of the impassioned examination of motives and attitudes on the part of Solana and the narrator, as they toss back and forth their ideas about why they bother trying to help other people. Solana fumes at the welfare- and aid-dependency culture. For Solana you make choices: either get away from the bottom or get submerged. Her rage wants to drag losers into line. The narrator muses that losers cannot help it, and that is why they band together with others who are also having difficulty. For the narrator, '[l]osers look out for one another. That's why I like them' (214).

There is no transformation, no false hope, for anyone in the story. It finishes with Solana singing what she thinks are positive things to Tirana's baby – 'Your daddy's rich . . . and your mama's good-looking' (217) – as if trying to counter the images of squalor and dependency the child will grow up surrounded by. Even if Solana is less resigned and cynical than she proclaims, the story constitutes a grim depiction of realities in the United States that horrify Hospital, but which do not lead her to condemn, sympathetic to the marginalised as she is. While she approves of being marginalised but defiant, to be marginalised and beaten down makes her angry with the waste of it, and the story wonders whether both white and black well-wishers can be related to the notion of repair only despairingly.

By placing a white narrator at the centre, and including another white character, so that the story does not become the narrator opposed to the other voices, Hospital is careful not to turn the story into her speaking for black people. Moreover, Solana's criticism and suspicion of the narrator indicate that Hospital is well aware of the politicised territory she has entered, in which white motives are immediately suspected as being patronising and out of touch with underprivileged black people's realities. Ultimately, however, the story reaches an impasse, in which subverting a Western folk tale in the story of Snow White told by Tirana to her children, or a child's lullaby as sung by Solana, offers temporary pleasure, but writing the narrative of the future differently proves impossible. Individual acts of connection, assistance and solidarity cannot repair structural problems, but goodwill is in such short supply that to scorn it seems counterproductive. As with all of Hospital's stories dealing with angry, marginalised people, the frustration is palpable, but so is admiration for the spirited and thoughtful voices she chronicles. In fact, for a writer to live in the United States and not to respond to the realities of different social groups would constitute a greater dereliction than any potential error in tone or register, given that being ignored and written out of the American social fabric is something that black people have experienced all too often in American history.

The third story set in the South is one of the volume's title stories, 'South of Loss'. It is centred on a picturesque road off the beaten track that runs some of the way between Columbia and Charleston. In part, the meticulousness with which Hospital locates the scenarios of her stories and novels relates to the intensity with which causality operates in her work, so that location, and the characteristics of place, are among the determining factors in establishing the conditions by which events happen, and fates go in the surprising directions they do. In part also, it relates to an American enthusiasm for exact placement engendered by a restlessly active population that ranges over the whole continent in ways that Australians do not, a movement in which people are constantly explaining to others where they are, where they come from, places they have transited in their lives or that day. Much of this type of bonding relates to lines of communication, in that Americans commonly enter into vigorous conversations dealing with Interstates or airports, identificatory connectors through which a vast and complex nation is known by its population.

The unlikely rural auto-shop in the story is worked by the descendants of the early settlers and their erstwhile slaves, and is an example of evolutions in the nature of belonging in ways that are fascinatingly complex. The auto-shop's owner Zach's ancestor set up at that location in 1690, not only long before Australia was invaded by the British but before slavery in the United States. The simple binaries between white and black are denied by the family's being Jewish, a group that in the seventeenth century was itself marginalised and stigmatised, albeit one that nonetheless participated in enslaving others.

Into this world comes a woman whose car has broken down, an event which is unusual enough in itself, given that the auto-shop is too far from the Interstate to pick up trade from outsiders. Alma is not only from outside the county, she is French, although she has lived in the United States for many years. Zach is mesmerised by her foreign air and fragility, while she recognises that he has an emotional relation with fixing cars that ennobles and enriches him. They are also able to connect via the theme of their distant or estranged children.

The empathy between them leads Zach to help Alma with her work at the women's shelter in Columbia where she works, so he arranges an outing for a battered woman and her daughter through Alma, and takes them to Charleston. They think they have done something healthy and healing, something that reveals to the woman and her daughter that there are other things besides being locked into a fate with a violent man. Despite this, the woman takes her daughter back to the batterer. Disconsolate, Zach and Alma encounter a massive flock of purple martins, which makes them feel not so soul-weary. Earlier in the story the birds had emblematised the confusing swirl of emotions awoken in Zach's heart after meeting Alma. They also enact the inexplicability of nature, which speaks to the pain both Zach and Alma are feeling over the absence of those they love the most. It seems that it is in the order of things for events to occur that defy elucidation or reason.

The birds also point to the power of the local to evoke the baffling extremities of life, for the purple martins mass and gather in that small part of Calhoun County more than anywhere else in the world. One does not need to have large horizons to experience the intensities of existence. Children leave, women stay in abusive relationships, one ends up living in a foreign country, and none of these things seem to have a rational explanation, but it is not only estrangement and disjunction that are achingly mysterious. The fact that a rural Jewish auto-shop owner can connect luminously with a French war bride in out-of-the-way South Carolina forms a continuum with the rest of the inexplicable events in the story. A place that is perceived by garage worker Billy as 'nowhere' (219) resonates with the heights and depths of human emotion just as much as supposedly more momentous places. Zach comes from this 'nowhere', and Alma says she comes from '[n]owhere, really' (231), and yet between the two of them, between A and Z, the density and vertigo of being are suggested.

Stories and ends

The last story has a suitably apocalyptic title, 'The End-of-the-Line End-of-the-World Disco'. The tale takes place in an outback town reminiscent of Outer Maroo in *Oyster*, but, where Outer Maroo was threatened with fire, this town is facing an imminent and all-destroying flood. According to locals, the last flood was devastating, and supposedly swept the pub off its foundations and off to Cunnamulla, 'and then she came floating home on the backwash' (276); the rhetoric of exaggeration is part of what Hospital finds attractive in the rural demotic. The rhetoric is also biblical, activating the resonances of punishment and guilt. After all, local characters Flutie and Mike 'tell only the gospel truth' (276). As the waters converge and rise, and escape is impossible by land, revellers come to the disco to celebrate, to go out with a bang, or more specifically with a beer, the bonhomie of beer-drinking doing duty as the correct emotional and physical response to impending destruction. But the bluster and the retreat to upper floors of the hotel may not be enough, for this time there really might be no backwash to bring the pub home.

One end-of-the-line moment is that of confession, the true stories of the lost and the escapees who occupy far west Queensland, and Flutie wants to know Gladys's story before they are swept away. Gladys's fate had been a common one for the middle-aged woman, as her husband had run off with a younger woman, but Gladys feels this as a liberation. In fact, her sense of having cut loose from her former references merges into the desperate glee with which she contemplates the flood's carrying everything away, a myth of cleansing as flood myths always are.

Donna Davis persuasively considers that as Gladys is swept away in a rubber dinghy she 'becomes like nature . . . to the point that she merges, indeed mates, with it in a rapturous sense of freedom'.[19] Like 'Our Own Little Kakadu', this story suggests 'that the psychological and spiritual victory belongs to the characters who identify with nature and willingly surrender to her vital power'.[20] As in *The Ivory Swing* and *Charades*, characters who are associated with the profusion of nature are positive. Gladys's freedom, however, is not simply nature-induced but was already latent in her personality, as can be seen when she recalls a childhood experience, when her daring on the swing earned her a pair of broken legs. Gladys's bravado is more than the verbal beer-swilling joshing of the men, for hers is the bravado of sailing into the unknown, of leaving the earth behind and flying into the air, the freedom of the woman formerly hemmed in by responsibilities enjoying having no baggage or ties. The discourses and myths of decorum and retribution that have accompanied women throughout the centuries can be defied by the woman who is willing to cut her connections, to be unreachable. In the echo of T. S. Eliot from *The Waste Land*, others' voices are '*[b]uzz buzz* to reckless ears' (283), Gladys's being the reckless ears. In Eliot's poem, '"Jug Jug" to dirty ears' refers to a moment when the nightingale sings but is heard only as a dull clunking sound by those who cannot hear, while 'still the world pursues'.[21] The dull sound is the sound of the story of our lives in others' ears, the story that others insist on hearing but, when told, '[h]ow boring, how *embarrassing* a life is, once it slides down into the tacky skin of words', thinks Gladys (282; Hospital's italics). To the last, both Gladys and Hospital centre resistance on representation, conflating Gladys's defying the authority of convention with her refusing to tell her story to a man. This empowers her, apparent in the fact that it is her 'sheer indifference, her unreachability, that's been driving [Flutie] crazy' (282), an unreachability indicated at the end in her being swept away from Flutie just as he is trying to seduce her.

The alignment of a childhood memory with the moment of Gladys's epiphany indicates the crucial function of memory in stitching us together. Memory, however, is not simply an automatic process that we have access to in uncomplicated fashion. It is something that has to be nurtured, developed and processed. It can be squandered, and then we become reduced, as is happening with Bethesda's brother Gideon in 'North of Nowhere', whose 'memory is like a little heap of expensive white powder. He bends over it and breathes, and *pouff*, there's nothing but fog' (40).[22] Memory operates in Hospital's work as a sign of value, in that anything that exists in memory demands our attention, nothing is irrelevant or extraneous, however apparently disjointed. As Suzanne Nalbantian observes with such writers as Borges or Octavio Paz, memory partly operates as 'a kind of "jouissance", or pleasure of linguistic signifiers presenting polyphonic voices of the subconscious in a grammar of its own making';[23] but unlike the attention to memory of those writers, memory in Hospital also asks moral questions, as it demands the constant recalibration of the meanings of our stories as compared with those of others, and hence the constant reassessment of how we relate to others, what we owe them, and what we owe ourselves.

CHAPTER 11

Living astride death
Due Preparations for the Plague

THE TIME OF THE END, seems just going to lay its Arrest upon us. May we now Awake unto it, KNOWING THE TIME!

Cotton Mather[1]

American nightmares

Between 1982 and 1996 Hospital published no fewer than nine and a half demanding books, so it was a surprise when seven years passed between the publication of *Oyster* and her next novel, *Due Preparations for the Plague*. This length of time can be explained by her uprooting herself from Canada and relocating to the United States, where she succeeded James Dickey in an endowed chair at the University of South Carolina in Columbia. The gap, however, meant that *Due Preparations*, begun well before the Al Qaeda attack on New York's twin towers in 2001, appeared to have been written in response to that outrage. Nevertheless, although the book deals with the hijacking of an aeroplane by terrorists, along with the shadowy manipulations that led up to it, and the repercussions many years later on a small group of survivors and others related to the event, it clearly continues Hospital's career-long fascination with groups or mechanisms that engender or facilitate violence. These interests can be seen in *The Ivory Swing*, with political protestors in Kerala, with Quebecois separatists in *The Tiger in the Tiger Pit*, with the shadowy collusion between the American right wing and murderous Central American regimes in *Borderline*, with class-based privilege in Australia ruthlessly maintaining and feeding off a manipulated underclass in *The Last Magician*, and with the psychology of a cult leader and his followers, along with the tendency of inward-looking rural communities to police and suppress difference, in *Oyster*. Also in line with her earlier work, *Due Preparations* is closely concerned with the operation of causality and the human need for pattern, and how these concerns intersect as the impact of violence spreads and resonates. As befits a Hospital novel, the roles that memory and language play in establishing and affirming these patterns are central, particularly the ways in which they propagate the effects of violence unexpectedly.

It is noticeable that *Due Preparations* is written in a more accessible style than her earlier novels. After the typically dense and allusive first page, the novel becomes almost racy in its plot, taking on much of the pace and mystery of the conspiracy narrative, with all the paraphernalia of secret tapes, a drop-off point in an airport locker, suspicious deaths and shadowy government figures. The narrative moves along breathlessly, as if responding to the urgency with which we need to deal with the fact that various forms of the plague are overtaking the contemporary world. That plague is partly a willingness to murder innocent people in the interests of an ideological agenda, and also a specific crime, for the terrorists who hijack an aeroplane in the novel's central event call either themselves or their act 'the Black Death' and 'return of the plague'.[2] It is also, however, the disabling fear that is spreading as the sense of the shadowy threat of terrorist death invades official discourse and decision-making. This has been described as one consequence of the movement from an industrial society to a risk society, in which '[t]he onus of decision-making is no longer on the production and distribution of "goods", but on the prevention of "bads"'.[3] In this transformation, our principal project becomes to keep something out, and not to believe in the possibility of removing barriers to understanding, or to move outwards in the direction of others.[4]

The book's plot revolves around the connection to the hijacking of two characters: Lowell Hawthorne – who has tried to suppress any memories of the event – and Samantha Raleigh – who has been restlessly investigating it. The name Lowell, particularly in conjunction with Hawthorne, invites comparisons with Robert Lowell,[5] whose work reacted against his Puritan inheritance, as did the work of fellow New England writer Nathaniel Hawthorne. In both authors' deep understanding of Puritanism it can, however, be seen that they have not been able to escape its protocols for reading the world, in particular a sense or a fear that everything around us constitutes some sort of test. Part of our readiness to face up to this test is to be able to read the encoded signs that make up reality; but it is an enterprise in which we will always be found wanting, given that the generator of the signs is so far beyond human understanding.

Lowell Hawthorne's father, even more improbably, is named Mather Lowell Hawthorne, referencing the seventeenth-century Puritan Mather family. Cotton Mather, who is the most famous member of the family, his father, Increase, and his grandfather, Richard, are stereotypical Puritan figures in American culture, evoking a prescriptive sternness and a polarised discourse of those who are saved and those who are not. An all-seeing Puritan God, for whom everything is a test of our faith, has mutated in twenty-first-century American culture into an all-seeing official presence whose justification is to protect the homeland, or the faithful, from the depredations of shadowy death-dealing outsiders. Among Cotton Mather's influential efforts to shore up Puritanism's hold on the population was that of redirecting energy away from self-lacerating accusations of straying from the path and on to the need to combat enemies external to the polity, 'forces of evil outside the garden [who] had jealously attempted to wreck God's plan'.[6] One result of this leads us to inhabit an ever-present discourse of the test, in which everything we do becomes a potential trial of our loyalty and worthiness to be saved. From lists of the library books we have taken out to the internet sites we have visited to opinions we utter in public places, few things about anyone are now safe from the distrustful assessment of the American government and its multiplying security agencies. Both this official paranoia and public suspicion of it contribute to the widespread contemporary circulation of conspiracy theories, which, in John Byrne's words, 'seem to be inherently suited to the "information overload" of the postmodern world'.[7]

Not for nothing is Samantha a student of American history and government at the iconically named Georgetown University (named after George Washington) in the centre of American political power, Washington DC. As she becomes increasingly caught up in the machinations of this power, an ironic gap is signalled between her being a student of American history and being the object of the attentions of official American authority. Her father, Jonathan Raleigh, comes from one of the long-established families in that symbol of the Southern establishment, Charleston, so that between them Lowell and Samantha represent both the North and the South in America's complex moral inheritance.[8] Thus it is that the novel takes place mostly in America, and is constantly focused upon America, moving right away from the Australian focus of her previous two novels (although there is an important Australian character later).[9]

The signs of death

The presence of signs and portents is highlighted by the fact that the present action of the narrative takes place almost entirely in the ominous year, 2000, with a brief section at the end of the book on the threshold of that millennially portentous act, the destruction of New York's twin towers. A little way into the novel, Lowell has to pick up confidential material from an airport locker, Locker B-64, which echoes the flight on which his mother died – Air France 64 – while the phrase 'Locker B' he repeats to himself recalls Lockerbie, the town in Scotland where the terrorist-destroyed Pan Am plane fell to the ground in 1988 (the beginning of the end for the airline once emblematic of global American reach and technical know-how). In this world, once the Puritan reading practice is activated, everything '*could* mean something. It might mean something' (35; Hospital's italics). Every person becomes a potential bearer of messages or threats, usually the latter, a situation chillingly activated in the official American view of the world by 'responsibilizing and regimenting everybody in the war on terror. Citizens are to be vigilant, attentive to any sign of suspicious behaviour'.[10] Once Lowell has been induced by knowledge of his father's life to enter into this relationship with reality, everything becomes a source of anxiety. The driver of the next car in the Logan Airport carpark 'wears a plaid shirt and has a bald patch. Lowell waits for him to leave, analyzing the plaid: vertical stripes and horizontal, green, black, gray, a thin vertical red line' (36). The pattern on the shirt appears to mean nothing, but one can never be too careful; only by scrutinising everything can we be sure whether or not there is information to be processed. Even then, we still need to interpret the data, giving rise to a spiralling process in which, as in Claudia Aradau and Rens van Munster's summary of the official response to the fear of terrorism: '9/11 has given way to more pro-active surveillance of suspect populations, leading to a surplus supply of data and an over prediction of threats'.[11]

Lowell is the son of one of the people on an airliner that was first hijacked on the 8th of September 1987 and then blown up on the 13th of September. The book opens as an anniversary of the event approaches, a time that often accentuates guilt in survivors. This survivor guilt is heightened in Lowell because at the time he had been so angry with his mother for her relationship with a man who was not her husband, and with whom she had been travelling, that he had wanted them to die. Since they did die, he has suffered from guilt. He is trying to blot out the apparent wish fulfilment, but death will not be blotted out, the novel tells us; it calls for a response. And death begins to intrude into the novel's present almost immediately. Lowell's father is killed in a car crash, on the ninth day of the ninth month of the year, an incident that he soon starts to think may have been murder – on account of his father's knowledge of the circumstances surrounding Flight 64. As he tries to explain his father's death, as well as the hijacking in which his mother died, to his two young children, they have panic attacks, leading him to conclude that '[n]othing will shelter children from life. The young, the fragile, the vulnerable, all are at catastrophic risk' (13). Whenever his children appear throughout the novel, there is always a connection with death, whether through their fears induced by their knowledge of what happened to Lowell's parents, or their insistence that Lowell tell them what happens after we die (170). The symbolic futurity of children never escapes this shadow in the plague-ridden contemporary world.

What preparations can we then make, the novel asks repeatedly. One obvious answer is that due preparations cannot be made in an exact fashion. That is, only rarely can we know in any precise sense when and how death will occur; but one time we can be almost certain that we are doomed, and that our time is limited, is when we realise we have the plague. In Daniel Defoe's *Due Preparations for the Plague* and *Journal of the Plague Year* he depicts numerous examples of people's seeing they have the signs of the plague, and their feeling of certainty that they are about to die. No-one who finds out they have the plague believes they have any chance of survival, that they might be one of the lucky ones. This crushing prospect is one of the meanings of the plague: a finality we do not think we deserve, and that nothing we do can prevent.[12]

Given that apparently we cannot avoid dying once we have contracted the plague, the task becomes avoiding it in the first place. The problem is, of course, that causality is only partly controllable, since any chain of causes and effects also involves others who enact their own influence over events. The idea that one can ensure against enemies, and control the events around one, will always be only partly successful at best. Dolores Herrero points out that the novel's literary allusions 'all aim to highlight one single but crucial idea: we cannot control our lives, nor the obscure mechanisms that rule the complex world we live in'.[13] There is no controlling knowledge of the future, nor absolute control of information. Paradoxically, the more focused an intelligence network becomes, the more it breeds distrust, and the more impossible it becomes for its parts to work harmoniously. According to an insider in the American intelligence network,

Commander Michael Studeman, there are no fewer than sixteen organisations within the US government that perform 'National Intelligence functions': 'A healthy amount of overlap in the functions of the Intelligence Community is due largely to the nature of issues that cross jurisdictional boundaries, as well as a desire to avoid single points of analytic failure.'[14] Concentrating intelligence in one organisation, let alone one individual, invites the possibility of malfunction. In *Due Preparations*, once anyone reaches the pitch of paranoia required in the intelligence-gathering business, it becomes difficult to trust anyone, including those one works with, leading to inevitable breakdowns in the circuits of information. Signs and codes become concentrated in the individual decoder through 'the desperate need to know all' (251). Yet knowing all, rather than making one valuable within the system, makes one an object of increased distrust – a potential 'single point of analytic failure' – thereby heightening still further one's paranoid relation towards information and its circulation.

Samantha, who was actually on Air France 64 (the children on the flight were released), is engaged in a desperate quest for more and more information about the fateful flight. Information is a key currency in the novel. It is sought by members of the public and withheld by official bodies. Samantha attempts to understand why the event happened, who is to blame, who could have done anything to prevent it, as well as what it means to accumulate this knowledge. From the start, she introduces troubling connections by telling Lowell about a woman called Françoise who believes she is Lowell's half-sister (and gradually this is revealed to be true) and that Lowell's father probably knew about what was going to happen on Flight 64. One of the ways in which Samantha is determined to find out more about the flight is to keep the connection alive between the now grown-up children who were on the aeroplane, via the Phoenix Club. But the members of this club are also threatened, now that they have grown up and are also piecing together clues about what happened to them. One has already died in mysterious circumstances in Bombay, and Samantha's lover and fellow-survivor Jacob is becoming unhinged with the knowledge of his powerlessness in the face of menace. Samantha tells him that '[t]he key is being invisible' (199); but in a Western world of ever-increasing vigilance, it is more and more difficult to remain invisible. Soon Jacob disappears as well.

In Hospital's novels from *Borderline* on, characters and readers are both faced with an oversupply of information. Puzzles, clues, possible leads, hypothetical connections and alternative chains of cause and effect all need to be processed in order to make sense of events. One way to characterise Lowell's intelligence-gathering father, Mather, is as a professional decoder or a professional reader. Some of the codes that intrigued him were those of supposedly lost languages, which could 'weather storms in the ocean of time, like Ulysses . . . They go astray, they are shipwrecked, they come ashore in strange places, and everyone believes they are lost, but one day they show up again' (174). Obsessed with codes, Mather feels encircled by them, and by their principal vehicle, words. References to *Alice in Wonderland* evoke Lewis Carroll's perception of the nature of language and its ability to destabilise realities and identities. Codes, however, are more than abstractly intriguing to Mather; the fact that lost languages may show up again ensures they are a means of fighting against darkness, for they tell us 'that the truth will endure . . . a dangerous message can hide and bide its time until the message can safely be read' (175). In a way, this is the writer's contract as represented by Hospital throughout her career: to be the bearer of dangerous messages, to speak in code, to be vigilant. It also provides one of the central ironies of the critique of reading the world through the lens of suspicion, reproducing an irony apparent to Nathaniel Hawthorne as well in his critique of 'the policy of our ancestors to search out even the most secret sins, and expose them to shame, without fear or favor, in the broadest light of the noonday sun'.[15] While we may be nervous when this is done by those in power, both Hospital and Hawthorne lay claim to the writer's obligation to carry out precisely this search, and for their writing to constitute this very exposure.

Discovering that his father feared his own elimination, Lowell ruminates upon what can be said in a world where people who work in the ironically entitled activity known as 'Intelligence' cannot actually share their so-called intelligence with almost anyone, even their own family. Knowledge is pursued in order to be kept secret, in opposition to the brief of the writer. Lowell's father calls this part of 'the necessary rituals of risk' (27), which exist as part of a structure that supposedly protects the rest of us. This is a structure, however, that Hospital perceives as inextricably bound up with control rather than with any utilitarian quest for intelligence or knowledge. The agency Mather works for admits proudly that it is as dedicated to establishing the fiery realm of punishment spoken of by St Mark as it is to protecting anyone.[16] Control, nevertheless, is limited, for 'it is a given that chaos is all; that order is not only arbitrary but evanescent' (227). 'Chaos' is a key term in Hospital's work, and does not necessarily signify random disorganisation (although it might signify this to a character); rather, chaos is a type of order that exists when we are not aware of it or, when we become aware of it, the purpose of which remains mysterious and yet whose shape appears meaningful. In terms of how this impacts on our existence, Hospital's work repeatedly stresses that the absence of ultimate perceivable order does not license the absence of a concern with an ethical relation to the world.

The bag of classified information that Lowell's father leaves him contains material relating to Air France 64 and an operation named 'Operation Black Death'. Here we learn of an Arab terrorist and apparent mercenary code-named Sirocco (the hot and oppressive wind that blows from North Africa to Italy, referencing thus the principal origin of terrorists in the Western mind, as well as the suspected location of the plague alluded to via the mention of the *Decameron*).[17] Other coded identities are mentioned, particularly Salamander (an amphibian that mythically was able to survive fire),[18] who has been introduced already via the intra-chapter section-separating images throughout the book, the first on page 13, a buried code for the reader perhaps, beckoning us to enter a paranoid relationship with clues and signs.[19] According to Intelligence memos, Sirocco will recruit terrorists for either side, Israeli or Palestinian, and yet American Intelligence still felt he was reliable enough to be used to set up a hijacking which would be a ruse to concentrate a Parisian terrorist group in one place and enable them to be killed or captured and interrogated.

The confluence of Lowell's new-found attentiveness to signs and portents with Samantha's search for secrets and meanings is highlighted, in good conspiracy narrative fashion, when people related to the events begin to disappear (something we have already seen Hospital concerned with in *Borderline*). Lowell's father's death, for example, appears less and less accidental. Agit, a survivor from the event, grows up and publishes a book of short stories called *Flight into the Dark*, and then dies apparently mysteriously; he is actually eliminated by American Intelligence, as later admitted by Lowell's father. In the hijacking, Agit had been saved when Salamander's pressure had led to the hijackers' freeing the children. He is saved when one of the terrorists pushes him down the plane's escape chute; he is killed when pushed under a train by someone working for Salamander. One push echoes the other, as the fantasies of control on the part of terrorists and Intelligence parallel each other. Mather's widow, Elizabeth, feels threatened by national security agents, and later Lowell finds she has disappeared. His own apartment is repeatedly broken into and searched in his absence until parts of the classified material his father had left him are found and removed. Samantha's lover Jacob is found dead, the cause apparently suicide.

Searching for clues to the perpetrators of these events, Samantha discovers the existence of Salamander, but is still trying to piece together clues as to his identity, motives and actions. Salamander deals in information, which enables him to manipulate people. This results in a world that loses its solidity: '[y]ou have no idea how unreliable things are, or how suddenly the sky can turn to fire' (46), she thinks, invoking apocalyptic rhetoric for the controlling influence of those who manage the ever-increasing and ever-more-specific information we generate about ourselves in the modern world. For Samantha, we live in the illusion of solidity, but for anyone who feels this solidity losing its shape, 'we are forced to become scavengers of our own past, searching, finding, relearning, reassembling the self' (47).

One result of this activity is that inevitably we find only details and fragments, so that re-creation morphs into creation, as gaps are filled by our connecting imagination, a mixture of probability and desire. Moreover, as quickly as we assemble evidence the world forgets it, leaving the individuals involved to inhabit history at the same time as they watch it fading around them. The disjunction between the retrieved history and that which is accepted by others is experienced obsessively by those who take the trouble to reassemble. In his work dedicated to remembering in the United States, *Mystic Chords of Memory*, Michael Kammen shows exhaustively that the country inhabits a commemorative economy in which 'the more we read about memory, the more we also are reminded of amnesia'.[20] In such an amnesiac world, the significance of keeping certain events alive is more than personal. Hospital has been committed throughout her career to being suspicious of authority, and her work suggests that, she, like Samantha, believes that 'accountability for shady activity, even in wartime, was one of the pillars of our democracy' (72). Piecing together evidence and ensuring that the past does not go unrecorded should not be left to official bodies.

Within these memories, connections exist not simply in terms of obvious causes and effects but also along the axis of complex personal histories, which unravel into complications as soon as they are looked at. The more Lowell and Samantha look back, the more they keep discovering new links that dissolve the certainties they held about their origins and family reference points: for example, the father of Samantha's lover Jacob was having an adulterous relationship with Lowell's mother, Isabella Hawthorne. Samantha pursues these unlikely connections, for it appears that they defy 'statistical odds. It has to mean something' (81). Indeed, the novel takes place at this time in Lowell's and her lives (and not in all the years between the event and the present) because, as Samantha feels, 'critical mass has been reached ... the accumulation of data has hooked up isolated circuits' (82).

Two of the circuits linked up are Samantha and Lowell, who meet as those around them are erased. They flee the tentacles of (un)official violence, escaping to the marshes on the shores of Chesapeake Bay, to the east of Washington DC. The marshes are a location that is shifting, imprecise, unfixed, a place where they feel they may have a chance to elude their stalkers; it is also a place about which information is fluid and unfixable, a place that defies human control. For Mather, a quagmire is an appropriate metaphor for the despair and insecurity of his journey into darkness, into the Inferno. Watching the tapes about Operation Black Death that Mather has left Lowell in an obscure motel deep within the marshes brings knowledge, but also fear that with such knowledge of how others' deaths have served deathly purposes will come death itself for Lowell and Samantha.

Keeping death foreign

Book III takes us back to 1987, the year of the hijack, and introduces us to a new character, Tristan Charron, a literary publisher who has recently had a brush with Czechoslovak police (reminding us that the complexion of present international tension is scarcely natural, but obeys geo-strategic imperatives that are constantly shifting). As we meet him, he is obsessing about his Australian ex-lover, Genevieve,[21] and is unconcerned about having been pulled aside by the Charles de Gaulle Airport gendarmerie as he waits to board Air France 64 to New York. Hospital has a love of Paris and France, and places that she likes are often rewarded with starring roles in her work. The use of numerous expressions and sentences in French, which she speaks well, also attests to this predilection. In this case, Paris appears to exude some of the standard meanings of twentieth-century literary history – *l'amour fou*, the highbrow and literary, romance and philosophy, the city of the marvellous in the surrealist imaginary. Not for nothing is Tristan's publishing house called Editions du Double, and his fate is ironically decided by the doubled pair of

Salamander and Sirocco, the former referring to himself as the latter's 'split-twin counterpart in covert operations' (274).

As Tristan wonders why the police have stopped him, he recalls his former lover Genevieve, who was followed as his lover by Françoise, the same Françoise that Samantha tells Lowell is his half-sister, the room-mate of Samantha's Aunt Lou when the latter was a student in Paris. Tristan remembers how nervous the idea of Françoise's secretive and powerful American father – Mather – had made him, and how he could not live with the opaqueness and uncertainty behind her. The coincidences multiply alarmingly; the connections between Tristan's supposedly political writers and Flight 64 are numerous and suspicious to the police, although a mystery to Tristan. He had been following a message from Genevieve informing him she would be on that flight, an illustration that what may appear a set of linked occurrences may not be so at all in the way imagined by the observer (recalling the detectives' questioning of Lucy in *The Last Magician*), for Tristan and Genevieve have both been duped into being on the flight by Sirocco. Each believes they are following what the other wants, when it is Sirocco who wants them there, supposedly for publishing anti-Islamic authors in Tristan's case and carrying anti-Islamic material to secular forces in Islamic countries in Genevieve's case (although there is also an element of revenge for personal slights real or imagined that Sirocco had felt in Paris during his relationship with Genevieve).

Sirocco, whose real name may be the generic Mohammed, embodies some of the standard American fears of the Arab terrorist, but only some. For example, he is not connected at first with religion or jihad, although he is brutish and threatening even in normal daily contact. He is also sexualised, albeit not particularly favourably, in that his sexuality is flaunted aggressively and imbued with menace and violence. The menace is no illusion, for Sirocco and other assailants take the plane hostage soon after take-off, whereupon the action jumps forward to the consequences at some unspecified time in the future, by which time the plane has made several landings and take-offs. We learn that Muslim 'freedom fighters' (160) are at the centre of the operation.

The thinness of the portrayal of Sirocco, especially when compared with the detailed depiction of Salamander, has drawn some criticism. Brenda Niall suggests that '[i]t would be a better story if the author had given the same measure of complexity to the men on both sides'.[22] There are good reasons, nevertheless, why this has not happened. In the first place, ever since *The Ivory Swing* Hospital has been wary of assuming the voices of peoples whose relation to the politics of authority has become especially politicised. In *Borderline* the El Salvadorean woman around whom the plot revolves does not speak, while Jean-Marc ventriloquises the responses of others to their perception of her situation. With reference to *The Last Magician*, Fiona Coyle believes that Aborigines are the determinate absence at the centre of the quarry, although there is no Aboriginal voice in the novel.[23] Despite the significance of Murri people and their relation to place in *Oyster*, Hospital keeps Ethel's voice to a minimum so that the novel does not become the appropriation of a Murri story. Not wishing to speak for peoples who have a troubled relation with the ways the West has spoken for them does run the risk that they will seem insufficiently rounded, but it also reproduces the position of many Western observers with respect to such peoples. Hospital admits that '[i]t is extremely difficult for a novelist to portray a character who is truly baffling to the novelist' and that 'I think my bafflement, and my torment about the question of Sirocco's frightening absence of normal empathy, all ended up in the character Salamander, who really does wrestle with his conscience'.[24]

Preparing to be murdered

From within the consciousnesses of Tristan and Genevieve we discover that the final remaining hostages are eventually sequestered in an enclosed space and encased in gasmasks. If they remove them, they die. The masks ensure that people are deindividualised and the contexts for interaction diluted: 'Everyone looks the same; wearers cannot detect the gender or race of other wearers; a child cannot tell his father from his mother' (261). Standard ways of decoding others are absent and 'this absence of standard signifiers eventually causes dizziness, confusion of mental processes, and inability to concentrate' (261). The only defence, according to a training manual for secret service operatives, is mental – to enter an imaginative zone in which we have to perform a complicated task: 'mentally walking from New York to Los Angeles on B roads . . . or by re-visioning every house and every garden on [one's] childhood block' (263). These challenges involve setting things into a pattern, textualising things as it were, and withdrawing from confrontation with immediate reality so as to deny its hold over one.

There are ten hostages in this final group, taken off the plane which is then blown up with the remaining adults on it. These ten are kept by the terrorists to be exchanged for ten prisoners they want released, and whom we know, given the rigid protocols on this issue, will never be released by the French government. Ten is also the same number of people who isolate themselves from the Black Death in the *Decameron*. Boccaccio's ten well-born young people sealed themselves off against the outside; here the ten are sealed off by Operation Black Death against their will.

The main parallel is in the act anterior to Boccaccio's ten people taking themselves off to a secure place – it is Boccaccio who takes himself off to a removed place by devising the complex task of making ten people tell ten stories each in ten days, in order for him to deal with the enormity and devastation of the plague. This is, however, a defence not against the physical plague but against being inhabited by the mental bacteria, the despair, that the plague may bring. Salamander calls the record he makes of the Black Death operation his 'Decameron tape' (275), but it certainly does not offer him any removal, psychic or otherwise. In fact, it places him in danger from his superiors, and it is evidence of the mental torments that his involvement in the operation has caused. Nonetheless, it is a testament to the necessity of creating something when it seems that destruction reigns, to the necessity of art, '*[e]specially* out of atrocity' (285; Hospital's italics). As one of the hostages claims exultantly while he prepares for death, 'the horsemen of Death . . . gallop and still they fail utterly to extinguish wonder' (309).

Most of the ten have been chosen deliberately, not simply from the passenger list but before the flight, influenced, pushed to be on the flight by causalities that are as yet opaque. The point is that they are not there randomly, but that insidious forces and influences operate constantly in modern life on every individual, shaping our lives beyond our knowledge, certainly beyond our will (although such forces are not omnipotent, so that one of the final ten hostages seems to be more truly randomly present, the student Billy Jenkins). We witness the breakdown of Mather's conviction, for, where he had accepted 'that in times of crisis, triage may be necessary' (283), he now realises that entering the logic of control and manipulation is to abandon faith in other human beings, to have become part of the problem himself.

Triage has not just taken place under the responsibility of the terrorists but is implicit in the actions of rulers and manipulators of human beings everywhere.

In a long series of speeches, the characters remove their gas masks in order to have one final say, knowing they are going to die. These speeches constitute versions of Boccaccio's characters' stories, although in the *Decameron* the characters survive, while here they do not. Each offers comments on death, time and their lives. Yasmina Shankara, the Bollywood star, speaks a message of karma, of the cycle: 'Everything returns. Nothing can ever be lost' (306). While there is sympathy for all of her characters, and throughout her work Hospital has shown an interest in Indian philosophies of time without necessarily endorsing them, ultimately Yasmina's confidence appears hollow. The later death of her son Agit at the hands of the Americans seems to confirm a skeptical reading of her philosophy of cosmic justice, and yet the speeches by the dying hostages together form a mosaic of human defiance of the horsemen of Death. They are all versions of human ingenuity, courage and wisdom, and in all of them there exists a need for story, a need for what the Yiddish writer Daniel Schulz calls 'the land of *even so*' (310; Hospital's italics), for all of them wish to render accounts, to preserve memories, to present narratives. After Yasmina and Daniel, Billy Jenkins has no compensatory philosophy to offer; death means to him simply the end of the things he likes – 'football, booze, getting laid' (316). Not everybody faces death with an answer, and from one angle Jenkins's hedonistic focus depicts the blankness that death may offer; but in its denial of any sense of punishment or after-death consequences, this too constitutes a form of defiance. Jonathan Raleigh, Samantha's father, admits to family hypocrisy, referencing the use in the distant past, and also the recent past, of African-Americans by white men. Death becomes a means of rewriting wrongs, confessing truths, balancing. Avi Levinstein, the musician and secular Jew, discovers after all that he needs ceremony, that 'awe begins at death' (326), so he begins playing his violin while his lover, Isabella Hawthorne, Lowell's mother, speaks. Both of them conclude with somewhat sentimental homilies: in Avi's case about hearing the universe, and in Isabella's case how freedom only means something if there is someone to share it with. Victoria Goldberg, Avi's musical partner, sings (itself a valorisation of the artistic impulse), and the words of her song are a hymn to bravado in the face of death.

Homer Longchamp's professorial intervention interrupts the mixture of sentimentalism and self-pity as he summarises the situation. Ultimately, he indicates, 'we are talking to ourselves, which is where all arguments begin and end' (333). For Longchamp the greatest mystery is not that of death, or life, but of randomness, of causality, the patterns in which life and death are caught and through which we experience them. Referencing chaos theory by way of the Lorenz effect,[25] Longchamp mentions 'the maddening neatness of randomness . . . the geography of chance is the ultimate teaser, intellectually and morally, because of the sheer enormity of divergence that results from a micro-change here and a micro-change there' (333). The randomness effect demands of us a heightened attempt to decode, as we trace the only apparently random chain of cause and effect, which Longchamp terms 'translation' (335); that is, we observe things and translate them into the terms by which we can understand or process them. He recalls observing two men conversing in Paris and that he formed suppositions about them, something that human beings constantly do in any event, with greater or lesser degrees of investment. A small error in translating others' actions or words, however, can have wildly unpredictable and momentous consequences. Homer's interest in following up on an absorbing interaction he witnesses in a restaurant leads to his trailing Sirocco to a Moroccan bar and arousing the latter's suspicion, whereupon he is led into accepting a commission from Sirocco that sends him on the fatal flight. The causes of this do not lie simply in that evening but in the whole train of circumstances that led to his becoming a professor in the first place, thereby having money to travel, being in Paris and so on.

The last passengers to speak are Tristan and Genevieve. They are led by Homer's ruminations into examining the operations of causality further. Even beyond the machinations of conspiracy, says Homer, there is 'something awesome about the patterns of chance, something mysterious, and we need that mystery' (342). Tristan and Genevieve's apparently final reflections, bringing things back to a personal level, are about their meeting, stolen passion, the significance of memories that are private, a network of connections that do not posit final explanations or ultimate meanings but which confirm the bonds between them, the way they spent their lives, and not the meaning of life for human beings in general.

The past as future

Finding out about what happened during the last minutes of the hostages' lives acts as an intense test of Samantha and Lowell's resilience, and not for nothing is one of Book V's epigraphs from the Book of Job: 'And I only am escaped alone to tell thee' (217). This is uttered by one of the messengers who come, one after the other, to tell Job of the series of disasters that has befallen him, suggesting the role of Lowell's father in the accumulation of evidence that Samantha and Lowell discover as the book goes on. The other epigraph is taken from Borges's tale 'The Other', significantly set in Cambridge, Massachusetts, and which relates the meeting of Borges in the present with himself in the past, except that, of course, the action of each on the other means that each version of Borges begins to become destabilised.[26] To come across details of yourself in the past changes not merely your image of your past self, which is the only past self you possess, but who you are in the present. Knowledge, even about so intimate a thing as your own history, is never effectless. Book V also begins by referring to split selves and is told by Lowell's father, Mather, who, we finally discover for certain, is also Salamander. In his professional role Mather has become increasingly absorbed into the pragmatic agent Salamander and increasingly divorced from his role as Mather Lowell Hawthorne. As Salamander, he would teach trainee agents that there is no retiring from the world of intelligence-gathering and the social manipulation consequent upon this role; to lose belief in this world is to invite erasure – about which he is proven correct. It also means that his only mode of cancelling his role in that world is to use the information he had gathered as Salamander, thereby confirming that he cannot step outside his history after all.

The plague is a metaphor not simply for death or even for mass death but for a type of death that we feel indiscriminately threatened by and which has the power to infect us imaginatively. This fear poisons our relation with the world, and accelerates and intensifies our decoding responsibilities to the point where daily life is transformed into nightmare, and all human beings into potential carriers of the plague. In 'Young Goodman Brown' Nathaniel Hawthorne created a classic chilling depiction of what it means to be drawn into such a relation with the world. Young Goodman Brown makes contact with the devil out of curiosity, out of a need to know better in order to be on his guard; but what happens is that he learns that his readings of the people in his village have been partial, that human beings are not perfect, and he is unable to be happy from that point on; he is unable to have Faith (the name of his wife) as before. Too much knowledge destroys his ability to interact with the world happily. The tale shows us that we cannot visit the Devil on our terms, we cannot call in on the Devil without becoming infected by and with him. In Hawthorne's repeated critique of the Puritan life, becoming obsessed with signs, codes, indeed with *knowing* about others, is destructive.

In resisting this obsession with the surveillance and control of others, Camus is another key reference, being cited twice: before the contents page, and later as Mather contemplates the fate of the ten last passengers. Facing up to the plague in *Due Preparations*, however, differs from the strategy suggested in novels such as Camus's *The Plague* or Geraldine Brooks's *Year of Wonders*:[27] the cloistered sufferers in Hospital's work are not a whole community, and they all know they are going to die. This allows solidarity to develop between them, whereas in Camus's Oran and Brooks's Derbyshire village, as in Defoe's London, communities partly crack and fall apart. There are always some inhabitants who attempt to circumvent controls, attribute blame or give up caring about others, and there are always some who try to control others viciously and hysterically in the effort to avoid being exposed to the plague. Hospital relates how her approach to the characters' response to their situation became the main alteration to the book following the events of 9/11: she had expected that people trapped in this way 'would be frantic, fraught and angry', but she discovered, through accounts of the mobile phone calls made by people in the twin towers who knew they were going to die, that instead they had 'passed through some kind of gateway where all the usual narcissistic concerns just flew away from them and they became these radiant benign beings'.[28] Hospital's inclusion of this life-affirming section renders it distinct from other fiction that takes terrorism as its subject, which Margaret Scanlan sums up as 'that most pessimistic of genres'.[29]

The last sections of the novel are concerned not only with the situation and experience of the final ten hostages but also with Mather's record of his response to their ordeal and death. Their deaths are recorded by Sirocco in line with the exposure of the private that has become one of the stock-in-trades of industries of the image: reality shows expose people's most intimate and unguarded moments, while news shows are predicated on the visuality of disaster. Recording and showing death – already a staple of fictional images far in excess of people's exposure to death in their daily lives – thus participates in the dominant logic of the visible, a fact that is manipulated by Sirocco at all moments in the final stages of Operation Black Death. As he is imagined to be saying, 'I am setting up shop in your nightmares' (283), except that this is a world in which we invite the nightmares into our living rooms, we have permitted them to become part of our own daily lives, and we are not innocent. Indeed, like any novel dealing with the subject, *Due Preparations* itself may be seen as contributing to the circulation of terrorism as spectacle. Dolores Herrero outlines how an 'act of violence is also an act of communication',[30] but that what this paradoxically enacts above all is a breakdown in the possibility of useful communication at all. This is supported by Richard Rubenstein, who begins *Alchemists of Revolution: Terrorism in the Modern World* by tracing one of the conditions for terrorist action to a losing of faith in the efficacy of language.[31]

In an ironic demonstration of how images and their circulation can be managed by those in power, Sirocco's attempt to make the final stage of Operation Black Death public is outflanked by American officials who deny the images' veracity and downplay them. The extreme control that Sirocco exercises over the location and therefore the production of the images ironically enables opposing forces to deny them, to brand them a hoax, to cancel out his control, for only multiple versions make history. This fact serves both Sirocco and American Intelligence at different stages of the process, but in this instance it hampers Sirocco, and at all times it constitutes a source of anxiety and paranoia for both sides. It is the knowledge that it was not a hoax that American Intelligence is so desperate to cover up, in addition to wanting to destroy evidence that they had lied when they claimed that the terrorist cell had been eliminated, when in fact its members had withdrawn and regrouped in Afghanistan. In a sarcastic aside on the inability of those who manipulate us to know what they are doing, it is imagined by US security agencies that, holed up in Afghanistan, they can do no harm to anyone.[32]

Despite the attempts by faceless forces to neutralise Lowell and Samantha's efforts at locating information, piecing it together and exposing it, Lowell and Samantha manage to preserve some of the material Mather left for Lowell, to evade capture, and finally to smuggle the tapes and printed material to Paris via Samantha's Aunt Lou, from where they finally reach the public. France is probably a place that represents the most sustained opposition to America in the developed world, despite the fact that, as Samantha says, '[a]nything coming out of France can be ignored here' (382). Indeed, proving Samantha's assertion, when the information finally comes out it is discounted, and its significance almost entirely disregarded, in the United States. Lowell and Samantha's efforts have been both a success and a failure in terms of immediate effects, but alternatives to official versions have been preserved, which is crucial. Samantha's Aunt Lou optimistically observes that '[t]he past leaves traces that eventually come to light. No one can stop them' (383). The dead signify differently for the two women, but the point is that they must not be ignored.

The end of the book reveals that the traces of the past have certainly come to light in the sense that Samantha finds out that Lou is really her mother, not her aunt; that Samantha's father and Lou had had sex at his and Lou's sister's engagement party, and that he and his wife Rosalie had adopted Samantha at birth and covered up her real origins. It was an act of abnegation, in defiance of the strict family proprieties of the established Charleston families they come from, but also an act of separation. The end of the book therefore constitutes a moment when origins are clarified and connections affirmed. Lowell had begun the book and Samantha ends it (there is also a tidy romantic connection between them by the end, yet another indication of connection and suture), in an image of continuity that reminds us that '[t]he dead are always with us; they are close; but we must cling to the living' (390). Holding on to this is the problem, for anything may fragment it at any moment; they have this conversation in a graveyard after all. How can we prepare for the plague, the novel asks again at the end, and the question reverberates in the air of New York in late August 2001, the destruction of the twin towers only days away.

CHAPTER 12

The broken chords of home
Orpheus Lost

Music is the imagination of love in sound . . . But take away love from man, and what is he?

W. J. Turner[1]

Finding and losing Orpheus

Given the sustained intensity with which the contemporary world experiences the threats and results of terrorism and state-sponsored violence, Hospital's latest novel, *Orpheus Lost*, continues to focus on these issues, as she had in *Due Preparations for the Plague*. Moreover, as if reproducing the urgency with which we experience these topics, there is a breathless forward movement to the novel, with Hospital's tendency to build a narrative by way of allusions, apparent digressions and speculations employed less. The time scheme remains typically broken up into contextualisations of the characters' positions and obsessions by depictions of their childhoods or important family members, but within these sections the narrative drive is also urgent and linear. Certainly Hospital had often demonstrated her command of the resources of the linear plot line – in the childhood sections of *The Last Magician*, for example, or while Samantha and Lowell are attempting to avoid detection in *Due Preparations*, not to mention in *A Very Proper Death* – but her ability to drive the plot forward is more evident here for longer periods than in her other books. Hospital's allusive suggestiveness is still apparent, partly through her citing of the works of high culture, mostly classical music,[2] and partly through her ability to construct a network of clues or references that is dense and ominous with meaning, but whose connections remain opaque until near the end. These elements are, however, utilised in a tightly focused fashion, and tend to be centripetal rather than centrifugal, working continually to heighten the tension of the novel's multiple psychological and physical dramas in what Peter Craven terms admiringly a 'fully-articulated, thrillerlike plot'.[3]

As is usual in Hospital, some form of hermeneutic responsibility that complicates the outline supposedly provided by linearity or clarity of exposition lies at the heart of the book, and this is evident in the first paragraph when Leela laments that '[t]he trouble was that the interpretation was obvious only in retrospect'.[4] The failure to interpret will thus become a constituent part of the story, implicitly challenging readers to be on their guard. Leela's capacity to crack mathematical codes has been insufficient to decode her lover, Mishka Bartok, an Australian music student she encounters at an underground station in Boston, where his music transfixes hardened commuters. After they have been lovers for some time, she will be forced to admit that '[s]he knew everything and nothing about Mishka' (97). By the end, she will be desperate to know simply what has happened to him: 'It's not knowing that's so unbearable. I think I could handle any kind of news, but I need to know' (338). Knowing someone and knowing what has happened to them are different types of knowing, and the novel will explore the cracks and connections between those different ways of knowing, and between different ways of speaking knowledge, set against the special category of knowledge provided by our experience of music.

Hospital tells in interviews that the initial visual impulse behind writing the book was the sight of a musician in the Boston underground railway system, a version of Orpheus in the underworld.[5] With typical suggestiveness, this character's surname becomes nothing less than Bartok, aligning him with an extreme of musical talent, appropriately enough if he is to be equated with Orpheus, but which also aligns him with a musician whose career was shaped by his opposition to tyranny. Hospital is not one to allow readers to miss the ambition of her principal parallels or allusions, and Leela summons up Orpheus almost immediately: 'He has the eyes of Orpheus at the moment when Eurydice is bitten by the snake' (10), the eyes, thus, of someone who has had something vital snatched away from him. She even tells him she could call him Orpheus. Nonetheless, the novel constantly plays variations upon the myth, and the parallels are skewed right from the beginning, inasmuch as Leela is not inhabiting any underworld from which Mishka tries to rescue her, and of course they both emerge above ground and live together. In fact, Leela occupies the Orpheus role for most of the book, as Hospital points out in an exploration of the Orpheus theme,[6] in that she has the sense that she cannot live without Mishka (frequently repeating Orpheus's line from Gluck's *Orfeo ed Euridice* – '*Que farò senza Euridice?*'; What will I do without Eurydice?).[7] She has the task of descending into more than one underworld to search for Mishka: the underworld of the subway system; the labyrinth of his melancholy; and later when he is being pulled away from her into the orbit of his fanatically Islamist Lebanese family, not to mention when he disappears into the bowels of the American interrogation network in Iraq, literally represented as a miasmic underground labyrinth. Mishka as Orpheus becomes lost, lost in the city, lost to Leela, and lost to his mythical role as the creative principle engaged in the quest to bring its inspiration into the light. His becoming lost to his role is signalled early on when he asks his Eurydice not to follow him as he moves not upwards but down 'into the subway tunnels' (4; also see 107).

Mishka is mysterious from the outset, albeit in ways that appear to relate to the awkward lack of social ease of the driven genius, and this is the interpretation Leela makes. He is a recluse, he says; he lives for his music, and is 'no good at anything normal' (13). He reminds Leela of the intensity of a childhood friend in South Carolina, Cobb, who will become one of the book's principal characters, and these resonances of childhood appear to locate Mishka within 'the sense of an interlocking part' (13). Mishka, on the other hand, gives no sense of believing he interlocks with anything; even his name, he laments, 'isn't part of me' (14); but whether he is referring to Michael, Mishka or Bartok, or all three, is unclear. Later, it will be discovered that he has yet another name, Mikael Abukir. He has come to feel that his surname is not connected with him because it is not his father's surname.

The principal male figure who might counter the powerful pull of the absent father is ironically also absent – Mishka's Uncle Otto, whose image appears to Mishka at moments of great stress, as if calling him back to the positive realities associated with his mother's side of the family, and above all to the realities of music. Otto is also a further Orpheus figure in the novel, for although he is dead he is experienced by his family as if he had returned from the underworld, his music living on in their daily rituals and reference points as they relax after dinner and 'listen' to him playing in the upstairs room. Mishka's musical genius participates in the metaphor, for his talent is 'like Otto restored' (180), his mother claims, as though through the sublimity of music death may be defeated. When Mishka first touches the Persian stringed instrument called a *barbat*, '[h]e had a sense of touching simultaneously his father and his grandfather Bartok' (199); the 'act of reverence' (199) brings together the Muslim and the Jewish sides of himself, while at the same time it eliminates the difference, as, in the Orpheus myth, music eliminates the greatest difference of all: that between the living and the dead. The parallels and suggestions thrown up by the use of Orpheus are numerous, for, like all significant Greek mythic figures, varying and conflicting stories have accreted around him. In the most widely known, Orpheus fails to bring Eurydice back from the underworld; but there also exists the story in which he succeeds, as his mentor Dionysus succeeded in bringing back Dionysus's mother, Semele, from Hades. To follow all of these possible implications would not necessarily be helpful, however, since we know that Hospital launches off flashes of visual and thematic stimulation rather than constructing parallels systematically.

There is one more significant Orpheus figure in the book, and that is Leela's childhood friend and rival, Cobb, who is directly involved in Mishka's disappearance into the hell of an underground prison in Iraq. Cobb wishes to atone for his involvement in an intelligence-gathering operation gone wrong, but he also wishes to atone for a life of resentment dedicated to erasing Leela's effect on him, an effect in which he is overpoweringly drawn to Leela, but in which he also feels constantly bitter about the power she has over him. The final Orpheus in the book is thus Cobb in his mission to rescue Mishka from illegal incarceration in Baghdad, 'Operation Underworld' (350). As it happens, Cobb also rescues his own image in this operation, for, in exposing the barbaric mixture of intelligence-gathering, sectarian revenge and extortion through kidnapping that has driven the torture complex, his own besmirched reputation is recuperated. In this case he becomes an incomplete Orpheus, one who has sung as a whistle-blower on military atrocities, and who travels into the underworld never to return, being killed in the operation. The novel presumes that such exposure of clandestine horrors will be rewarded by the system, inasmuch as Cobb is laid to rest in Arlington cemetery, so that the knowledge he brought above ground survives, while the figure who went down to get it is buried. His actions are also rewarded in that he does manage to get Mishka out alive, as well as helping to bring his own father out of the underworld of remorse and bitterness in which he has lived since Vietnam.

Although there are, then, various candidates for the role of Orpheus, and although the role is played in differing forms by different characters, the Orpheus who is most obviously lost is Mishka. Despite being physically rescued by Cobb, and having a projected future being nursed back to health by his mother's family in Queensland, Mishka is not actually represented after his rescue, and his trajectory in the novel takes him through a chain of losses. His first loss is the truth of Uncle Otto, when it is revealed to him that Otto does not exist, at least not physically. This is followed by the loss of the connection to his mother when she tells him the story of how he was conceived, and some of the background of his father, about whom he had known almost nothing until he was a teenager. Finally he loses both Leela and his music as he tries to find out about and make contact with his father in Lebanon. In the quest to make contact with his father, who he had learnt was a fanatical Islamist bent on jihad against the West, Mishka had naively imagined that he could both connect with him and bring him back from the dogmatic mental underworld he inhabited, if only he could play music to him or in some way repair his former love of music. This is a version of Hell, however, that is resistant to the pleasures of music. Marwan Abukir, Mishka's father, 'abhors music' (207). For Marwan, '[b]eauty is dangerous [. . .] It is a trap' (255). When Orpheus is unable to make that beauty work for him it signals a darkness so profound that it is no wonder he becomes lost. To desire to cancel music is to desire to cancel a realm that lies outside dogma, one through which people can speak to each other when they have no other language in common. To communicate outside language is, however, to communicate outside the possibility of being told what to think, what to do and what to be. For those who wish to control other human beings, this is anathema, and the novel introduces such characters only briefly, as if lending them voice were to allow their mental underworld too much exposure, as if for the narratorial voice to descend too far into such a world were too frightening to bear. For if there is one thing the novel is in no doubt about, it is the wonder and the necessity of music.

Music, codes and reading

Leela and Mishka are connected in terms of their mirrored obsessions, given that Leela is a mathematician, her special area of research the mathematics of music. Music and mathematics are intimately linked via their investment in measurable patterns, systems and the pleasures of arranging the units of their respective notational codes. Nevertheless, while for Leela mathematics is beautiful and inspires pleasures related to those of music, for Mishka music is 'always and only about loss' (18). Despite claiming to be happy with Leela, he always looks sad, and becomes defensive when his apparent sadness is probed. Later in the book, when Leela is despairing of ever seeing Mishka again after he has disappeared into the torture chambers of American security agencies in Iraq, she loses her sense of the beauty of numbers, telling her mathematical mentor at MIT: 'I no longer believe there's any code. It's just static. It's scrambled noise and scrambled numbers. Nothing makes sense to me' (300). This trajectory underlines the inescapability of hermeneutic positioning, even in our relation to patterns that are supposedly non-social, for, while two and two must always make four, this fact can be lived in varying ways (for example as a sign of beauty and order or as a prosaic restriction). Moreover, while music and mathematics are areas of endeavour centred on codes and patterns, music is very definitely social, and it is insistently engaged with on cultural and personal levels in ways that connect it with other experiences, cultural affirmation or positioning, not to mention the nature of the divine. Whatever the truth of Stravinsky's famous assertion that 'music is, by its very nature, essentially powerless to *express* anything at all',[8] the fact is that, as Derrick Wright sums up, 'all musical meaning is the result of the interpretation of that music by the listener'.[9] The hermeneutic imperative runs through the world of Hospital's fiction, in which nothing exists innocently or transparently, so it is no surprise that '[m]usical meaning, like all meaning, is not the intrinsic property of an object, but arises out of the relationship between the object and the observer'.[10] Mishka's attempts throughout the novel to bring together the violin and the oud (a stringed Persian instrument) certainly indicate an awareness of music as culture and not simply as abstract notation. As an example of how this operates, when Mishka hears about Cobb's having spent time in Iraq, he puts away his violin and begins playing the oud. In retrospect, this can be seen as the sort of clue Leela had been unable to read, a sign of protest over what is happening in

Iraq, as Mishka moves to an instrument that derives from what we will later learn is (and is not) his father's culture.

Music constitutes the most troubling interface between many things in the novel. It becomes a site of the clash of world views, and is thus centrally implicated in culture. At the same time, music exists via notational codes that, like mathematics, may be said to operate outside culture, although different musical traditions exist in ways that do not happen with mathematics, so that, as J. Peter Burkholder elaborates, 'just as in language, *meaning depends on what the listener knows*'.[11] In addition, music also enters culture as soon as it is associated with words, and much of the music referred to in the book is associated with words in opera. Gluck's *Orfeo ed Euridice* references a story whose characteristics are known independently of the music, so Mishka's grandfather is able to speak of it as 'a song of the utmost grief and pain' (169), through which, when Orpheus 'sings his grief, he touches her again' (169). Mishka's Syrian music teacher in Brisbane, whose brother was killed for political reasons in a way that Mishka links to the death of Uncle Otto, executed in a concentration camp for stealing food, also considers that '[f]or loss, we have music' (202).

Music further exists in the novel as an interface between the living and the lost dead, picking up on how Orpheus was able to face up to 'the King of terrors, the stone heart no prayer can tame', in one translator's resonant version of Virgil.[12] The Bartok family reconnects with Otto and their lost homeland, indeed with a whole way of being, via music, in which the lost are felt to be present once again. While much of the music in the book is allied with words, ultimately it is the music that gives the words their significance rather than vice versa, a form of translation whose operation is mysterious. Leela's love of music is allied to a fascination with its codes and patterns and the ways they unite and intertwine, but the production of emotional effects occurs in the listener, and is not guaranteed by those patterns.

In Leela's sister Maggie's understanding, Leela follows the clues suggested by numbers, 'picking up numerical crumbs and magic as she went' (138), which echoes their Evangelical father or any seeker after ultimate truth: 'pressing on toward the heart of the labyrinth and the radiant answer to some vast riddle' (138). Leela's intoxication by numbers is depicted positively as an awareness of the complexity and interlocking vectors that characterise anything when examined in enough detail. Her father, on the other hand, is portrayed as lovable but misguided in his extreme Evangelism, summed up at one point as 'magic numbers' (113), numbers which do not lead to an expanded sense of the mysterious multifariousness of the criss-crossing lines of reality, but which lead instead to a dogmatic certainty about meaning and divine purpose. When a letter arrives for her father from Leela in Cambridge, he reasons that as it was posted on the sixth day of the sixth month, and it is Leela's sixth letter since she went north, it carries the '[m]ark of the beast in the Book of Revelation' (129), so he throws it into the fire unread. The letters he does read are decoded by means of 'marking off seventh letters and seventh words' (134), a form of realisation that the surface meanings of words are not their only meanings, and that there are hidden meanings that we need to know how to process if we want to perceive the world aright. In this, Southern Pentecostal and literary analysis are agreed: texts require interpreting, and no text can be accepted at face value. Any deviation from what is expected summons the need for analysis, so that when Leela's mentor Berg holds her wrists, for example, she looks down at his fingers as 'symbols that had to be decoded' (301). An indication that she has not given up on meaning as much as she claims is that she continues to try to relate what has happened to mathematical structures, and defiantly claims that '[i]n math, we accept strange loops' (303). On one occasion, after she has found out that Mishka has disappeared, she visits a tarot card reader rather than a therapist, drawn to the mysteries of the interpretation of formal codes rather than anything else.

Cobb forms a triangle with Leela and Mishka inasmuch as his principal talent also involves the deciphering and rearrangement of codes. A childhood prodigy at mathematics like Leela, there is nonetheless a difference between them: Leela 'seemed to find numbers themselves – the ciphers and cryptic symbols – strangely beautiful and full of narrative mystery', while Cobb's fascination with numbers occurs only 'after he had applied them to moving parts and tangible structures' (43). Mathematics for Leela is supposedly what 'makes the world go round' (44), with the great advantage that 'you can learn what his [*sic*] secrets are' (44). As has been seen, however, mathematics is a code that offers little certainty in the constant decoding of human beings, whether individually or en masse. Given that secrets are ever-present in the novel, and that keeping them or finding them out has results that can destroy or save, the activity of deciphering and reading the connections between causes and effects is of decisive significance. This sort of decoding requires an alertness to connections and ordering on the one hand, but, as with anything involving human beings, being able to read the fractal and the irregular, the unexpected and the paradoxical, is crucial.

Interpretation of different types of evidence is accordingly scrutinised, and what can be seen is that human beings are spectacularly bad at interpreting each other. It is precisely because Leela's father is aware of human fallibility that he has recourse to a system whose authority and shaping supposedly come from outside himself, from God, who thus enters reality as the ultimate encoder and the ultimate code at the same time. Claude Lévi-Strauss affirms categorically that 'it is absolutely impossible to conceive of meaning without order', and that meaning itself is nothing less than 'the ability of any kind of data to be translated in a different language', by which he does not mean into a foreign language, but into 'different words on a different level'.[13] Music and mathematics question this to some extent, in that meaning seems to exist *as* order, or rather order exists as meaning, with reference being added by the listener. For example, even if a piece of music is universally felt to evoke sadness, it is the listener who decides how to process that sadness, whether in terms of a personal memory, a group reference (what happened to our people) or something more generic (we all have to die). In this openness to interpretation, music is further related to the other principle type of translation examined in the novel – photographs.

One of the key sites of interpretation that characters have to negotiate is that of photographs, generally photographs involving violence, whose enigmatic power continues to fascinate Hospital. It is the existence and interpretation of photographs that have made Cobb's father embittered and hostile, an attitude of suspicion towards the world that his son has inherited. Cobb's life has been bound by the ironclad southern imperatives of his fire-breathing father, named, with pugnacious symbolic resonance, Calhoun Slaughter, whose hates and categories reverberate with the unresolved clamour of the Civil War. He also brings an older generation's set of references to the issues of war and honour, for he had fought in Vietnam and, according to local rumour, 'shot prisoners in the back of the head' (48), reminding us that American atrocities in Iraq are hardly without precedent.[14] Even this action, however, is not what assails Slaughter's conscience and dreams, for he has also been guilty of grenading a hut full of Vietnamese children.

The photographs that have damned Slaughter in the eyes of the world concern the shooting of prisoners in the back of the head, while the more horrific act goes unnoticed because there are no photographs to tell of it. When Cobb examines the photographs that do exist, showing the events on either side of his father's actions, he is able to delineate a different narrative from the one implied by the photograph that became iconic.[15] For newspapers, '[c]ontext meant nothing . . . visual drama was all' (232), so that typically photographs are presented as evidence as though the moment they represented needed no framing, when for Hospital framing provides the condition for meaning itself. Even the absence of apparent framing is a framing device, in that it still establishes a visually absent but nonetheless signalled narrative whose direction the reader is encouraged to infer. In the sequence as reconstructed by Cobb, his father's actions can be justified, for although Slaughter shot a man lying on the ground in the head, it was a split-second decision made in the heat of being ambushed. Cobb tells him, '[y]ou couldn't have known' (326) whether the man was pretending to be injured or not, in a scenario where mimicry, pretence and subterfuge were the norm. When dealing with enemies, the necessity to mistrust appearances, along with the possibility of error, becomes heightened. There is, however, a further sinister connection linking Slaughter's trial-by-photograph during the Vietnam War to his son's belief in controlling access to photographs, for since the first Gulf War the United States has tried to ban unofficial photographers from its theatres of operation. In Fred Ritchin's summary of the consequences of this, 'When the US government announced that it did not want "another Vietnam," it effectively erased wounds and death from the visual vocabulary of war',[16] thus concealing even the type of flawed evidence contained in the photography of conflict.

Leela makes the connection between Cobb's interest in Mishka and Cobb's understanding of his father's experience, in that information out of context can easily seem like a truth. Such truths, however, tend to be not only diminished and skewed but too readily placed into an easily understandable causal sequence. As David Simpson points out: 'Images always come with or quickly lead to words when sense begins to be made of them, but any image that fits too happily into verbal translation should be suspect.'[17] Through Cobb's own erroneous interpretation of photographs of Mishka, he will compound the domino effect of interpreting items without knowing enough about the gaps between them, damning Mishka to incarceration and torture. At the same time, as in *Charades*, photographs, rightly framed, can aid in the struggle against the forces that aim to dictate their own narrow and destructive narrative to the rest of the world. After Mishka is swallowed up by outsourced American interrogation and intelligence agencies, one hope that the truth about his fate will emerge is provided by the fact that '[g]uards and soldiers take photographs' (289). This has already been revealed earlier, when soldier Benedict Boykin (from the same town as Leela and Cobb) delivers photographs of American atrocities to Cobb, his superior officer. On that occasion, Cobb had failed to pass them on. Later it transpires that one reason Cobb had been unwilling to bring Boykin's photographs to the attention of higher authorities is because he wishes to spare his father (or possibly himself); that he wanted to restrict the connections that would be made between his involvement in atrocities and his father's disgraced military record. He is proven correct when he later decides to send the photographs to the newspapers, as all aspects of his military career, personal life and father's history are vilified by former colleagues and the media. In *Due Preparations* information is sent to the newspapers, but it is denied, minimised and ignored by those in power. We know, however, from the publicity surrounding events at the Abu Ghraib prison in Baghdad, not to mention the harrowing photographs of Nazi concentration camps, that photographs can help to convict wrongdoers.

Cobb's use of photographs is conditioned by his profession, which revisits that of Lowell's father in *Due Preparations*: Cobb works in the area of intelligence-gathering, and he has the power to decide on the consequences of his interpretations of the 'evidence' he finds. In the course of his surveillance of radical Islamists in Boston, he has occasion to have Leela brought into custody and interrogated, a process whose existence is an admission that people cannot easily be decoded. Cobb's annoyance that 'certain kinds of people were so casual, so unaware' (50) resonates with a sense of reality as requiring constant vigilance and deciphering. For both of them numbers 'were secret codes' (54), positive indicators of patterns that lie waiting to be elucidated. Like music, however, numbers and patterns possess no moral direction in themselves, their meanings being constructed by human beings according to pre-existing imperatives. Cobb's capturing of Leela derives from his suspicion that she 'possibly without her own knowledge – was being used to encode information of a dangerous kind' (54); her departmental supervisor, Berg, a Jew who is being anonymously harassed, also wonders whether Leela 'might have been used' (121). Ironically, Cobb's suspicion is followed by his remembering when he had had racist Southern icons tattooed onto his body, encoded information of a dangerous kind whose secret is that he does not realise how poisonous or how dangerous it is. For Cobb the symbols are 'heritage' (56), a noxious pride that will be ironically echoed in Mishka's father's relatedly destructive belief that 'heritage' justifies murdering those whose 'heritage' is opposed to yours. Dangerously powerful codes in fact seep through everyone's culture, and even our interest in the apparently neutral codes of harmonic notational systems does not remove us from the turbulence of competing moral systems.

Cobb has his own decoding skill, which he feels to be 'a sixth sense' (229). It consists in being able to intuit connections, an activity in which '[h]e had never been wrong' (229). This type of deciphering connections has as its aim 'forestalling acts of mayhem' (239), an act of narrative projection into the future, when Cobb knows that how connections become established cannot be predicted. Despite his confidence, Cobb's plan to observe Mishka's meeting in Beirut with his father, Marwan, and then to apprehend them separately goes disastrously wrong, and both of them are captured and taken to Baghdad, where private security teams act under the official radar. Connections spin dangerously out of control, as wise music professor Dr Siddiqi disappears in Boston, presumably taken by shadowy Intelligence forces, despite the fact that he was in America because he had had to flee the Iranian theocracy; but at least the system can sometimes read people sympathetically, as Siddiqi is released unharmed. Once decoding starts to operate without a honed awareness of the larger frameworks or the pitfalls of interpretative excess, however, it disfigures the social fabric, its simplistic logic mirroring the essentialist frames it is supposedly combating.

Family as connection, family as secrets

Mishka's elusive despair, which so troubles Leela throughout the beginning parts of the novel, seems at first as if it has to do with his mother's family history, that of Hungarian Jews traumatised by the Holocaust and displaced in Australia after World War II. Mishka's Uncle Otto remains in his upstairs room and never appears in front of the family, speaking to them only by playing music. A version of this family had already appeared in Hospital's story 'The Last of the Hapsburgs', in which the Jewish Weiss family, immigrants from the Austro-Hungarian empire, live in a fancifully constructed dwelling in the Daintree rainforest just like the Bartok family. Apart from the importance of music in the household, there is also a reclusive son, Leo, who is claimed to play the violin from within his room but, it is intimated, does not actually play anything and perhaps does not exist or has died. Initially, the visiting schoolteacher, Miss Davenport, hears only the noises of the rainforest, but then, inexplicably, she hears the absent music along with the Weiss family.[18] This eccentric, melancholy, displaced family has been greatly extended and rewritten in *Orpheus Lost*. In the story and the novel Rebecca and Mishka respectively are reticent about discussing their family with outsiders, a defence mechanism in response to the treatment of difference in Australia.

From an early age, connections have been broken in Mishka's life, and one of the larger implications of the novel is perhaps nothing less that that this is the world's problem: we cannot perceive the connections that make us family, and, in the self-destructive intensity of the family, we keep trying to hurt and punish those who have failed to live up to the impossible codes of love and/or obedience that we imagine make up the perfectly functioning family. Broken and sundered families lie at the centre of the book: Mishka's fate is tied to the desire to make contact with the father he has never seen, while Cobb and Leela's lives have been structured by dealing with obsessive fathers, in turn damaged by the loss of their wives as well as by their feeling that the rest of the world does not know how to interpret correctly. When Cobb decides to try to make amends for what has happened to Mishka, he recalls being on a verandah with Leela when they were seven years old, shortly after his mother had died: 'How was it that a memory from so far back could be more intense, in all its particulars, than last week?' (334). The intensities of the family are so compelling that it is as if we spend most of our lives attempting to repair the breaks and damage that occur in childhood, a causally overdetermining power whose logic Hospital examines compulsively in all of her books from *Tiger* on.

The most perfect family in the novel exists through a mixture of shutting everyone else out, enclosure within nature, and the presence of a member who is dead. This is the family of Mishka's early childhood, while he is still living in the north Queensland rainforest with his mother and grandparents, when 'everything seemed to him to flow into everything else and to be on the same page and to be part of a river of feeling without a name . . . until he would believe that the pressure of so much beauty would lift him off his feet and loft him into the rainforest canopy' (171). The family house built by his Hungarian Jewish grandfather in the late 1940s is a mixture of a tropical dwelling with 'anomalous European flourishes' (158), a hybrid mixture of influences and adaptation that both responds to the environment and creatively adds something to it as well. Something of a metaphor for a Hospital novel itself, the house is lovingly portrayed in its mixture of imagination, practicality and beauty, and even the vegetation that 'seemed intent upon swallowing the house' (158) can be seen to metaphorise once again the undergrowth of allusion and story that entwines most of Hospital's narratives. The mysterious upper floor, not usually a feature of houses in the region, serves as an indication of the difference of Mishka's family and thus of 'the story that was not supposed to exist in north Queensland' (160).

One story that does exist in contemporary Australian narrative is that of migration as loss and victimisation at the hands of a punishingly normalising Anglo-Australia. While Hospital does not minimalise the loss, and writes evocatively of the consuming absences experienced by the migrant, she is also thoroughly committed to the idea of displacement as opportunity as well. From early short stories such as 'Happy Diwali' or 'You Gave Me Hyacinths',[19] she has enjoyed depicting displaced people who have come to new understandings out of the adjustments they have had to make to altered situations. The pain of dislocation has led important characters to evince heightened sensitivity and story-telling power as they try to hold on to the meanings of where they came from as well as to communicate them to others, from the Turners of 'The Bloody Past, the Wandering Future'[20] to the Bartoks in *Orpheus Lost*. It is sometimes overlooked in present-day Australia how grateful to be in Australia many migrants once were, coming from war-blasted countries in which getting enough to eat, finding work or the chance to buy a house, let alone making a dwelling to house one's mysteries, had been next-to-impossible for large sections of the population. Hospital is attentive to the situation of migrants to Australia in the 1940s and 1950s in her touching portrayal of Mishka's grandparents, who have brought some things from where they came from, adapted to others, and made a home for themselves which is a creatively positive mixture of music, integration with the environment and central European *gemütlichkeit*. Mishka's description sums it up radiantly as:

> safety, belonging, connectedness . . . a river that rose and rose in its banks like the Daintree in the Wet season until it washed his body with warmth and rushed all around him, foaming and splashing him with Gluck and Mendelssohn and Uncle Otto's violin and bird cries and fragrant night-blooming flowers. (163)

At the same time, Mishka's grandparents' environment has been constructed as a refuge, and scarcely engages with Australian society at all. The family's central references are back in Europe, and the music they love can be included here. While loss and displacement structure their emotional lives, they have no awareness of the loss and displacement the presence of Europeans in Australia has forced upon the country's original inhabitants, or that the history of the nation since colonisation involved absence and exile on a massive scale. The historical rupture of the Holocaust has used up the family's connections with human beings. Their cocooned existence becomes one of the possible contexts for Mishka's susceptibility to social estrangement, to being able to step outside the bonds that tie human beings together. Kept apart from other children until he attended school at age six, and keeping himself apart from others throughout his school years and beyond, Mishka lives in a 'limbo of not-here and not-now' (182). All he really feels connected with is his family, their house and the rainforest, along with music. This upbringing means that it is easy for him to live parallel lives, in which the principal rule is to 'keep things separate' (200), something he attempts to do in Boston with disastrous results.

A puzzling feature of the household is Uncle Otto, who plays music to them from his room but who has apparently been so psychically damaged by the war that he never emerges from his room. A once-famous musician, whose genius Mishka has inherited, Otto was formerly accused 'of being unpatriotic because he was interested in the folk music of the Slovakians and the Romanians' (167), the sort of description that can slip past the reader in a Hospital novel but which, on reflection, is always reverberating against the novel's principal themes. What does it mean to be patriotic, to 'belong' so much to a culture that being interested in other cultures is considered inappropriate or worse? These are not conundra merely of today, and Hospital is constantly probing human beings' tendency to compartmentalise, exclude and punish on the basis of supposed cultural loyalties. Although Mishka's family is not related to the composer Béla Bartók, the name is hardly accidental: Bartók 'believed passionately in the brotherhood of mankind . . . refused to perform in Nazi Germany' (168), and fled to America instead.

The story of Mishka's mother's relation with his father is told halfway through the book. A Lebanese student in Sydney, he was also passionate about music; just as Leela is attracted to Mishka through his music, Mishka's mother and father became lovers after she was entranced by hearing him play the oud. Upon hearing that Mishka's mother had become pregnant, he returned to Beirut to tell his family; three months later she received a letter to say he had died in a car crash. Mishka's response on hearing this story is to feel intense anger towards and rejection of his mother, whom he walks away from and does not see again during the rest of the novel. In a mental rearrangement that smacks of youthful bloody-mindedness, he reclassifies his whole identity: 'I'm an Abukir, not a Bartok' (193), as if his father's genes determine who he is rather than the experience of his whole life until that point.

The desire to touch his father has as a consequence that the most memorable area of his life as a student in Brisbane is his contact with Mr Hajj, a Syrian teacher of classical Middle Eastern music, who understands both loss and the need to keep one's life safely compartmentalised. Mr Hajj and, in particular, Mishka's Iranian music teacher at Harvard, Dr Siddiqi, are learned men for whom Islamist fanaticism is anathema. Dr Siddiqi laments that such people 'have no interest in history' (267), which results in their inability to contextualise or relativise knowledge, so that all their interpretation proceeds from predetermined conclusions. Mishka's compartments begin to leak into each other more seriously in Boston when he meets Jamil Haddad, a Lebanese student who claims to know Mishka's father. Jamil represents an extreme Islamism for which '[m]usic is licentious. It is forbidden' (206). Mishka is repelled by Jamil's simplistic creed of Islamic purity, but Jamil has information about his father which Mishka craves. This information is alienating in the extreme, for Jamil reports that Marwan Abukir, Mishka's father, 'abhors music' (207) and has trained in Afghanistan for jihad against the West. Nonetheless, Mishka is so desperate for contact with this side of himself that he moves into the orbit of a radical Islamist faction. Knowledge of his father's existence 'was like one of those double-edged treasures in Scheherazade's tales: a jewel that brings death to the finder' (211).

The echo of *Charades* connects Charade's search for her father with that of Mishka, but his 'desire to know the Abukir side of myself' (155) possesses quite other contours than Charade's quest. For a start, there is no suggestion in *Charades* that Charade might be in any danger, or that her search for her father is locked into the fault lines of current geopolitical events. Charade's search is linked to speculations on the nature of origins and how we represent them or live in terms of what we imagine they represent, and this allows the narrative to be playful and teasing, as well as serious and ambiguous. Mishka's absent father also enables the book to ask questions about origins, but the fractures of family history here, including that of the human family as a whole, do not allow playfulness or suture.

Underworlds

Orpheus Lost deals with various types of sundered relations, relations figured as a set of interlocking ways by which we are connected to the world, and whose rupture presents human beings with challenges as large and as perilous as a descent into the underworld. These relations involve Leela and Mishka on the most obvious level, but also the Bartoks and history, Mishka and his father, Cobb and his father, even human beings and nature; but perhaps the most shocking may be the break between Islamists and music. This break does duty for what in cruder hands might be positioned as a 'clash of cultures'. Hospital, however, has an investment in human beings as so inextricably involved in each other that an insistence on the solidity of one's 'culture' can become more divisive than useful, a type of underworld itself that the contemporary world is in, and out of which it needs to extricate itself. For cultures to consider themselves lost to each other is as poignant as Orpheus's loss of Eurydice.[21]

The novel thus refuses to oppose Muslims to the West, and traces various trajectories along which underworlds of different types may be entered. These underworlds are both literal and metaphorical, as well as both at the same time. The first suicide bombing in Boston leads to 'the first night that Mishka disappeared' (28), figured at this stage as a descent into a mental underworld, but later as possibly an immersion in the murky networks of Islamist jihad. The bombing is one of a series that the novel imagines as having been happening throughout major cities in the United States,[22] to which Americans react with the customary determination not to have their lives obstructed: '[i]t won't make me avoid the Callahan tunnel' (29),[23] someone claims; entering the Callahan tunnel also enacts an echo of the defiance of the underworld, from which the driver will emerge at the other end into the confident assertions of the Boston city centre. From this point, nevertheless, Mishka's life becomes increasingly disrupted, as he appears to respond to the horror of the attacks by absenting himself from the apartment, disappearing to play music in places where he cannot be contacted, needing to be alone to respond to the outrage. Leela reads his traumatised response in terms of his mother's family's history, and Mishka appears to take his place among those characters in Hospital's work who have been formed by their relation to the Holocaust, from the Weiss family to Rachel and Verity in *Charades*. This reading contains intense historical ironies, given the linking of the bombings in the novel to Islamist terrorists, with Jews and Islamists two groups destined, it seems, to deny each other's victim status while claiming that status centrally for themselves.

Mishka becomes a victim when he first attends school and encounters the relentless normalising pressure of the other children (ironically articulated by a boy whose family were or are migrants from Europe themselves – Tony Cavalari). This pressure dilutes the clarity of the page he has drawn of his life, and the main thing it brings him to realise is the absence of his father. The line repeated in the novel – *Que farò senza Euridice* – comes to Mishka to mean that the great loss and absence in his life is that of his father. Among other things, the metaphor is foreshadowed here by which Mishka's father is in the underworld, and in this trope Mishka becomes an Orpheus who now begins a long, arduous quest to find a way into this underworld and bring his father back above ground. This absence becomes conflated with the other great absence in his family life, that of Uncle Otto, who exists in photographs and family ritual, but who is otherwise unknown to Mishka. Indeed, it is Tony who flings open the door to Uncle Otto's room on his first visit to Mishka's house to reveal that the room contains only photographs. The experience leads to Mishka's feeling that he is falling 'to where a vast underground cavern opened up' (179). A Hades awaits us when the connections that bind our existence together are sundered, but does this mean that believing in the existence of something that is not there might be healthier than opening the door?

When the door is thrown open, Mishka begins to move from a relation to an authority figure who is not materially present and whose authority is spoken through music, a code which does not tell anyone to do or to think anything, to a search for the materially present authority figure of his father, who denies music and who speaks instead through commandment and prohibition. This is not an opposition between West and East. Indeed, the first cultural reference to the Muslim world in the novel is to a musical instrument, the oud, and there are sympathetically drawn Muslim characters who feel the value of music deeply. Nevertheless, the first obvious reference to Islam comes when Cobb reveals that Leela had been going in the direction of a mosque in Cambridge, Massachusetts, following Mishka, who Cobb calls Mikael Abukir, and who he claims is 'involved with a Muslim Youth Association which has ties to Hamas and to assorted extremist groups' (73). As Leela thinks of Mishka as Jewish, and believes him to be neither religious nor political in the slightest, she disbelieves Cobb's assertions and suspects that photographs of Mishka with the suicide bomber are doctored.

Mishka's twinned heritage as Muslim and Jew also participates in Hospital's perception of the irrevocably mixed discourses we inhabit, along with the inevitable ambiguities and multivalence of any identificatory manoeuvres we make. It is the refusal either to recognise this or to attempt to live up to its potential for richness and tolerance that becomes destructive.

Leela equates herself with Eurydice in her version of what must have happened when Orpheus was leading her out of Hades: he must have called back for reassurance, 'are you still there?', and for whatever reason she had failed to answer, or to answer quickly enough to Orpheus's overwrought state of mind, and in a panic he had looked back, losing her forever. Leela also had failed to answer Mishka, failed to reassure him; but it is Mishka who disappears back into the realm of death. From this point the novel becomes Leela's attempt to locate and rescue Mishka, including a chilling sequence in which she tries to see him in an Australian holding camp for refugees, more like a high-security prison than anything else. The lawyer who is helping them wishes to be called K, and the processes involved in getting through the bureaucracy to see Mishka are certainly Kafkaesque. The parallels between unaccountable American detention camps and official Australian ones are clear: Australia is no better than America, and is perhaps nothing but a slavish imitation. The process of getting through the camp's procedures recalls K's attempts to have his case dealt with in *The Trial*, but it is also a quest into an underworld where normal rules do not apply. In the end, the man they manage to see is not Mishka at all.

Promised lands?

While the novel is replete with underworlds of various kinds, it also contains many types of promised lands. The final section is named 'Promised Land', and there is a place actually called Promised Land in the novel (as there is in South Carolina). The name of the town in South Carolina where Leela, Cobb and Benedict Boykin come from speaks of a desire that has not been fulfilled, in the disjunction between the resonance of the name and the backwater the town has become and indeed always was. Promised lands in the novel, as in Hospital's work, inevitably establish a fissure between the desire for meaning that cannot be challenged and the complex, messy, multi-meaninged realities of human existence, to which Hospital is irrevocably committed. Leela's ability to live in a world of multivalent possibilities had infuriated Cobb as a child, and he had always 'wanted her to know precisely this: the shameful suck of hopeless wanting, the dead weight of things that nothing could change' (339). On many levels, however, the book affirms that change is possible, and ultimately Cobb comes to believe this as well.

The deathly imperatives of those who hate and wish to control others are counterposed to various versions of promised lands, and the one that is the most attractive is the one that is inflected the least with theology and the most with creative adaptation: that of Mishka's grandparents, for whom their portion of Australia at least is referred to as 'the promised land' (163). In this land it is hard not to feel that Mishka's perception when a child of the way things belong together is a healthy, suturing one, so that his grandmother's painting of botanical illustrations in which a plant is separated from the contexts in which it lives becomes an early vision of adult reductiveness in which disconnection is central. How can we draw the quandong tree without birds, for 'there are *always* birds in the quandong trees' (170; Hospital's italics), Mishka points out. More than this, '[i]t seemed to him that not only the birds but his grandparents and his mother and himself and Uncle Otto's music and Gluck's aria and their house also belonged on the page' (171). The fact that this page includes a figure who Mishka has never seen requires further explanation. It seems apparent that the family's relation to Uncle Otto evokes a version of a relation to the divine; even Otto's palindromic name, begun and completed by perfect circles, possesses the symmetry of the numinous. It is a relation in which the figure is materially absent, but in which the family acts towards him as if he were present, and from which they clearly draw sustenance. This figure lives above them in a space whose characteristics suggest somewhere out of the ordinary, and from which the family derives the sensation of contact with music, which is one of the principal forms most religions use to make contact with or express a yearning for the divine. Uncle Otto, however, did exist, and he was a brilliant musician, so the suggestion seems to be that of a divine being who was once present to human beings, but who has now become a metaphor, one that we might experience as a physical absence, and know to be symbolic, but which we might also know that we need after all if our lives are be connected to that which is meaningful for us.

Significantly, the book does not end with any revelation of this nature, and it is necessary that Uncle Otto's physical absence become apparent halfway through, for the book is interested in what human beings do when they know they have to make an effort to hold on to meaning. The absent father figure as someone who remains absent but about whom we continue to need stories had been central to *Charades*, and the narrative had led up to this as one of its final, albeit buried, implications. In *Orpheus Lost* the question of this loss needs to be flagged earlier so that varying responses may be followed. When Mishka finds out that Uncle Otto is not living in the upstairs room, he is unable to hear

Otto's music any more; not only that, he glimpses the possibility that the rest of his family do not hear it either, or not as he had thought they had. As he observes his mother with his eyes open during Uncle Otto's music for the first time, what he sees is 'resignation' (178), and this is one strategy: we live resigned to the absence, we keep up appearances because to do otherwise would be to forget a connection we once believed in, and then it would indeed be lost forever.

Another form of resignation occurs when Leela's sister Maggie remembers rifle shots being directed at black neighbour Esau Boykin's house, and her father asking Esau about the effect of constant racist violence: 'How come I don't never see you down?' (144). Esau's answer refers to his faith in the Lord, but his young son, Benedict, had retorted: 'It ain't right not to be angry' (144). Later, he will complain to Cobb, his commanding officer, about violations of human rights in Iraq, but his evidence will be suppressed. Much Western writing dealing with these issues is attempting to modulate just how one can be angry without essentialising the objects of one's anger or damaging one's own values. From *The Ivory Swing* until the present, Hospital's favoured protagonists are notable for getting angry and for fighting back against violence and murder, generally at great risk, and even at the cost of being murdered themselves, as happens to Cat and probably to Charlie and Gabriel in *The Last Magician*, or to Felicity in *Borderline*, not to mention various characters in *Due Preparations*. Throughout her work, moreover, the people or forces that are to be fought against are often diffuse, secretive, difficult to identify and locate. For the most part, these have been official or in league with official agencies, and, even though terrorists have entered her last two novels, it is semi-official channellers and instigators of violence who continue to figure centrally. Ironically, most of the violence that is actually carried out against the inhabitants of Western countries is felt by many to come from their own governments, and the development of repressive state controls that threaten civil liberties and private pleasures in increasingly restrictive ways.[24]

Promised lands inflect the foundation of America (in contradistinction to Australia) with a rhetoric of social decency and liberty that is brought into question by developments since 9/11. Hospital has been examining the cynical and hypocritical actions of official and semi-official American and Australian authorities since *Borderline*, so that *Orpheus Lost* takes its place in a coherent reading of the Western societies she knows best; it is not simply an opportunistic response to Islamist jihad or Western reactions to terrorism. In this reading, or indeed in the fact itself of writing such a reading, Hospital is determined to highlight the misfit between the lands our traditions promise us and the uses public officials put them to. In this sense, writing the book may be related to *New Yorker* journalist Mark Danner's campaign to put before the public the evidence concerning the Abu Ghraib case, and the evasive responses of members of the American military and governing bodies. As Danner says in the foreword to his compendium of photographs and documents, *Torture and Truth: America, Abu Ghraib, and the War on Terror* 'it is not about revelation or disclosure but about the failure, once wrongdoing is disclosed, of politicians, officials, the press, and, ultimately, citizens to act . . . It is not about information; it is about politics'.[25]

Mishka is an Orpheus who tries to bring back from an underworld nothing less than music itself. To the extent that he fails to convince his father of the value of music, and that he fails to convince American surveillance that his relation to music does not signal a terrorist plot, his fate demonstrates how lost and simplistically polarised both Western and Islamist readers of reality may become. Despite this, the book finishes on a note of both redemption and return. Cobb has redeemed himself in Leela's eyes as well as in those of the wider polity. Calhoun Slaughter appears to have been calmed by his son's sacrifice, while Mishka has been brought back from Hell and faces a future being nursed back to health in his beloved Daintree rainforest. The crazed interrogators in Iraq had read Mishka's living the world through music as a code for a plot to booby-trap musical instruments. Early on in the novel Mishka had told Leela that '[p]eople learn to do without whatever they have to do without' (33). Learning to do without music, however, represents the loss of something so intrinsic to our humanity that the novel will not sanction it by confirming the possibility even in narrative. Otto and Orpheus – whose names begin with the unusual beginning letter for a name in English of O, both plenitude and zero – are not lost but restored in some way to the rainforest, itself a metaphor of continual rebirth, as is the myth of Orpheus itself.[26] For American reviewer Donna Rifkind, 'Hospital's novel about music also aspires . . . to be music, or at least to mimic the solace it can offer. Lushly orchestrated, *Orpheus Lost* answers grief and fear with an emotional expressiveness more visceral than words, with the candor of music – and of myth'.[27] And ultimately, the book suggests, we need some version of the myth of renewal as we need music itself.

ACKNOWLEDGEMENTS

Thanks are due for financing provided at the different stages of this project, particularly by the Portuguese Foundation for Science and Technology (FCT) – grant BSAB/528/2005. The University of Aveiro, through the Centre for Languages and Cultures, has also permitted numerous short research trips.

The project began with an approach from Tony Hassall, who, far beyond the call of duty, has read every chapter at more than one stage of its preparation, making careful and numerous suggestions which have greatly contributed to making the book more fluent and consistent. Without Tony's encouragement and labours, it is doubtful whether the book would have been completed, for which I cannot thank him enough.

Thanks are due to the helpful librarians at the Fryer Library at the University of Queensland, the State Library of NSW, and the National Library of Scotland in Edinburgh. My tireless mother, Dawn Walton, has become more familiar with the State Library of NSW than she ever imagined, and is a much more dogged researcher than I am.

In my approach to Australian literature and culture over the years I have especially benefited from the encouragement and stimulation of Mary-Lynn Broe, Ruth Brown, Ian Craven, Marc Delrez, Catherine Dunne, the late Bernard Hickey, Graham Huggan, Lars Jensen, Toni Johnson-Woods, Peter O'Neill, Helga Ramsey-Kurtz, the late Robert Ross, Selina Samuels, and Deborah Torkko.

My partner Andreia Sarabando has discussed every phase of the book as well as helped with the research, despite having her own complicated projects to complete. The name Janette Turner Hospital is indelibly engraved in the minds of my forbearing children, Nicholas and Kate.

On the last straight, the people at UQP got me to the finishing line, particularly Madonna Duffy, Nikola Lusk and Felicity McKenzie.

Finally, Janette Turner Hospital herself has been a model of writerly recitude as the object of this study. Putting up with all my fussy questions, she has not tried to direct my conclusions or force any explanations on me.

Permission from the following to use, adapt and dismember work previously published is gratefully acknowledged: *Antipodes: A North American Journal of Australian Literature*; *Ariel: A Review of International English Literature* and the Board of Governors, University of Calgary, Calgary, Alberta, Canada; *Australian Studies*; *Critique: Studies in Contemporary Fiction*; *Tulsa Studies in Women's Literature*; the Sir Robert Menzies Centre for Australian Studies, London; and Stauffenburg Verlag, Tübingen, Germany.

NOTES

1. Displacement, interpretation and responsibility

1. 'A man who is tired of Swiper's Creek is tired of life', *Hunting the Wild Pineapple*, Melbourne: Thomas Nelson, 1979, p. 175.
2. 5 October 1986, p. C8. 'Hospital' is Janette Turner Hospital's husband Cliff's surname. By retaining her own surname, even if followed by her husband's surname, Hospital makes a feminist point which was extremely uncommon in 1966 when she got married. Many critics and reviewers accordingly refer to her as 'Turner Hospital', and I have done so myself elsewhere. She has said, however, that she does not mind which version of her name is used, so in this work I will be using 'Hospital' in order to save words. The typescript of her first novel, *The Ivory Swing*, has as a running header: Janette T. Hospital. Fryer Library, University of Queensland Library, Papers of Janette Turner Hospital, UQFL 255, Box 1.
3. Luckily Hospital resisted the early temptation to call Charlie 'Sushi' in *The Last Magician*. Papers of Janette Turner Hospital, Box 5.
4. *Borderline*, St Lucia: University of Queensland Press, 1987, p. 152.
5. *Orpheus Lost*, Sydney: Fourth Estate, 2007, p. 87.
6. I have expanded upon this in 'Rainforest narratives: Janette Turner Hospital and the ethics of interference', *Antipodes*, 15.1, June 2001, pp. 31–5. The rainforest is also dealt with in Sue Lovell, 'The "psychic space" of Queensland in the work of Janette Turner Hospital', *Queensland Review*, 11.2, December 2004, pp. 11–23.
7. The situation is mirrored in the difficulty people often have in writing or pronouncing Hospital's first name correctly. Despite her telling people she is JanETTE, introducers will stand up five minutes later and present JANet to the audience, while knowledgeable academics who admire her work have nonetheless referred in print on occasion to Janet, or Jeannette. See John McLaren, 'The boundaries of the audience', *Span*, 30, April 1990, p. 15; Silvia Albertazzi, 'Beautiful travellers: notes on postmodern fiction', *Commonwealth: Essays and Studies*, 11.2, 1989, p. 54.
8. *Dislocations*, 2nd edn, St Lucia: University of Queensland Press, 1987, pp. 9–21; *Isobars*, St Lucia: University of Queensland Press, 1991, pp. 150–63.

9. 'The inheritance of difference: an interview with Janette Turner Hospital', *Imago*, 1.1, March 1989, p. 8. Interview conducted by Sue Lovell.
10. Tom Adair, 'Vultures return to pick over the bones of lost childhood', *Scotland on Sunday*, 28 June 1992, p. 38. Review of *Charades*.
11. Laurie Clancy, 'Only the writing is certain', *Age*, 24 September 1988: Saturday Extra, p. 12.
12. 'Litany for the Homeland', *North of Nowhere, South of Loss*, St Lucia: University of Queensland Press, 2003, p. 257.
13. There is evidence that Hospital's work has been edited at times for non-Australian readers. For example, in *The Last Magician* Lucy is talking with Robinson Gray about 'a glass or two of Four-X *beer*' (St Lucia: University of Queensland Press, 1992, p. 261; my italics). The 'beer' is redundant as information for an Australian reader, and unrealistic as dialogue, for no-one in Australia would refer to 'Four-X beer', including Hospital, and even Four-X instead of XXXX seems a concession.
14. *The Last Magician*, p. 331.
15. 'Janette Turner Hospital and the National Dilemma', in Kate Burridge, Lois Foster & Gerry Turcotte (eds), *Canada-Australia: Towards a Second Century of Partnership*, Ottawa: International Council for Canadian Studies/Carleton University Press, 1997, p. 427.
16. ibid., p. 428.
17. 'Litany for the Homeland', p. 266.
18. *Dislocations*, pp. 43–56.
19. *Charades*, St Lucia: University of Queensland Press, 1988, p. 48.
20. On this subject, see James Jupp, *The English in Australia*, Melbourne: Cambridge University Press, 2004.
21. *Oyster*, Sydney: Knopf, 1996, p. 257.
22. *Reading Images: Narrative Discourse and Reception in the Thirteenth-century Illuminated Apocalypse*, Cambridge: Cambridge University Press, 1995, p. 13. The embedded quote is from Gay Clifford, *Transformations of Allegory*, London: Routledge, 1974, p. 38. Hospital's Queen's University (Canada) MA thesis was 'The hero and his destiny: a study of thirteenth and fourteenth century, pre-Chaucerian Middle English romance'.
23. *Reading Images*, p. 338.
24. 'Borderline magic: Janette Turner Hospital and transfiguration by photography', *Studies in Canadian Literature/Études de la littérature canadienne*, 16, 1991, p. 184.
25. See, for example, Alberto Manguel, 'Around the universe in 304 pages', *Quill & Quire* [Canada], February 1989, p. 20, review of *Charades*; or Marion Halligan, 'Countdown to the Millenium', *Australian Book Review*, October 1996, pp. 40–1, review of *Oyster*.

26. 'The truth, the whole truth, may be anything *but* the truth', *The Writer* [Boston], April 1987, p. 19.
27. *The Burden of Representation: Essays on Photographies and Histories*, Minneapolis: University of Minnesota Press, 1993, p. 4.
28. '"Multiple exposures": spatial dilemma of postmodern artistic identity in the fiction of Janette Turner Hospital', in Anne Luyat & Francine Tolron (eds), *Flight from Certainty: The Dilemma of Identity and Exile*, Amsterdam: Rodopi, 2001, p. 182.
29. *Words in Reflection: Modern Language Theory and Postmodern Fiction*, Chicago: University of Chicago Press, 1987, p. 108.
30. *Oyster*, p. 39.
31. Durham: Duke University Press, 1993, p. 19.
32. ibid., p. 20.
33. *Last Magician*, p. 349.
34. 'Wild child turns tedious in Sydney', *Los Angeles Times Book Review*, 24 December 1989, p. 2.

2. 'They are not *my* rules': *The Ivory Swing*

1. *Life in Common: An Essay in General Anthropology*, (trans.) Katherine Golsan & Lucy Golsan, Lincoln: University of Nebraska Press, 2001, p. ix.
2. An interest owing much to the phenomenal success of Salman Rushdie's *Midnight's Children* (1981). On the Western response to writing from India, see Graham Huggan, *The Post-Colonial Exotic: Marketing the Margins*, London: Routledge, 2001, pp. 58–82.
3. Janette Turner Hospital, *The Ivory Swing*, St Lucia: University of Queensland Press, 1991, p. 9. Further citations will be included within the text.
4. In the novel's first draft, the characters are American, from Boston, suggesting that the Western side of the comparison was rather more generic than the Indian side. See Fryer Library, University of Queensland Library, Papers of Janette Turner Hospital, UQFL 255, Box 1. While all critical considerations of the novel inspect Hospital's representation of India suspiciously, few show any interest in her depiction of Canada; the principal example of this is Graham Huggan's 'Orientalism reconfirmed? Stereotypes of East–West encounter in Janette Turner Hospital's *The Ivory Swing* and Yvon Richard's *Les silences du corbeau*', *Canadian Literature*, 132, 1992, pp. 44–56. In Kingston, however, the novel sparked vigorous debate, in which Hospital's status as a local resident was central; for example, Tim McNamara, 'Trapped between two poles', *Whig-Standard Magazine*, 2 October 1982, p. 19.
5. *Literary Theory and the Claims of History: Postmodernism, Objectivity, Multicultural Politics*, Ithaca: Cornell University Press, 1997, p. 131.

6. Huggan critiques this strongly for being an instrumentalisation of the East 'as the pretext for a specious rationalisation of Western anxieties'. 'Orientalism reconfirmed?', p. 46. Indeed, the whole article constitutes a stern condemnation of the novel as 'reinforcing the very prejudices [it sets] out to attack', ibid., p. 53.
7. The first title, however, was 'The Flute Player', recalling one of the traditional images of Krishna, and privileging both male beauty and male centrality – somewhat denied by the events of the novel – as well as referencing Prabhakaran, at the bottom of the social hierarchies in the book. It had to be changed because Hospital's US publisher was bringing out then high-profile Welsh novelist D.M. Thomas's novel of the same name. See Diana Brydon, 'The stone's memory: an interview with Janette Turner Hospital', *Commonwealth Studies in English*, 4.1, Spring, 1991, p. 23.
8. Margaret Schramm, 'Identity and the family in the novels of Janette Turner Hospital', in Mickey Pearlman (ed.), *Canadian Women Writing Fiction*, Jackson: University Press of Mississippi, 1993, pp. 84–98.
9. Mulk Raj Anand, to take an Indian example, had also activated epic tropes in the construction of his harijan hero Bhakha in *Untouchable* (1933), a deliberate attempt to enact such epic characteristics in an unexpected context and also to question them. Coral Ann Howells, however, thinks that '[t]he fairy-tale quality of the story and its strong mythic typologies where Yashoda can be seen as an image of the goddess Radha or a demonic Yakshi living in a forbidden forest . . . is a measure of the simplifications that are only possible when a culture is unfamiliar'. *Private and Fictional Words: Canadian Women Novelists of the 1970s and 1980s*, London: Methuen, 1987, p. 135.
10. The sense of lost opportunity David perceives here becomes the central obsession of the principal male character, Edward, in Hospital's next novel, *The Tiger in the Tiger Pit*. In general, however, David rejects this position, looking forward to '[l]uminous years, no matter what lay ahead' (84).
11. Maureen Clark's 'Grim wit and family outings in Janette Turner Hospital's *The Ivory Swing*' considers women's complicity in such constructions and finds that 'the image of the swing is treated ironically to undermine not only the "sacredness" of history but also the myth of male sexual dominance'. *New Literatures Review*, 37, Summer, 2000, p. 3. Clark's article finds irony to be central to many of the novel's issues, and even that Yashoda is not supposed to be a realistic depiction but 'a parody of the archetypal, sexualised representation of woman' (p. 6).
12. This is one of the events in the novel that Keralan reviewer Mathew Zachariah sees as highly unlikely, 'an unthinkable breach of etiquette'. 'Janette Turner Hospital's passage to India: a critique of *The Ivory Swing*', *Toronto South Asian Review*, 4.1, 1985, p. 59.

13. Marc Augé, *A Sense for the Other: The Timeliness and Relevance of Anthropology*, trans. Amy Jacobs, Stanford: Stanford University Press, 1998, p. 34.
14. 'Janette Turner Hospital's passage to India: a critique of *The Ivory Swing*', p. 60.
15. Rana Kabbani, *Europe's myths of Orient: devise and rule*, London: Pandora Press, 1986, p. 10.
16. ibid., p. 10.
17. This part of the novel began life as Janette Turner Hospital's first published fiction, a short story entitled 'Waiting', which appeared in the prestigious *Atlantic Monthly* in March 1978, pp. 110–14.
18. Some of this opposition colours the picture of Shivaraman Nair also, who is generally represented as a simplistic buffoon, even childlike, as in 'he clapped his hands with pleasure like a child' (124).
19. See Huggan's 'Orientalism reconfirmed?' for an unsympathetic reading of this relationship as conventionally orientalising sentimentality.
20. 'The Stone's Memory', p. 19.
21. Candida Baker, *Yacker 2: Australian Writers Talk about Their Work*, Sydney: Picador, 1987, p. 271. Also see Brydon, 'The Stone's Memory', p. 19.
22. Janette Turner Hospital, 'The truth, the whole truth, may be anything *but* the truth', *The Writer* [Boston], 1 April 1987, p. 19.
23. See Baker, *Yacker* 2, pp. 256–7. It needs to be said that the book is not a close autobiographical account of Hospital's time in Kerala, which should be obvious from some of the events narrated. Mathew Zachariah, despite finding the novel 'seriously flawed' on account of what he perceives as errors in the representation of Keralan realities, also sums up the book as one 'in which the complexity of our human condition reveals itself in a crosscultural setting', and comes to the conclusion that 'Hospital deserves our appreciation for taking such a risk'. 'Janette Turner Hospital's passage to India: a critique of *The Ivory Swing*', pp. 58, 57, 61.
24. *Yacker* 2, p. 257.

3. Anger mismanagement: *The Tiger in the Tiger Pit*

1. *The Ethics of Memory*, Cambridge, Massachusetts: Harvard University Press, 2002, p. 5.
2. Janette Turner Hospital, *The Tiger in the Tiger Pit*, St Lucia: University of Queensland Press, 1990, p. 7. Further citations will be included within the text. The quotation from *Coriolanus* comes from Act IV, Scene II.
3. Six chapters, including the first, are named Edward, while seven chapters, including the last, are named Elizabeth; their children, Emily, Jason and Victoria, have one named chapter each, while grandson Adam has two; there are also five chapters that mix points of view, including that of a narrator.

4. The classic opposition to this tendency is Salman Rushdie's '"Commonwealth literature" does not exist', *Imaginary Homelands: Essays and Criticism 1981–1991*, London: Granta, 1991, pp. 61–70, first published in 1983. The issues remain capable of arousing violent debate from unexpected angles; for example, the clause stipulating that the recipient of the Miles Franklin Prize should be a novel that represents Australian life has led increasingly to several high-profile works by Australian authors being rejected for consideration, since Christopher Koch's *The Year of Living Dangerously*, Melbourne: Thomas Nelson, 1978, set in Indonesia.
5. For example, Patricia Morley, 'Hospital may be great novelist', *Ottawa Citizen*, 1 October 1983, p. 42; Doris Ober, 'Powerful novel brings together a divided family', *San José Mercury*, 20 May 1984, p. 26. For Ober, the novel 'has the rare ability to write consecutive pages of people doing nothing more than just *thinking* and make these pages as alive and colorful as all the others' (Ober's italics). In 1990 Hospital observed that the novel had 'generated more private letters from readers than any of my other books'. Fryer Library, University of Queensland Library, Papers of Janette Turner Hospital, UQFL 255, Box 5.
6. Diana Brydon, 'The stone's memory: an interview with Janette Turner Hospital', *Commonwealth Writing in English*, 4.1, 1991, p. 19.
7. 'Borders', *Saturday Night* [Canadà], April 1986, p. 57.
8. As one of the epigraphs to the book indicates, the allusion is to T. S. Eliot's poem 'Lines for an Old Man', in which an irascible old man wallows in his rage and claims access to emotional depths denied to the young; see *Collected Poems 1909–1935*, London: Faber, 1936, p. 153.
9. Hospital mentions affectionately that her own father 'speaks in a mosaic of Shakespearian and King James Bible English'. Diana Brydon, 'The stone's memory', p. 20.
10. Sue Lovell notes that '[t]he step forward creatively in [*Tiger*] is the introduction of a metaphor of creativity for each of the characters', not just Elizabeth's music-making but Emily's music-playing, Jason's psychiatry, Victoria's escapism and Edward's rewriting of history. These creative strategies become acts of 'compensation' for the family disharmony, and only out of their conjunction is a fuller picture possible. 'The Pygmalion factor: creativity in the novels of Janette Turner Hospital', *Literature in North Queensland*, 17.1, 1990, pp. 80, 82.
11. Prospero, nevertheless, is also one of Shakespeare's embittered authority figures, having engineered shipwrecks, altered the course of people's lives, and even raised the dead to enact revenge for his brother Antonio's usurpation of his power.
12. 'A shared depository of wisdom: connection and redemption in *Tiger in the Tiger Pit* and *Possession*', *Southerly*, 53.2, June 1993, p. 124.

13. Diana Brydon, 'The stone's memory', pp. 21–2.
14. In *North of Nowhere, South of Loss*, St Lucia: University of Queensland Press, 2003, pp. 77–95, and pp. 256–72.
15. Hospital shows she has no illusions about this in, for example, the story 'Bondi', in *Isobars*, St Lucia: University of Queensland Press, 1990, pp. 68–81, not to mention *The Last Magician*, St Lucia: University of Queensland Press, 1992.
16. This is a perspective that, it should be noted, was revised some time ago with the rise of cultural studies and a greater appreciation of the intensities and pleasures of suburbia. See John Fiske, Bob Hodge & Graeme Turner's seminal *Myths of Australia: Reading Australian Popular Culture*, Sydney: Allen & Unwin, 1987, or Ian Craven's detailed examination of *Neighbours*, 'Distant neighbours: notes on some Australian soap operas', *Australian Studies*, 3, December 1989, pp. 1–35.
17. This may allude to T. S. Eliot's *The Waste Land*, also quoted in Hospital's early story 'You Gave Me Hyacinths', in which the appearance of a girl with her arms full of hyacinths leaves the observer speechless but conscious that she is in the presence of something momentous, a moment of grace. See *Dislocations*, 2nd edn, St Lucia: University of Queensland Press, 1987, pp. 23–31.
18. Margaret Schramm, 'Identity and the family in the novels of Janette Turner Hospital', in Mickey Pearlman (ed.), *Canadian Women Writing Fiction*, Jackson: University Press of Mississippi, 1993, p. 89. Since Schramm wrote her piece, *Due Preparations for the Plague* has also demonstrated a related resolution, albeit only after much death and suffering.

4. Tuning the telling: *Borderline*

1. *Regarding the Pain of Others*, New York: Picador, 2004, p. 21.
2. Elspeth Cameron sums up the changed level of response to the novel: '*Borderline* is a coup for Hospital. She brings to the fore political issues that seemed slight and redundant in her first two novels.' 'Borders', *Saturday Night*, April 1986, p. 58.
3. 'Letter to a New York editor', *Meanjin*, 47, 1988, p. 560.
4. Janette Turner Hospital, *Borderline*, St Lucia: University of Queensland Press, 1987, p. 11. Further citations will be included within the text.
5. 'Hospital's latest nears new frontiers', *Quill & Quire* [Canada], November 1985, p. 23.
6. As is usual in English with names from other languages, she also loses any accentuation she might have; in this case, the name should be 'Márquez'.
7. 'Borders', p. 58.
8. Hospital recounts how 'Jean-Marc' 'is deliberately named for two of the

Gospel writers who, from fragments, similarly try to put together the truth of what happened'. *Writers in Action: The Writers' Choice Evenings*, Gerry Turcotte (ed.), Sydney: Currency Press, 1990, p. 72.

9. 'The improprieties of Janette Turner Hospital: strategic punning in *Borderline* and *Charades*', in Shirley Chew & Lynette Hunter (eds), *Borderblur: Essays on Poetry and Poetics in Contemporary Canadian Literature*, Edinburgh: Quadriga, 1996, p. 86.
10. 'Introduction', Janette Turner Hospital, *Borderline*, London: Virago, 1990, p. 6.
11. 'Letter to a New York editor', p. 560.
12. 'Letter to a New York editor', p. 563; Hospital's italics.
13. 'Identity and the family in the novels of Janette Turner Hospital', in Mickey Pearlman (ed.), *Canadian Women Writing Fiction*, Jackson: University Press of Mississippi, 1993, pp. 89–90.
14. 'Beautiful travellers: notes on postmodern fiction', *Commonwealth: Essays and Studies*, 11.2, 1989, p. 59; Albertazzi's italics.
15. 'Borderline magic: Janette Turner Hospital and transfiguration by photography', *Studies in Canadian Literature*, 16.2, 1991, p. 186. Stead observes that Gus's 'long-suffering wife is Therese, near-namesake of that St Teresa of Avila who was so ardent a follower of Augustine that she names no other author in her autobiography' ('The improprieties of Janette Turner Hospital', p. 86).
16. Rather than the unstable borderlines of stories, Geraldine Stoneham sees 'the central issue of *Borderline*' as being 'the obscurantist and imprisoning effect of narrative'. 'Dislocations: Postcolonialism in a postmodernist space', in Jane Dowson & Steven Earnshaw (eds), *Postmodern Subjects/Postmodern Texts*, Amsterdam: Rodopi, 1995, p. 246.
17. Arthur Miller's Willy Loman, in *Death of a Salesman* (1949), also makes a mess of his personal life, and can have a certain weary grandeur (depending on how he is played), but his fate is as generic as the unnamed product he sells, beaten down by the logic of capitalism, which corrodes relations on all levels.
18. This is also, of course, related to Pentecostal intensities with respect to the signs and meanings that surround us.
19. 'The fictional daughter: Janette Turner Hospital's *Borderline*', *Literature in North Queensland*, 17.1, 1990, p. 55. Perkins's article develops the idea that Jean-Marc represents a form of patriarchal control over a woman's story, a woman he would like to possess sexually but is denied access to. This, in turn, inflects the narrative with parallel patriarchal relationships, so that '[b]oth Canada and El Salvador assume the status of the female in a patriarchy controlled by the United States' (p. 52).
20. In one of the most powerful, MIT, Hospital has been writer-in-residence, while in the most powerful, Harvard, her husband studied and she worked part-time in the library.

21. 'Letter to a New York editor', p. 560.
22. Hospital's detective novel set largely in Boston, written under the pseudonym Alex Juniper, *A Very Proper Death* (Toronto: Random House, 1990), should be read alongside *Borderline*. Some of Hospital's anger at inequalities in the city, and the shadowy interfaces between developers, drug-dealers and indifference, has been transported to the mystery novel, with its much clearer narrative line and narratorial point of view. Her delight in unpicking the social faultlines of Boston is also much expanded upon in *A Very Proper Death*, of which Alistair Stead notes that 'though comparatively stable generically, [it] is fiercely critical of virtually all the pejorative significances of the proper in the socio-political sphere' ('The improprieties of Janette Turner Hospital', p. 76).
23. 'The fictional daughter', p. 58.
24. This is exacerbated by the absence from his life of Jean-Marc's real mother. Indeed, there are very few stable pairs of parents in Hospital's work from *Borderline* on. Parents are either separated, missing, or one of them is dead. This heightens the awareness of absence on the part of major characters, leading to the repeated quest-motifs in Hospital's work, where what is being sought is some form of re-connection with a missing part of one's self, and, as a consequence, some way to make sense of oneself and one's place in the world.
25. See Christine Hamelin, 'Novelist as urgent quester: an interview with Janette Turner Hospital', *Australian and New Zealand Studies in Canada*, 9, June 1993, p. 106.
26. This accident happens between the minor town of Carthage and the small city of Utica in New York state, and, although Gus is travelling on back roads, placing Augustine in Carthage (the home of St Augustine) is admitted as a flourish of invention on Jean-Marc's part, an admission that the attractions of pattern, echoes, connections and irony may make meaning work better than plain attention to fact.
27. 'Borders', p. 58.
28. 'Borderline magic', p. 195.
29. 'Identity and the family in the novels of Janette Turner Hospital', p. 92.
30. As Lee Grove assesses the characters: 'Felicity and Gus forsake their pride, their jobs, and are willing to lose everything. Jean-Marc . . . turns his back on nearly everyone and opts out of loving, is a victim of his own vanity and in the end loses more than anyone.' 'Star-crossed', *Boston*, 77.12, December 1985, p. 125. While Jean-Marc cannot really be said to lose 'more than anyone', given that he does not die, he generally fails to gain readers' sympathy, representing the borderline between telling and what is told that all narratives establish, and that readers are constantly attempting to forget. Jean-Marc thus becomes as popular among readers as border control officers are popular among travellers.

5. Out of the comfort zone: *Dislocations*

1. *Postmodernity and Its Discontents*, Cambridge: Polity Press, 1997, p. 89.
2. Janette Turner Hospital, *Dislocations*, St Lucia: University of Queensland Press, 1987. This is the 2nd edition, in which the last three stories have been added to the 1st edition (Toronto: McClelland and Stewart, 1986). All further citations will be included within the text. The volume *Collected Stories 1970–1995* (St Lucia: University of Queensland Press, 1995) contains *Dislocations*, *Isobars* and seven stories under the heading 'North of Nowhere'. 'Tri-tree' (*Dislocations*, 192) has been corrected to 'tea-tree' (*Collected Stories*, 164). 'Capetown', however, remains uncorrected (*Dislocations*, 172; *Collected Stories*, 147).
3. 'Necessary idiocy and the idea of freedom', in Sneja Gunew & Kateryna O'Longley (eds), *Striking Chords: Multicultural Literary Interpretations*, Sydney: Allen & Unwin, 1992, p. 6.
4. 'Body maps', review of Mary Gordon, *The Rest of Life*, *London Review of Books*, 7 April 1994, p. 23.
5. 'Words that fly up', *Canadian Forum*, 66.764, December 1986, p. 38.
6. 'Lives in truthful disorder', review of *Dislocations*, *The Age*, Arts & Books Section, 28 November 1987, p. 15.
7. 'Waiting', *Atlantic Monthly*, 241, March 1978, pp. 110–14.
8. 'The distinctive terrain of Janette Turner Hospital's stories', review of *Collected Stories 1970–1995*, *Australian Book Review*, 175, October 1995, p. 29.
9. Conceptions of the nature of the short story are usefully anthologised in *The New Short Story Theories*, Charles E. May (ed.), Athens, OH: Ohio University Press, 1994. In May's summary: 'If . . . one feels that immanent in the everyday exists some other reality that somehow evades him, if one's view is religious in the most basic sense, then the short story is more "realistic" than the novel can possibly be' ('The Nature of Knowledge in Short Fiction', ibid., p. 141).
10. Review of *Dislocations*, *Queen's Quarterly*, 94.3, Autumn 1987, p. 693.
11. ibid., p. 692.
12. Hospital chose 'Happy Diwali' (1985) to be the first story in the volume, rather than following the chronological order of the stories, in which the second story in the volume, 'You Gave Me Hyacinths' (1970), was the published story she wrote first.
13. A Hindu festival invocating Lakshmi, the goddess of wealth, and by extension a range of types of wealth we might wish for, such as strength or health, knowledge, the balancing of accounts and generosity towards others.
14. See, for example, a string of novels by one of the best-known Indian immigrant writers in Canada (subsequently the United States) – Bharati Mukherjee – for whom emigration may easily offer as much as it takes

away, if not more: *The Tiger's Daughter*, Boston: Houghton Mifflin, 1972, *Jasmine*, New York: Grove Weidenfeld, 1989, *The Holder of the World*, New York: Knopf, 1993, or essays such as 'A Four-Hundred-Year-Old Woman', in Philomena Mariani (ed.), *Critical Fictions: The Politics of Imaginative Writing*, Seattle: Bay Press, 1991, pp. 24–8.

15. *The Trouble with Community: Anthropological Reflections on Movement, Identity and Collectivity*, London: Pluto Press, 2002, p. 48.
16. ibid., p. 86. Hospital claimed in 1990 that 'After Long Absence' was her only really autobiographical story to date, although autobiographical details are clearly apparent elsewhere as well. See 'Janette Turner Hospital: *Dislocations*, *Borderline*, *Charades*', in Gerry Turcotte (ed.), *Writers in Action: The Writers' Choice Evenings*, Sydney: Currency Press, 1990, p. 67.
17. 'Dislocation and memory in the short stories of Janette Turner Hospital', *Journal of Modern Literature*, 20.1, Summer 1996, p. 85.
18. *Inside Culture: Re-imagining the Method of Cultural Studies*, London: Sage, 2000, p. 92
19. The attempt to bridge the puzzling disturbances created by different cultures is also at the centre of one of Hospital's first stories, 'Waiting', which subsequently became incorporated into *The Ivory Swing*, and which has been dealt with in the chapter on that book. There are some differences of detail, however. The character known as 'Jennifer Harper' here is a young student, while 'Juliet' in *The Ivory Swing* is a married woman accompanying her academic husband to Kerala. At the end of the story, Jennifer leaves India. A central character in the story is the Air India clerk, Chandrashekharan Nair, whose ideas about Jennifer are partly carried over into Prem but largely subsumed into the expanded argument between world views that constitutes the novel.
20. Review of *Dislocations*, *Literature in North Queensland*, 17.1, 1990, p. 162.
21. Martha Ann Mueller, however, finds that at least Williamson's self-regard enables him 'to stare down death, and continue making his life into art in his own noble and pathetic, but ultimately comical, fashion', review of *Dislocations*, *Queen's Quarterly*, p. 693.
22. Robyn Groves believes that the attempted reassembly of the self in the forest makes this story 'the most Canadian' in the volume. 'The appreciation of grace: fictions of the global village', review of *Dislocations*, *Australian Book Review*, December 1987 – January 1988, p. 11.
23. *The Feeling of What Happens: Body, Emotion and the Making of Consciousness*, London: Heinemann, 1999, p. 25.
24. 'Dislocation and memory', p. 94.
25. *Remembrance of Things Past*, vol. 1, (trans.) C. K. Scott Moncrieff & Terence Kilmartin, Harmondsworth: Penguin, 1983, p. 47. Proust's depiction and analysis of the nature of memory provide many absorbing points of

contact with Hospital's interests. Proust's work is generally translated now as the more appropriate *In Search of Lost Time*, privileging the more active process indicated in the original title, in consonance with Hospital's own approach.

6. Particles, waves and stories: *Charades*

1. Thomas Mendip, affecting to be the Devil, in Christopher Fry's *The Lady's Not for Burning*, 2nd edn, Oxford: Oxford University Press, 1950, p. 54.
2. As she says, 'the two dominant influences on my prose [are] the King James Version of the Bible and the Queensland rainforest'. Gerry Turcotte (ed.), *Writers in Action: The Writers' Choice Evenings*, Sydney: Currency Press, 1990, p. 81.
3. 'The improprieties of Janette Turner Hospital: strategic punning in *Borderline* and *Charades*', in Shirley Chew & Lynette Hunter, *Borderblur: Essays on Poetry and Poetics in Contemporary Canadian Literature*, Edinburgh: Quadriga, 1996, p. 75.
4. Janette Turner Hospital, *Charades*, St Lucia: University of Queensland Press, 1988, p. 3. Further references will be included within the text. This was the first of Hospital's books to be initially published in Australia.
5. An earlier title for the book was 'The 1,001 Speculations of Charade and Professor King'. See Fryer Library, University of Queensland Library, Papers of Janette Turner Hospital, UQFL 255, Box 2.
6. Briefly, the Uncertainty Theory argues that the activity of observing or measuring anything affects some of the states of what we are observing in ways that are unpredictable. In terms of the atomic scale of the order of reality that Heisenberg was talking about, this means that the instruments used to measure would affect the momentum of what they were measuring. This was widely extrapolated by writers and theorists in the twentieth century as proof that reality cannot be disassociated from the observer. Another consequence of the theory is that the more we know about the position of anything, the less we know about its momentum and vice versa. Although developed to account for what happens when measuring sub-atomic particles, this too can be extrapolated to suggest that reality depends on the type of question we want to ask, and that in any event reality is unable to be fixed or described in all of its aspects.
7. For Betty Birskys, Koenig's name is another irony, in that he 'approaches regality only in his science, in all else he is a "little man"'. 'Principles of uncertainty', *Imago* 1.1, March 1989, p. 47.
8. The 'ashkenazim' is a Yiddish term that refers to the Jews of the diaspora. The name Verity is clearly a tease for such an unstable reference, as she is the least verifiable character in the novel, and her surname is one she has

adopted, dropping her 'real' name, Acier (although there is uncertainty about this name as well).

9. Investigation of earlier drafts of the novel only complicates the picture; see Fryer Library, University of Queensland Library, Papers of Janette Turner Hospital, UQFL 255, Box 2. Not only is Kay called 'K' at one point, conflating her with Koenig and Kafka's K, but she is also called 'Jaye' (J), and Hospital has said that 'Kay's childhood in *Charades* is pretty much mine' (*Writers in Action: The Writers' Choice Evenings*, p. 80). Alistair Stead's 'The improprieties of Janette Turner Hospital' deals well with the multiple names and masks of the characters.
10. 'Are women's novels feminist novels?', in Raoul Granquist (ed.), *Major Minorities: English Literatures in Transit*, Amsterdam: Rodopi, 1993, p. 41. Laurel Bergmann explores this issue in 'Janette Turner Hospital's radical re-writing: oedipal Charades', *Australian Literary Studies*, 17.4, October 1996, pp. 364–72.
11. 'Are women's novels feminist novels?', p. 41.
12. 'Identity and the family in the novels of Janette Turner Hospital', in Mickey Pearlman (ed.), *Canadian Women Writing Fiction*, Jackson: University Press of Mississippi, 1993, p. 93.
13. Cook's striking the east coast of Australia is generally seen more heroically, as in Kenneth Slessor's 'Five Visions of Captain Cook', in which Cook's daring decisiveness takes him where earlier navigators had been too timid to venture. One of the consequences of Cook's choice in Slessor's vision is nothing less than that now 'men write poems in Australia', another version of Hospital's wonder at the unexpected ramifications of events. See Slessor's *Selected Poems*, Sydney: Angus & Robertson, 1977, p. 68.
14. The butterfly effect is also central to the story by Borges which provides one of the epigraphs to the novel, 'The Other Death'; see Jorge Luis Borges, *Collected Fictions*, (trans.) Andrew Hurley, New York: Penguin, 1999, pp. 223–8.
15. Just as in Borges's fable 'The Library of Babel', the library contains all the books that have been or could be imagined, along with their refutations. This story provides a good gloss on the issues in *Charades*. See *Collected Fictions*, pp.112–18.
16. No reputable historian believes that the Holocaust was a hoax, but it is agreed that it was certainly manipulated by Zionist leaders to achieve the establishment of Israel. See David Cesarini (ed.), *The Final Solution: Origins and Implementation*, London: Routledge, 1994.
17. In an earlier draft of the novel, Charade plans to go back to her history degree instead of studying physics, suggesting that more useful knowledge about reality can be approached, after all, in the consideration of human beings in messy, lived time than in the unifying theories about the building

blocks of the universe. See Fryer Library, University of Queensland Library, Papers of Janette Turner Hospital, UQFL 255, Box 2.

18. Verity may be outside expected social patterns in the present of the novel, but the experience of being treated as an outsider was as common to Hospital as a child as to the Jewish children in one of the books Hospital mentions as having had an impact on her writing of this novel, Claudine Vegh's *I Didn't Say Goodbye: Interviews with Children of the Holocaust*, (trans.) Ros Schwartz, New York: Dutton, 1984. Several details from this book have found their way, transmuted, into *Charades*, such as Verity's pocketing of raisins, here Jean's automatically putting walnuts in his pocket, Vegh, pp.127–8. More than such details, however, Vegh's book chronicles the difficulties of mourning when there is no definite evidence for what one believes to have been the fate of one's parents. Verity's inability to insert herself back into history derives from this unmooring from her origins, and her slide into insanity and the inability to bring up her daughter are not critiqued by the novel. Indeed, in Bea's loyalty to Verity we witness a necessary solidarity with the irremediably damaged.
19. *Literature and Feminism*, Oxford: Basil Blackwell, 1993, p. 28.
20. An observation I owe to Cynthia Fortner, AAALS Conference, University of Tulsa, 1995.
21. Review of *Charades*, *Literature in North Queensland*, 17.1, 1990, p. 157.
22. From the moment Wilhelm Conrad Röntgen sent Henri Poincaré photographs of the bones in someone's hand in 1896, leading to the discovery of radioactivity and ultimately to the whole area of sub-atomic reality, photographs and their interpretation were often at the centre of twentieth-century physics.
23. Sigmund Freud, 'The Uncanny' [Das Unheimliche], in James Strachey (ed. & trans.), *The Standard Edition of the Complete Psychological Works of Sigmund Freud*, vol. 17, London: Hogarth, 1955, pp. 217–56.
24. '*Charades*: searching for Father Time: memory and the Uncertainty Principle', *New Literatures Review*, 21, Summer South 1991, p. 75.
25. 'Writing back from another centre: *Charades* by Janette Turner Hospital', in Alwin Fill, Sonja Bahn-Coblans, Heidi Ganner-Rauth & Helga Ramsey-Kurtz (eds), *New-Found-Lands: Festschrift für Harro Heinz Kühnelt*, Tübingen: Gunter Narr, 1993, p. 150.
26. ibid., p. 154.
27. 'The telltale art of Janette Turner Hospital', interview with Missy Daniel, *Boston Phoenix: Literary Section*, 28 April 1989, p. 16.
28. 'The 1,001 Australian nights', *Los Angeles Times Book Review*, 23 April 1989, p. 7.
29. 'Writing back from another centre', p. 165.

30. On the history of the search for grand unified theories and the chimera of the end of physics, see Robert P. Crease & Charles C. Mann, *The Second Creation: Makers of the Revolution in 20th-century Physics*, New York: Macmillan, 1986, one of the books Hospital credits as having stimulated her. The most recent candidate for a unified theory has been String Theory, but that too has failed to establish itself. See Lee Smolin, *The Trouble with Physics: The Rise of String Theory, the Fall of a Science, and What Comes Next*, New York: Houghton Mifflin, 2006.
31. 'Identity and the family in the novels of Janette Turner Hospital', p. 94.
32. As in one of the epigraphs to Part 1, by J. Robert Oppenheimer, the founder of the Los Alamos research and development centre where the atom bomb was developed. This can be found in another of the books Hospital states has been influential in her writing of the novel: Fritjof Capra, *The Tao of Physics: An Exploration of the Parallels between Modern Physics and Eastern Mysticism*, 4th edn, Boston: Shambhala, 2000, p. 154.

7. 'All the signs on Four Mile Beach': *Isobars*

1. *El laberinto de la soledad y otras obras*, New York: Penguin, 1997, p. 227; my translation.
2. Canadian reviewer Louis Mackendrick felt that the North American stories were 'less apt to fracture time and voice . . . less lyric in manner, less playful'. 'Clever by far', review of *Isobars*, *Essays on Canadian Writing*, 48 (Winter 1992–93), p. 55. While this is not borne out by an examination of the volume, given that almost all of the stories tend to fracture time and voice, and playfulness seems to be distributed throughout the volume as well, it does indicate a tendency on the part of reviewers to try to distinguish between Hospital as an Australian writer and Hospital as a North American writer.
3. *Australian Short Fiction: A History*, St Lucia: University of Queensland Press, 2002, p. 270.
4. *Isobars*, St Lucia: University of Queensland Press, 1990, p. 1. Further citations will be included within the text. The Canadian edition began with the three last stories from the Australian edition of *Dislocations*: 'The Mango Tree' ('After Long Absence' renamed), 'Morgan Morgan' and 'The Bloody Past, the Wandering Future', in that order. *Isobars*, Toronto: McLelland & Stewart, 1991. This displaces the introductory piece 'Isobars' to a much less prominent place and somewhat dilutes the coherence of the volume, leading to the conclusion that the Australian editions of both *Dislocations* and *Isobars* should be considered as preferable. The US and UK editions are the same as the Australian edition: *Isobars*, Baton Rouge: Louisiana State University Press, 1991, and *Isobars*, London: Virago, 1992.

5. 'Emptiness and isobars – the mapping of isolation', *Southerly*, 51.1 (1991), p. 163.
6. 'Interview', *Literature in North Queensland*, 17.1 (1990), p. 19.
7. This introductory meditation is analysed in depth by Joan Davis in 'Come on in, the water's fine: Janette Turner Hospital's short prose fiction, *Isobars*', *Literature in North Queensland*, 17.1 (1990), pp. 109–13.
8. A version of this family will reappear in much greater detail as the Bartoks in *Orpheus Lost*.
9. Thea Astley's dark story also set in Far North Queensland, 'Ladies Need Only Apply', horrifyingly depicts the endpoint to which male control of women aspires. *Hunting the Wild Pineapple*, Melbourne: Nelson, 1979, pp. 111–44.
10. 'Come-By-Chance', *The Man from Snowy River & Other Verses*, introduced by Jonathan King, Sydney: Angus & Robertson, 1995, pp. 174–6. Paterson wrote the poem after hearing of a place of this name; the place, however, turns out to be a crossroads rather than a town. See King's notes, p. lxii.
11. 'Dislocation and memory in the short stories of Janette Turner Hospital', *Journal of Modern Literature*, 20.1 (Summer 1996), p. 91.
12. 'Letters of the law: women, human rights, and epistolary literature', in Marjorie Agosín (ed.), *Women, Gender, and Human Rights: A Global Perspective*, New Brunswick, NJ: Rutgers University Press, 2001, p. 303. This article contains a full analysis of 'Dear Amnesty'.
13. *Australian Short Fiction*, p. 272. Hospital admits that 'the naming of characters has always been profoundly important for me. They nearly always have some allegorical significance, and at the very least are meant to evoke multiple specific associations'. Letter to American academic D'Arcy Randall, 25 February 1988, Fryer Library, University of Queensland Library, Papers of Janette Turner Hospital, UQFL 255, Box 7. What these names do not do is map exactly or clearly to whom or what they are alluding, existing to excite the reader into following further connections along our own isobar, rather than obliging us to import close associations with a name's possible source.
14. Helen Daniel (ed.), *Expressway*, Ringwood: Penguin, 1989. The volume contains stories responding to the urban brutalism of the Cahill Expressway in Sydney. Hospital's story occurs on pp. 252–61.
15. 'Dislocation and memory in the short stories of Janette Turner Hospital', p. 85.
16. 'Dislocation and memory', p. 89.
17. 'Emptiness and isobars', p. 161.
18. 'Dislocation and memory', p. 88.

8. There is no straight way: *The Last Magician*

1. *Unclaimed Experience: Trauma, Narrative, and History*, Baltimore: Johns Hopkins University Press, 1996, p. 6.
2. Janette Turner Hospital, *The Last Magician*, St Lucia: University of Queensland Press, 1992, p. 85. Further references will be included within the text.
3. Hospital admits that 'people always tell me they find my books difficult, especially with *The Last Magician*'. Kevin Connolly, 'Threads of order: an interview with Janette Turner Hospital', *Paragraph* [Canada], 19.2 (Fall 1997), p. 7.
4. Some readers of the book had rejected these strategies as overfamiliar by 1992, Australian writer Eden Liddelow going so far as to claim that '[s]elf-reflexivity in texts has come to resemble dishonesty' ('Repeating the cataclysm', *Modern Times*, July 1992, p. 32). Jonathan Coe also feels Lucy's garrulous allusions 'do nothing except guarantee the sacrifice of credibility on the altar of a pointless intertextuality' ('Sydney's Inferno', *London Review of Books*, 24 September 1992, p. 22). The most sustained critique of this aspect of the book is Kate Temby's 'Gender, power and postmodernism in *The Last Magician*', *Westerly* 40.3 (Spring 1995), pp. 47–55.
5. Alistair Stead confirms the same thing with respect to the intertextual use of Dostoevsky in the novel, in which Hospital is 'much more concerned to borrow and rework a resonant metaphor and fundamental situation than to excite a close comparison of character or plot' ('Notes from underground: *The Last Magician* and Janette Turner Hospital', in Selina Samuels (ed.), *Janette Turner Hospital*, London: Sir Robert Menzies Centre for Australian Studies/University of London, 1998, p. 21).
6. Margaret Schramm, 'Identity and the family in the novels of Janette Turner Hospital', in Mickey Pearlman (ed.), *Canadian Women Writing Fiction*, Jackson: University Press of Mississippi, 1993, p. 85.
7. On the so-called 'hermeneutic circle', in which the *way* we interpret anything becomes a part of the interpretation itself, see David Couzens Hoy, *The Critical Circle: Literature, History and Philosophical Hermeneutics*, Berkeley: University of California Press, 1982.
8. Sue Lovell, 'Janette Turner Hospital's *The Last Magician*: "a feminist's nightmare"?', *Hecate* 28.2 (2002), p. 59. This article is a rejoinder to Kate Temby's, see note 3 above.
9. See Janette Turner Hospital, 'Margins within margins: an interview with Francine Ringold', *Nimrod: Poetry & Prose* [Tulsa, OK], 36.2 (Spring/Summer 1996), pp. 27–32.
10. Fiona Coyle notes that there are only two direct references to Aborigines in *The Last Magician* (297, 351) but manages to make an argument for their significance, buried in the text as the quarry is buried under the city. For

Coyle, the quarry is nothing less than 'both a metaphor for Aboriginal land claims in Australia and the material manifestation of chaos'. See 'A third space? Postcolonial Australia and the fractal landscape in *The Last Magician* and *Oyster*', in Jamie Scott & Paul Simpson-Housley (eds), *Mapping the Sacred: Religion, Geography and Postcolonial Literatures*, Amsterdam: Rodopi, 2001, p. 111.

11. See Dante Alighieri, *The Divine Comedy 1: Hell*, (trans.) Dorothy L. Sayers, Harmondsworth: Penguin, 1949, p. 181. This is the translation most consulted by Hospital.
12. Aamer Hussein, 'Trial by triage', review of *The Last Magician* and *Isobars*, *Times Literary Supplement*, 3 July 1992, p. 25. Alistair Stead places the quarry in a tradition of novelistic investigations of the underworld ('Notes from underground', pp. 21–2).
13. Hospital, 'Margins within margins', p. 28.
14. 'Sydney's Inferno', p. 22.
15. Aritha van Herk, 'Fiction', *University of Toronto Quarterly*, 63.1 (Fall 1993), p. 29.
16. Sue Lovell, 'Janette Turner Hospital's *The Last Magician* in "an expanded field"', *AUMLA: Journal of the Australasian Universities Language and Literature Association*, 104 (November 2005), p. 128.
17. I am convinced by Sue Lovell's preference for this word over 'excess', with the latter's suggestion of an unusable or supplemental excrescence. See 'Janette Turner Hospital's *The Last Magician*: "a feminist's nightmare"?', p. 63.
18. Helen Daniel, a fervent supporter of Hospital's work, wrote in her reader's report on the novel: 'any sections regarding literary criticism always seemed to me intrusive here'. See Fryer Library, University of Queensland Library, Papers of Janette Turner Hospital, UQFL 255, Box 4.
19. See Papers of Janette Turner Hospital, UQFL 255, Box 5.
20. Later, Hospital suspected she might have conflated Green Falls and Cedar Creek Falls, or that the lower part of Cedar Creek had been lusher in the 1950s. See Papers of Janette Turner Hospital, UQFL 255, Box 5.
21. 'Natural imaginings: the literature of the hinterland', in Patrick Buckridge & Belinda Mackay (eds), *By the Book: A Literary History of Queensland*, St Lucia: University of Queensland Press, 2007, p. 105.
22. This term also appears in *The Tiger in the Tiger Pit*, where, however, it refers pejoratively to what appears to Jason as his disturbed sister Victoria's psychic instability (p. 225). The issues of shapeshifting and difference are covered more fully in David Callahan, 'Becoming different in Janette Turner Hospital', *Ariel: A Review of International English Literature*, 28.2 (April 1997), pp. 23–34.

23. 'Fiction', p. 29.
24. In Eliot's 'Burnt Norton' (1935), the first of the meditations on time and meaning contained in *Four Quartets*, the lines go: 'human kind / Cannot bear very much reality'. T. S. Eliot, *Four Quartets* [1944], London: Faber: 1954, p. 14.
25. James Gleick, *Chaos: Making a New Science*, New York: Viking, 1987, p. 307.
26. Susan Sontag, *On Photography*, Harmondsworth: Penguin, 1979, p. 19. This could be derived from Émile Zola's famous 'you cannot claim to have really seen something until you have photographed it', quoted in Sontag, p. 87.
27. Julian Cowley, '"Violent times": Janette Turner Hospital's art of memory and the history of the present', in Sarah Sceats & Gail Cunningham (eds), *Image & Power: Women in Fiction in the Twentieth Century*, London: Longman, 1996, p. 180.
28. '"Violent times"', p. 180.
29. *On Photography*, p. 3.
30. *On Photography*, p. 5.
31. Silvia Albertazzi, 'The Australian landscape in Janette Turner Hospital's *The Last Magician*', in Susan Ballyn, Doireann MacDermott & Kathleen Firth (eds), *Australia's Changing Landscapes*, Barcelona: University of Barcelona, 1995, p. 17. This article is more a stimulating discussion of the uses of photography in the novel than an enquiry into landscape. The use of photographs as enabling links to be maintained with the absent is significant in *Borderline*, where an underground operative, Angelo, says of a photograph: 'We all need a piece of magic to keep going' (206).
32. '"Violent times"', p. 181.
33. 'Notes from underground', p. 27.
34. Elza Adamowicz, *Surrealist Collage in Text and Image: Dissecting the Exquisite Corpse*, Cambridge: Cambridge University Press, 1998, p. 11.
35. ibid., p. 11.
36. ibid., p. 193.
37. Christine Hamelin, '"Novelist as urgent quester": an interview with Janette Turner Hospital', *Australian and New Zealand Studies in Canada*, 9 (June 1993), p. 110.
38. *Surrealist Collage in Text and Image*, p. 195.

9. 'What branches grow out of this stony place?': *Oyster*

1. *The Road to Botany Bay: An Essay in Spatial History*, London: Faber, 1987, p. 99.
2. Associated with the doomed expedition of Burke and Wills in 1860–61.

3. Outer Maroo is to be imagined somewhere in the area near where the Queensland border with South Australia makes a right-angled turn, and near Cooper's Creek, being north-west of Eromanga and south-west of Windorah.
4. From which comes the title of this chapter: *Collected Poems 1909–1935*, London: Faber, 1936, p. 61.
5. Janette Turner Hospital, *Oyster*, Sydney: Knopf, 1996, p. 4. Further citations will be included within the text.
6. Richard Carr has drawn attention to the confluences between *Oyster* and one of the finest Australian works to read the nation's spiritual absences in the context of its relation to the land, Randolph Stow's *Tourmaline* (1963): 'the residents of Tourmaline and Outer Maroo, in refusing to address their alienation from their environment and themselves, ensure the disaster that closes both novels. In seeking easy answers to complex questions of self and spirit, residents of Tourmaline and Outer Maroo find not salvation but annihilation' ('"Just enough religion to make us hate": the case of *Tourmaline* and *Oyster*', *Antipodes*, 18.1 (June 2004), p. 9).
7. Markman Ellis feels that the novel 'explodes [the] settler myth of an organic community of pioneers bringing civilization to the unexplored interior', although this is a myth that has not had any currency in Australian literary fiction or historical studies for some time ('In the back of the outback', *Times Literary Supplement*, 13 September 1996, p. 22). In Patrick White's iconic *Voss* this is marked when Voss's expedition moves inland, from the cultured and thoughtful environment at Rhine Towers to the brutalised racism of Jildra (Harmondsworth: Penguin, 1976), pp. 123–88. Peter Carey's ironic summary of the violent progress of 'pioneers' through the countryside in *Oscar and Lucinda* (London: Faber, 1988), in the form of violent expedition-leader Mr Jeffris's report on his achievements, well represents contemporary attitudes to the activity of 'civilisation-bringing' by the time Hospital wrote *Oyster*.
8. Anja Müller explores ramifications of Oyster's name in 'Travels in no-man's-land: closure and transgression in Janette Turner Hospital's *Oyster*', in Liselotte Glage (ed.), *Beings in Transit: Travelling. Migration. Dislocation*, Amsterdam: Rodopi, 2000, p. 147. The most likely suggestion is that an oyster is 'a hermetic enclosure breeding an object of singular perfection and value', from which various interpretative possibilities are seen to follow.
9. Kevin Connolly, 'Threads of order: an interview with Janette Turner Hospital', *Paragraph* [Canada], 19.2 (Fall 1997), p. 4.
10. Janette Turner Hospital, *Isobars*, St Lucia: University of Queensland Press, 1990, p. 41.
11. Just who the narrator is is itself a shimmering, uncertain point. While the Prologue is told by Jess, when Book 1 – 'Outer Maroo' – starts the narrator

becomes Mercy Given, a teenage girl. Later, more briefly, we appear to be reading the perspectives of Sarah, Nick or Major Miner. All are united in their opposition to what Oyster has come to stand for. Canadian reviewer Anne Steacy feels that there are only two narrators: Jess and 'a compassionate, all-seeing narrator who slips into characters' minds or seems to breathe right beside them'. 'This microcosm is her *Oyster*', *Books in Canada*, 25.9 (December 1996), p. 20. Russell West perceptively suggests that the 'collapsing of linear narratives into dispersed localised places where versions of reality are constructed perhaps accounts for the frequent switching between first, second and third-person narrative in Turner Hospital's fictions' ('"Multiple exposures": spatial dilemmas of postmodern artistic identity in the fiction of Janette Turner Hospital', in Anne Luyat & Francine Tolron (eds), *Flight from Certainty: The Dilemma of Identity and Exile*, Amsterdam: Rodopi, 2001, p. 183).

12. 'This microcosm is her *Oyster*', p. 21.
13. See *Alice in Wonderland*, Chapter 1.
14. 'Travels in no-man's land', p. 150.
15. Susannah's name recalls the virtuous figure from the Book of Daniel whom two elders attempt to violate. When repulsed, they bear false witness against her, leading to her being condemned to death. In Outer Maroo, however, there is no Daniel to see that justice is done, suggesting that this is a land without God's champions, for here the elders who control the town are able to have Susannah put to death. Susannah's story occurs in Daniel 13, which can be found in Catholic Bibles but not in Protestant ones, a buried indication of the variable nature of stories, even within the canon. Moreover, Daniel secures Susannah's freedom by exposing the inconsistencies between the elders' stories, so that Susannah's name gestures towards the repeated conundrum in Hospital's work: sometimes different versions are enriching, but at other times they are dangerous.
16. In the most negative review of the novel, Marion Halligan finds fault with the 'gorgeous words and lilting cadences' for having 'glamorised and trivialised' the serious issue of evil in repressive communities ('Countdown to the millennium', *Australian Book Review*, October 1996, p. 41). For the most part, however, reviewers responded like Valmai Howe: 'Its Biblical cadence draws us into a savage world shimmering with language as prismatic as the fabulous opals of the doomed reef' ('Seduction and opals in the outback', *Globe and Mail* [Toronto], 26 October 1996, p. D10).
17. *Apocalypses: Prophecies, Cults and Millennial Beliefs Throughout the Ages*, London: Pimlico, 2000, p. 151.
18. This blind spot is not peculiar to remote Australia. In Margaret Atwood's *Cat's Eye*, when the protagonist finds out her Toronto neighbours are

Jewish, she remarks: 'I've seen the word *Jew*, the Bible is full of that word, but I didn't know there were any live, real ones, especially next door to me' (New York: Doubleday, 1989, p. 142).

19. There is another disturbing instance of this in Thea Astley's novel *An Item from the Late News*, St Lucia: University of Queensland Press, 1982, also set in the mining-crazed interior of Queensland, in which the local inhabitants of Allbut refuse to believe that recent arrival Wafer does not know more about where to find sapphires than he is letting on; they prevent him from leaving the area, torture him and eventually murder him.
20. In 1993, shortly before Hospital began writing *Oyster*, she made a writers' tour of the United Kingdom in the company of Sam Watson, outspoken Murri author of *The Kadaitcha Sung*, Ringwood: Penguin, 1990, whose views made a strong impact on her. Even more significant, however, was to be contact with the Aboriginal community in Cunnamulla, a contact made through her husband's nephew, Thom Blake, former Methodist pastor in the town.
21. In Hospital's earlier novels Aborigines are largely invisible, but in some of her most significant short stories they are centrally important, particularly 'The Second Coming of Come-by-Chance', 'The Last of the Hapsburgs' (*Isobars*) and 'Our Own Little Kakadu' (*North of Nowhere, South of Loss*). In no case, though, does Hospital occupy an Aboriginal speaking voice or attempt to tell their stories for them. Of the six works mentioned in the bibliography at the end of *Oyster*, the first three deal with Indigenous issues.
22. 'A third space?', p. 128.
23. Private communication, 7 January 2007.
24. Anja Müller, 'Travels in no-man's-land', p. 149. The character in *Catch 22* is actually Major (his rank) Major Major Major (his given names plus surname), who becomes trapped by the pleasure his absurd name gives others, unable to be promoted because the pattern would be lost. All he wants is to escape the exceptionalness his name confers, and to evade being noticed.
25. The first part of his citation is from Leviticus 10, but the second is not, Prophet pontificating as though his own words were scripture. Lest the surname be thought overdetermined, the head of one late twentieth-century US apocalyptic sect, the Church Universal and Triumphant, was one Elizabeth Claire Prophet, and renaming characterises many extreme sects.
26. Hospital admits that Mercy's father is 'based fairly closely on my own father' (Connolly, 'Threads of order', p. 5).
27. For Koresh, an apocalyptic fiery immolation was part of the script he had written for the sect, leaning on the book of Revelation, whereby he and his followers would be restored to stand beside the lamb of God. In such a script, his earthly destroyers – the FBI – can be seen as fulfilling a role

Koresh had written for them. See Kenneth Newport, *The Branch Davidians of Waco*, Oxford: Oxford University Press, 2006. It may be that Oyster was making use of a related script, although he is represented as cynically manipulative of scripture rather than eschatologically inspired.

28. 'Eclipsing the constitutive power of discourse: the writing of Janette Turner Hospital', in Elizabeth St Pierre & Wanda S. Pillow (eds), *Working the Ruins: Feminist Poststuctural Theory and Methods in Education*, London: Routledge, 2000, p. 195.
29. Jane Campion explores similar themes in her film *Holy Smoke*, 1999, Miramax, and in the novel written by her and her sister Anna Campion, *Holy Smoke*, London: Bloomsbury, 1999. On this, see Rebecca Pannell, 'Making the sign of the Cross: interdisciplinary intersections in theology, Australian studies and postcolonial studies', *Kunapipi*, 22.2, (2000), pp. 64–74.
30. Revelation 1.3.
31. 'Multiple exposures', p. 183.
32. 'Ideas of order in Janette Turner Hospital's *Oyster*', *Critique*, 48.4 (Summer 2007), p. 382.
33. ibid., p. 386.

10. A moment out of place: *North of Nowhere, South of Loss*

1. *On Longing: Narratives of the Miniature, the Gigantic, the Souvenir, the Collection*, Durham: Duke University Press, 1993, p. 13.
2. *North of Nowhere, South of Loss*, St Lucia: University of Queensland Press, 2003, p. 167. Further citations will be included in the text.
3. *Empathic Vision: Affect, Trauma, and Contemporary Art*, Stanford: Stanford University Press, 2005, p. 11.
4. *S/Z: An Essay* [1970], (trans.) Richard Miller, New York: Hill & Wang, 1974, p. 55.
5. A version (one later set to music by Percy Grainger) can be found at: www.recmusic.org/lieder/get_text.html?TextId=16987.
6. *Memory in Literature: from Rousseau to Neuroscience*, Houndmills, Basingstoke: Palgrave Macmillan, 2003, p. 138.
7. In *Orpheus Lost*, the principal character, Leela, is compared positively to a bird, in that she is restlessly curious (Sydney: FourthEstate, 2007, pp. 40–1).
8. Laura Trevelyan, in White's *Voss*, is drawn to him out of a sense of intellectual kinship she is unable to find in colonial Australia. She is also left irremediably disturbed by Voss's actions and fate.
9. *The Shell and the Kernel: Renewals of Psychoanalysis*, Chicago: University of Chicago Press, 1994, p. 171.
10. Katherine Golsan & Lucy Golsan (trans.), *Life in Common: An Essay in General Anthropology*, Lincoln: University of Nebraska Press, 2001, p. 84.

11. *Dark Side of the Dream: Australian Literature and the Postcolonial Mind*, Sydney: Allen & Unwin, 1990, p. 25.
12. 'Postmodern issues in Janette Turner Hospital's nature-dominated short stories "The End-of-the-Line End-of-the-World Disco" and "Our Own Little Kakadu"', in Farhat Iftekharrudin, Joseph Boyden, Joseph Longo & Mary Rohrberger (eds), *Postmodern Approaches to the Short Story*, Westport, CT: Praeger, 2003, p. 66.
13. ibid., p. 73.
14. In this Hospital is in tune with increasingly widespread sentiments in contemporary Australia, often articulated in terms that reference Aboriginal attitudes to nature, as in the work of Judith Wright. To take one well-known example, 'At Cooloola' brings together a desire to be more caring for the environment with an awareness that it was precisely the poet's ancestors who came to disrupt Indigenous relations with the land. *Collected Poems: 1942–1985*, Sydney: Angus & Robertson, 1994, pp. 140–1.
15. King's confident arguments are outlined in *Being Pakeha: An Encounter with New Zealand and the Maori Renaissance*, Auckland: Hodder and Stoughton, 1985. In contrast, an apologetic tone is noticeable throughout an Australian anthology of essays stimulated by King's book: Duncan Graham (ed.), *Being Whitefella*, Fremantle: Fremantle Arts Centre Press, 1994.
16. The friendship that provided raw material for this group of stories is described at length in Hospital's autobiographical reflection 'Old Friends Are Best', in Mickey Pearlman (ed.), *Between Friends*, Boston: Houghton Mifflin, 1994, pp. 214–35. There, Hospital remembers her friend Patrick saying of his scientific research: 'it's not the careful calculations that matter. It's imagination, intuition, dreams', to which Hospital answers: 'that's what writing a novel is like', p. 225.
17. 'Partridge wings', review of *North of Nowhere, South of Loss*, *Australian Book Review*, August 2003, p. 50.
18. Biblical support for this comes from Mark 16:18: 'They shall take up serpents; and if they drink any deadly thing, it shall not hurt them.' The rest of the verse goes on: 'they shall lay hands on the sick, and they shall recover', implying a link between healing and the ability to survive danger unharmed.
19. 'Postmodern issues', p. 66.
20. ibid., p. 66.
21. *Collected Poems 1909–1935*, London: Faber & Faber, 1936, p. 64. Just before these lines, the *Waste Land* also alludes to Ovid's tale of Philomela, raped by her brother-in-law Tereus and subsequently mutilated (for which Tereus pays a suitably terrible price), a possible hint of the centuries of male violence that lie behind Flutie's attempted seduction. See Book VI, *Metamorphoses*.

22. Fog tends to be a negative reference in Hospital's work, whether doing duty as the lack of solidity of a life, as in 'North of Nowhere', or as an extended metaphor for mental anxiety, as in 'Nativity'. In the latter story fog embodies an anxiety derived from Jonathan's feeling disconnected from the people he should feel connected to. When he learns that his daughter Stacey has missed him, 'he notes a thinning of the fog that fills the room' (187).
23. *Memory in Literature*, p. 117.

11. Living astride death: *Due Preparations for the Plague*

1. *A Midnight Cry, an Essay for Our Awakening out of That Sinful Sleep, to Which We Are at This Time Too Much Disposed* (1692), quoted in Sacvan Berkovitch, *The Rites of Assent: Transformations in the Symbolic Construction of America*, New York: Routledge, 1993, p. 114.
2. Janette Turner Hospital, *Due Preparations for the Plague*, Sydney: Fourth Estate/ HarperCollins, 1993, p. 157. Further citations will be included in the text. The title of the novel is taken from Daniel Defoe's book of the same name, published in the same year as his more famous *A Journal of the Plague Year* (1722).
3. Claudia Aradau & Rens Van Munster, 'Governing terrorism through risk: taking precautions, (un)knowing the future', *European Journal of International Relations*, 13.1 (2007), p. 92. The theorisation of a risk society can be found in the work of Ulrich Beck, principally *World Risk Society*, Cambridge: Polity, 1999.
4. One of Defoe's purposes is to argue strongly against the oppressive policing and militarisation of control of the populace that the plague often occasioned on the part of frightened governments. See *Due Preparations for the Plague as Well as for Soul and Body*, Boston: Dana Estes & Company, 1904, pp. 9–10.
5. Robert Lowell is also linked to Hawthorne in that he wrote a triptych of plays focused on delusional beliefs about the legacies of American history, based on nineteenth-century American literature, in which two of the plays were rewritings of short stories by Hawthorne – 'My Kinsman Major Molineux' and 'Endicott and the Red Cross' (*The Old Glory*, New York: Noonday Press, 1965). In Lowell's versions, the stories become even more withering denunciations of Puritanism. There are other candidates for the resonance of the name 'Lowell', such as the Massachusetts town of Lowell, centrally implicated in the early history of American social engineering, in which the fusion of mechanistic production lines and control of the workers through time and motion principles applied to contemporary factory environments was extended to the paternalistic control of industrial workers in all aspects of their lives. Lowell the town stands thus for a

well-meaning attitude to social control, but one whose rigid vision of society envisages it as a machine regulated in such a way that stepping outside the system is impossible. Representing these tendencies, Mather names his son Lowell. In addition, nineteenth-century writer James Russell Lowell knew Hawthorne, and much of his work was dedicated to exposing those in power, although focusing most often on the cause of anti-slavery, which would appear to have limited relevance here.

6. Quoted in Emory Elliott, *Power and the Pulpit in Puritan New England*, Princeton: Princeton University Press, 1975, p. 189. Cotton Mather was nevertheless insistent that New England had been chosen by God to achieve great things, and indeed that it was already well on the way to doing so.
7. 'An impossibly ordered scheme: conspiracy theories and interconnectedness', *EnterText*, 1.1 (Winter 2000), p. 31. Witness the rash of paranoid theories concerning 9/11, in which, supposedly, Bush, Rumsfeld and the CIA are supposed to have arranged missile attacks on the twin towers and the Pentagon in order to justify the ensuing military action, with secret operatives taking out Flight 77 or United 93. See, for example, Jim Marrs, *Inside Job: Unmasking the 9/11 Conspiracies*, San Rafael, CA: Origin Press, 2004, or David Ray Griffin, *Christian Faith and the Truth behind 9/11*, Louisville, KY: Westminster John Knox Press, 2006.
8. The allusion is probably to Sir Walter Raleigh, responsible for the first English colony in the south, Virginia. Moreover, Raleigh's venture grew out of a belief that 'England would remain a weak, impotent country unless it emulated the great superpower Spain with its rich American empire', an attitude comparable to that of the contemporary imperial insistence of those who wielded power in America when the novel was written. Citation from Karen Ordahl Kupperman, *Indians & English: Facing Off in Early America*, Ithaca, NY: Cornell University Press, 2000, p. 12. In addition, Samantha's name, in conjunction with its androgynous abbreviated form, captures 'both her aggressiveness and her feminine sexuality' (Janette Turner Hospital, Private correspondence, 11 April 2007).
9. One sly Australian reference is the film Lowell's daughter is watching as he examines the secret package left for him by his father (36) – *Babe* (Chris Noonan, 1995), a parable in which a creature marked for death – a pig – steps outside his fate by following a dream of difference, albeit one in which he performs tasks for a superior controller, the human farmer.
10. 'Governing terrorism through risk', p. 108.
11. ibid., p. 104.
12. This fate resonates with the consequences of the Puritan concept of prevenient grace, which averred that God had predetermined who was to be saved, and if one was not one of the elect there was nothing one could do to ensure one's salvation. Given that no human could know God's mind,

it was necessary to try to live as if one might be one of the elect, but at the same time this situation encouraged constant attempts to read the codes and signs through which God spoke, in order to attempt to discover clues with respect to one's fate.

13. '*Due Preparations for the Plague*: globalization, terror and the ethics of alterity', *Kunapipi*, 28.1 (2006), p. 26.
14. 'Strengthening the shield: US Homeland Security Intelligence', *International Journal of Intelligence and Counterintelligence*, 20 (2007), pp. 196–7.
15. 'Endicott and the Red Cross', in Michael Colacurcio (ed.), *Selected Tales and Sketches*, New York: Penguin, 1987, p. 219.
16. Hospital quotes from the Gospel of Mark, with a specific alteration, when referring to this hell: 'a place where their worm dieth not, and *their* fire is not quenched' (227); in Mark 9, where this is repeated three times (verses 44, 46 and 48), it is: '*the* fire is not quenched'. *Their* has the effect of rendering more personal the torments being suffered.
17. The origins and nature of the plague are, however, still vigorously studied and contested. The recent upsurge in contemporary scholarship on the plague suggests that it remains a mysterious historical event as well as a compelling metaphor for various contemporary phenomena, from HIV to bird flu. Norman F. Cantor's *In the Wake of the Plague: The Black Death & the World It Made*, New York: Free Press, 2001 was even a bestseller.
18. In the story 'Bondi', in *Isobars*, a character muses, 'Excitement, salamander style, comes slinking in through Cass's eardrum' (70).
19. Page 13 gives the numerological value of 4 (by adding together numbers until one is left with one digit), and the next time the image appears it is on p. 211, which also gives 4 (2 + 1 + 1). While this is likely to be as meaningless as the man's shirt at Logan airport, it can be pointed out that the number 4 is associated with death in Chinese culture, as the character for '4' sounds similar to the character for 'death'.
20. *Mystic Chords of Memory: The Transformation of Tradition in American Culture*, New York: Vintage, 1993, p. 9.
21. Genevieve is the only Australian character in the novel. She accretes a certain set of standard Australian meanings – the young Australian as a breezy traveller, both geographically and through life, carried here by her being a travel writer for a low-budget series of travel books clearly meant to suggest the Lonely Planet series (run from Australia by its English founders, Tony and Maureen Wheeler).
22. 'Loading the dice', review of *Due Preparations for the Plague*, *Australian Book Review*, June/July 2003, p. 38. Dolores Herrero argues the same point in 'Globalization, terror and the ethics of alterity', pp. 35–6.
23. 'A third space? Postcolonial Australia and the fractal landscape in *The Last Magician* and *Oyster*', in Jamie Scott & Paul Simpson-Housley (eds),

Mapping the Sacred: Religion, Geography and Postcolonial Literatures, Amsterdam: Rodopi, 2001, pp. 111–30.

24. Jessica Jernigan, 'Interview: The story of what is happening: Janette Turner Hospital on terror and resilience', at www.bordersstores.com/features/feature.jsp?file=hospital. Defoe captures Salamander's condition well: 'it is a double terror to the dying person [Salamander knows he will not be allowed to survive by his own organisation] to have the work of dying and the work of repentance both upon his hands together. Oh, sinner! remember that the terrors of thy conscience will be a weight too heavy to be borne at the same time with the terrors of death' (*Due Preparations for the Plague as Well as for Soul and Body*, p. 98). Cotton Mather, in Berkovitch's words, 'cast himself in the image of a suffering Savior', believing that 'his special capacity for vision and insight rendered him the unacknowledged legislator of his world' (*Rites of Assent*, p. 99). It is precisely this hubristic belief that led Mather/Salamander to set up the Black Death operation in the first place, and its failure that has left him in anguish.
25. A condition in which research meteorologist Edward Lorenz perceived 'order *masquerading* as randomness', in James Gleick, *Chaos: Making a New Science*, New York, Penguin, 1988, p. 22; Gleick's italics. This is also known as the Butterfly Effect, understood not as unstructured accident but as 'sensitive dependence on initial conditions' (Gleick, p. 23).
26. *Collected Fictions*, (trans.) Andrew Hurley, New York: Penguin, 1999, pp. 411–17.
27. Albert Camus, *The Plague* [1947], (trans.) Stuart Gilbert, Harmondsworth: Penguin, 1960; Geraldine Brooks, *Year of Wonders: A Novel of the Plague*, Sydney: Fourth Estate, 2001.
28. Jane Sullivan, 'The thrills in Turner Hospital', *The Age*, 31 May 2003, Review, p. 3, www.theage.com.au/articles/2003/05/30/1054177726457.html. The attack on the twin towers also meant that Hospital had to move the date of the action back from her planned 2002, given that the world post-9/11 would have responded differently to the events of the novel in ways that would have interfered with the narrative. Hospital also confirms that the tone of the ending was made more optimistic. See Eleanor Hall, 'The world today – book *Due Preparation* [*sic*] *for the Plague* explores death, terrorism', at: www.abc.net.au/worldtoday/content/2003/s860328.htm.
29. *Plotting Terror: Novelists and Terrorists in Contemporary Fiction*, Charlottesville: University Press of Virginia, 2001, p. 155.
30. 'Globalization and terror', p. 175.
31. New York: Basic Books, 1987, pp. 8–11.
32. Corroborating Hospital's sarcasm, a special report in *The Economist* on Intelligence reform in the United States and the United Kingdom following 9/11 came to the conclusion that 'America's secret world is inefficient

and demoralised, and has been for some time', while the CIA in particular 'is burdened by a miserable run of failures' ('America's intelligence reforms: can spies be made better?' *Economist*, 19 March 2005, p. 27). This has been confirmed by the exhaustive research of Tim Weiner in his *Legacy of Ashes: The History of the CIA*, New York: Doubleday, 2007, a devastating account of agency ignorance, bungling and ideological blindness.

12. The broken chords of home: *Orpheus Lost*

1. *Orpheus or the Music of the Future*, London: Kegan Paul, 1926, p. 3.
2. In a mostly harsh review, Andrew Riemer referred to this aspect of the novel 'as decorative, rather than fundamental to the characters' intrinsic selves'. *Sydney Morning Herald*, 4 May 2007, www.smh.com.au/news/book-reviews/orpheus-lost/2007/05/04/1177788377833.html?page=fullpage#contentSwap1.
3. 'Beauty in terror: Janette Turner Hospital's *Orpheus Lost*', *Critique*, 48.4 (Summer 2007), p. 356.
4. Janette Turner Hospital, *Orpheus Lost*, Sydney: Fourth Estate, 2007, p. 3. Further references will be included within the text.
5. See, for example, the interview with Luan Gaines on the 'Curled up with a good book' site: www.curledup.com/intjthosp.htm.
6. 'Falling into the mirror, *Australian Literary Review*, 2 May 2007, pp. 6–7.
7. Many versions of this aria can be heard at www.youtube.com. An excellent recording of the whole opera is that by the Freiburger Barockorchester, conducted by René Jacobs (Harmonia Mundi 901742.43; 2 CDs, 2001).
8. *Chronicle of My Life*, London: Gollancz, 1936, p. 91; Stravinsky's italics.
9. 'Musical meaning and its social determinants', *Sociology*, 9.3 (1975), p. 420.
10. ibid., p. 421.
11. 'A simple model for associative musical meaning', in Byron Almén & Edward Pearsall (eds), *Approaches to Meaning in Music*, Bloomington: Indiana University Press, 2006, p. 101; Burkholder's italics.
12. 'Georgic IV', *The Aeneid, the Georgics, the Eclogues*, (trans.) James Rhoades, Oxford: Oxford University Press, 1962, p. 384.
13. *Myth and Meaning: Cracking the Code of Culture* [1978], New York: Schocken Books, 1995, p. 12. Lévi-Strauss delivered these lectures originally in English.
14. Symptomatic of the generalised sense that to begin to understand Iraq it is necessary to try to understand Vietnam, the National Book Award winner in the same year that *Orpheus Lost* appeared was Denis Johnson's massive and anguished novel dealing with the damage done to white American

manhood by Vietnam, *Tree of Smoke*, New York: Farrar, Straus & Giroux, 2007.

15. This echoes the condemnation of William Calley over the My Lai massacre in 1968. Documents from the court martial, and a contextualisation of the legal framework surrounding the trial of Calley, can be found at the University of Missouri law department site: www.law.umkc.edu/faculty/projects/ftrials/mylai/mylai.htm.
16. *In Our Own Image: The Coming Revolution in Photography*, New York: Aperture, 1999, p. xi.
17. 'Iwo Jima v. Abu Ghraib', review of *No Caption Needed: Iconic Photographs, Public Culture and Liberal Democracy* by Robert Hariman & John Louis Lucaites, *London Review of Books*, 29 November 2007, p. 27. The most iconic photograph of the war in Iraq so far is the 'Marlboro Marine' (James Blake Miller), taken by Luis Sinco in 2004. The image has been translated into a representation of American courage and forbearance, but Miller, now returned to Kentucky, is a broken man, unable to inhabit the famous image of himself. See Sinco's report in the *Los Angeles Times*, 2007: www.latimes.com/news/nationworld/nation/marlboromarine/.
18. *Isobars*, St Lucia: University of Queensland Press, 1990, pp. 11–27.
19. *Dislocations*, St Lucia: University of Queensland Press, 1987, pp. 9–21, 23–31.
20. *Dislocations*, pp. 181–9.
21. For Andrew Riemer, Mishka's attempt to bring together his twinned inheritance is the most impressive aspect of the novel: 'Where Mishka seeks to reconcile the two warring aspects of his heritage – European Jewish and Lebanese Muslim – by adding a devotion to the oud and to Sufi music and poetry to his immersion in Western musical culture, Turner Hospital manages, for several pages at a time, to give real substance to her writing, leading us into her character's perplexed mind and soul' (*Sydney Morning Herald*, 4 May 2007).
22. Hospital is tapping into a widespread American nightmare here, whose basic features, along with the battle lines between contending views on how to respond to such a scenario, are forcefully represented in the ambiguous Fox network television series *24*, particularly the sixth season (broadcast 2006). Andrew McGahan has transferred the nightmare to Australian soil in his sardonic dystopia *Underground*, Sydney: Allen & Unwin, 2006, while Richard Flanagan's *The Unknown Terrorist*, Sydney: Picador, 2006, bitterly critiques the hypocritical official interest in maintaining excessive levels of public paranoia, the better to license increased surveillance and control of all aspects of domestic life. Frank Moorhouse's long essay 'The writer in a time of terror' vigorously exposes the restrictions that are already in place in Australia, along with the serious damage they are doing to creative

activity, writing and the wider polity as a whole. *Griffith Review*, 14 (Summer 2006–07), pp. 11–60.

23. A major traffic route in Boston, and significantly the principal access to the city from the airport, one of the central reference points of 9/11.
24. Within Australia these fears have been widely expressed in differing registers. See, for example, Hannie Rayson's play *Two Brothers*, Sydney: Currency Press, 2005, first performed in Melbourne in April 2005; Peter Mares, *Borderline: Australia's Treatment of Refugees and Asylum Seekers*, Sydney: University of New South Wales Press, 2001; Anna Saulwick (ed.), *University of NSW Law Journal*, 27.2 (2004), an excellent special issue dedicated to 'Counter-Terrorism Laws'; or Thomas Keneally's spirited parable about a sinister, authoritarian state, *The Tyrant's Novel*, Doubleday: Milsons Point, NSW, 2003.
25. New York: *New York Review Books*, 2004, p. xiv.
26. Joseph Campbell includes in his *Transformations of Myth through Time* a suggestive cylinder seal from 300 AD in which Orpheus is represented on the Cross. New York: Harper & Row, 1990, p. 207.
27. *Los Angeles Times*, 4 November 2007: www.latimes.com/features/books/la-bk-rifkind4nov04,0,4407186.story?coll=la-books-center.

BIBLIOGRAPHY

1. Works by Janette Turner Hospital

This is a working bibliography of Hospital's publications, giving first publication and first Australian publication, where this is different. A full and fascinating publishing history can be found in Benjamin Franklin V's 'A Transcontinental Quest: A Janette Turner Hospital Checklist', *Critique: Studies in Contemporary Fiction*, 48.4 (Summer 2007), pp. 391–405. A good bibliography referencing the early part of Hospital's career, including listings of the first publications of many short stories, is Ron Store's 'Janette Turner Hospital: A Preliminary Bibliography 1973–1988', *Literature in North Queensland*, 17.1 (1990), pp. 148–159. Finally, AustLit is a good source for information about Hospital's own articles and reviews: www.austlit.edu.au.

Novels

The Ivory Swing, Toronto: McLelland & Stewart, 1982. St Lucia: University of Queensland Press, 1991.

The Tiger in the Tiger Pit, Toronto: McLelland & Stewart, 1983. St Lucia: University of Queensland Press, 1990.

Borderline, Toronto: McLelland & Stewart, 1985. St Lucia: University of Queensland Press, 1987.

Charades, St Lucia: University of Queensland Press, 1988.

The Last Magician, St Lucia: University of Queensland Press, 1992.

Oyster, Sydney: Knopf, 1996.

Due Preparations for the Plague, Pymble, New South Wales: Fourth Estate/HarperCollins, 2003.

Orpheus Lost, Pymble, New South Wales: Fourth Estate/HarperCollins, 2007.

Bibliography

Novel (as Alex Juniper)

A Very Proper Death, Toronto: Random House, 1990. Ringwood, Victoria: Penguin Australia, 1990.

Short stories

Dislocations, Toronto: McLelland & Stewart, 1986.

Dislocations, Second Edition, St Lucia: University of Queensland Press, 1987 [contains the Canadian edition plus three further stories].

Isobars, St Lucia: University of Queensland Press, 1990.

Isobars, Toronto: McLelland & Stewart, 1991 [the first three stories are the three last stories of the Australian edition of *Dislocations*].

Collected Stories 1970–1995, St Lucia: University of Queensland Press, 1995 [contains all of the Australian editions of *Dislocations*, *Isobars*, and seven stories collected under the title 'North of Nowhere'. These stories were later included in *North of Nowhere, South of Loss*].

North of Nowhere, South of Loss, St Lucia: University of Queensland Press, 2003.

Uncollected fiction (selected)

'A Dream of Isfahan', *Chateleine* [Toronto], 53 (July 1980), pp. 31, 42–5.

'Our Little Chamber Concerts', *Saturday Night*, 97 (June 1982), pp. 46–8, 50–3.

'Walking on Water', *Chateleine*, 55 (November 1982), pp. 64–5, 112, 116–17.

'Performances', *Toronto Life*, (October 1983), pp. 44–5, 116.

'Sometimes a Holding Pattern is Perfect', *Cosmopolitan*, 195 (November 1983), pp. 319–24.

'Adolescence by Any Other Name', *Chateleine*, 57 (February 1984), pp. 46, 86–94.

'Here Comes the Sun', *Cosmopolitan*, 198 (November 1984), pp. 299–302.

'Amazing Grace', *Ladies Home Journal*, 103 (June 1986), pp. 114–16.

'Expatriate', *Prairie Schooner*, 62.4 (Winter 1988), pp. 55–63.

'In the Beginning', *Good Weekend*, 10 September 1988, pp.61–5.

'Genesis, Genesis', *Queen's Quarterly*, 96.3 (Autumn 1989), pp. 625–30.

'The New Physics', *Descant 66/67*, 20.3-4 (Fall–Winter 1989), pp. 147–54.

'A Corpse at the Opera House', in Stephen Knight (ed.), *A Corpse at the Opera House: A Crimes for a Summer Christmas Anthology*, St Leonards, New South Wales: Allen and Unwin, 1992, pp. 203–34.

'Hurricane Season', in Peter Craven (ed.), *The Best Australian Stories 2003*, Melbourne: Black Inc, 2003, pp. 1–16.

'Blind Date', *The Monthly*, 2 (June 2005), pp. 46–9.

'The Prince of Darkness is a Gentleman', *The Monthly*, 7 (November 2005), pp. 44–8.

Manuscripts

Forty-two boxes of manuscripts, letters, reviews and miscellaneous material are held in the Fryer Library at the University of Queensland. This material relates to Hospital's career until *The Last Magician*.

Articles and reviews

Hospital has written a large number of articles and reviews. When her first novels were published and her career took off, Hospital accepted numerous commissions to write travel articles, commentary articles, and reviews. Soon she was swamped, and has in recent years restricted this type of activity. This list is a selection of some of the most interesting for the analysis of her work.

'Keneally's Reluctant Prophets', Janette Turner Hospital interviews Thomas Keneally, *Commonweal* [New York] 103.10 (May 1976), pp. 295–300.

'Sisyphus Laughs in Pakistan', rev. of Salman Rushdie, *Shame*, *Globe and Mail* [Toronto], 1 October 1983, p. E8.

'I Feel in Transit. I Don't Quite Belong Anywhere', *Australian Author*, 17.3 (September 1985), pp. 3–9.

'The Truth, the Whole Truth, May be Anything *But* the Truth', *The Writer* [Boston], 100.4 (April 1987), pp. 19–21.

'Violent Times', *Whig-Standard Magazine* [Kingston], 11 April 1987, pp. 8–10; reprinted in *Australian Literary Quarterly*, 6–7 June 1989, p. 9.

'In the Pioneer Tradition', rev. of fiction by Australian women, *The*

Women's Review of Books [Wellesley, MA], 4.10–11 (July 1987), pp. 10–11.

'Letter to a New York Editor', *Meanjin*, 47 (1988), pp. 560–4.

'Afterword', Brian Moore, *The Lonely Passion of Judith Hearne*, Toronto: McLelland and Stewart, 1988, pp. 241–5.

'Space Invaders', *The Women's Review of Books*, 5.10–11 (July 1988), pp. 3–4.

'The Expatriate Writer: A Case of Dislocated Perspective', *Australian Author*, 20.2 (July 1988), pp. 9–10.

'Angels in the skies above England', rev. of Salman Rushdie, *The Satanic Verses*, *Globe and Mail*, 22 October 1988, p. C9.

'The Whitefellas Don't Understand', rev. of Sally Morgan, *My Place*, *New York Times Book Review*, 19 February 1989, pp. 13–14.

'The Heroic Outsider', rev. of Anita Desai's *Baumgartner's Bombay*, *Toronto South Asian Review*, 7.2 (Winter 1989), pp. 66–70.

'An Expatiation on Expatriation', *Overland*, 114 (May 1989), pp. 35–9.

'On Being a Writer in Residence', *Sydney Review*, 16 (September 1989), p. 8.

'Strange Ships, and Biting Insights', rev. of recent Australian writing, *The Age*, 9 September 1989, Saturday Extra, p. 10.

'A Writer Comes in from the Cold', rev. of books by Amy Witting, *Sydney Morning Herald*, 14 October 1989, p. 80.

'The Verbal Web of Anorexia', rev. of Fiona Place, *Cardboard: The Strength Thereof and Other Related Matters*, *Australian Book Review*, 116 (November 1989), pp. 18–19.

'Voices of Stars and Rebels', rev. of recent writing by Australian women, 'The Wild Child Turns Tedious in Sydney', rev. of Robyn Davidson, *Ancestors*, *Los Angeles Times Book Review*, 24 December 1989, p. 2.

Age, 4 November 1989, Saturday Extra, p. 9.

'Letter to the Editors', in Libby Scheier, Sarah Sherad & Eleanor Wachtel (eds), *Language in Her Eye: Views on Writing and Gender by Canadian Women Writing in English*, Toronto: Coach House Press, 1990, pp. 146–7.

'Afterword', Sara Jeannette Duncan, *The Imperialist*, Toronto: McLelland and Stewart, 1990, pp. 311–6.

'Coming Home', *Courier-Mail*, 18 August 1990, Weekend, p. 4.

'The Writers' Train', *Australian Bookseller & Publisher*, 70.1009 (October 1990), p. 16.

'A country still in the making', rev. of V. S. Naipaul, *India: A Million*

Mutinies Now, *New York Times Book Review*, 30 December 1990, pp. 1–3.

'Author's Note', in Garry Disher (ed.), *Personal Best 2: Stories and Statements by Australian Writers*, Sydney: Angus & Robertson, 1991, pp. 1–4.

'Changes and the Things That Don't Change: India 1977 and 1990', in Robin Lucas & Clare Foster (eds), *Wilder Shores: Women's Travel Stories of Australia and Beyond*, St Lucia: University of Queensland Press, 1992, pp. 74–9.

'A Myth at Risk', rev. of Thomas Keneally, *Our Republic* and David Malouf, *Remembering Babylon*, *Courier-Mail*, 29 May 1993, p. 29.

'Aboriginal Encounters', rev. of a selection of books by Aboriginal authors or dealing with Indigenous issues, *Times Literary Supplement*, 20 August 1993, pp. 4–5.

'A transgressor of boundaries', rev. of works by May Sarton, *Times Literary Supplement*, 9 July 1993, p. 25.

'Old Friends are Best', in Mickey Pearlman (ed.), *Between Friends*, Boston: Houghton Mifflin, 1994, pp. 214–35.

'Why I Write', *Kunapipi*, 16.1 (1994), pp. 126–8.

'Bush High', *Courier-Mail*, 3 December 1994, Weekend, pp. 3–4.

'Body Maps', rev. of Mary Gordon, *The Rest of Life*, *London Review of Books*, 7 April 1994, p. 23.

'Grand Gestures', rev. of Thomas Keneally, *A River Town*, *London Review of Books*, 25 May 1995, pp. 22–3.

'Hybrid Heroes', rev. of David Malouf, *The Conversations at Curlow Creek*, *London Review of Books*, 12 December 1996, p. 27.

'A Walk Around the World: Home and Homelessness in the Work of Christina Stead', in Selina Samuels (ed.), *Janette Turner Hospital*, London: Sir Robert Menzies Centre for Australian Studies/University of London, 1998, pp. 1–16.

'Letter to a Younger Writer Met at a Conference', in Frederick Busch (ed.), *Letters to a Fiction Writer*, New York: Norton, 1999, pp. 179-88.

'Introduction', in Janette Turner Hospital (ed.), *Inheritance: Selections from the South Carolina Fiction Project*, Spartanburg, SC: Hub City Writers Project, 2001, pp. 3–11.

'An Accidental Nomad', *Bulletin*, 17 December–14 January 2002–03, pp. 66–9.

'Australia's Cultural Identity Now', *New Literatures Review*, 44 (October 2005), pp. 5–13.
'Giacometti's Foot and Proust's Madeleine', in Maurice Lee (ed.), *Writers on Writing: The Art of the Short Story*, Wesport, CT: Praeger, 2005, pp. 77–82.
'First Voice: Janette Turner Hospital', looking back at *The Ivory Swing*, *The Age*, 3 June 2006, A2, p. 27.
'Falling into the mirror', *Australian Book Review*, 2 May 2007, pp.6–7.
'Fugitive Days', rev. of Peter Carey, *His Illegal Self*, *The Monthly*, (February 2008), pp. 46–9.

2. Works about Janette Turner Hospital

Interviews

The following is a selection from the numerous interviews Janette Turner Hospital has given, namely those in print from earlier in her career. More recent interviews tend to be online and are easily locatable.

Baker, Candida, *Yacker 2: Australian Writers Talk About Their Work*, Sydney: Picador, 1987, pp. 248–78.
Brydon, Diana, 'The Stone's Memory: An Interview with Janette Turner Hospital', *Commonwealth Writing in English*, 4.1 (1991), pp. 14–23.
Connolly, Kevin, 'Threads of Order: An Interview with Janette Turner Hospital', *Paragraph*, 19.2 (Fall 1997), pp. 3–9.
Daniels, Missy, 'The telltale art of Janette Turner Hospital', *Boston Phoenix: Literary Section*, 28 April 1989, p. 16.
Greiner, Donald, 'The "God Itch": An Interview with Janette Turner Hospital', *Critique: Studies in Contemporary Fiction*, 48.4 (Summer 2007), pp. 331–43.
Hamelin, Christine, '"Novelist as Urgent Quester": An Interview with Janette Turner Hospital', *Australian and New Zealand Studies in Canada*, 9 (June 1993). pp. 106–11.
Hay, David, 'The Loneliness of the Long Distance Writer', *Bulletin*, 25 July 1989, pp. 132–6.
Jernigan, Jessica, 'Interview: The Story of What Is Happening: Janette Turner Hospital on Terror and Resilience', at: www.bordersstores.com/features/feature.jsp?file=hospital.
Lovell, Sue, 'The Inheritance of Difference', *Imago*, 1.1 (March 1989), pp. 8–9.

McKay, Belinda, 'Transformative Moments: An Interview with Janette Turner Hospital', *Queensland Review*, 11.2 (December 2004), pp. 1–10.

Metcalf, John & Leon Rooke, 'Janette Turner Hospital', in John Metcalf & Leon Rooke (eds), *The Second Macmillan Anthology*, Toronto: Macmillan, 1989, pp. 245–7.

Pearlman, Mickey, 'Interview with Janette Turner Hospital', in Mickey Pearlman (ed.), *Listen to Their Voices: 20 Interviews with Women Who Write*, New York: Norton, 1993, pp. 47–58.

Ringold, Francine, 'Margins Within Margins', *Nimrod: International Journal of Prose and Poetry* [Tulsa, OK], 36.2 (Spring/Summer 1993), pp. 27–32.

Turcotte, Gerry, 'Janette Turner Hospital: *Dislocations*, *Borderline*, *Charades*', in Gerry Turcotte (ed.), *Writers in Action: The Writers' Choice Evenings*, Sydney: Currency Press, 1990, pp. 65–85.

Criticism

(i) Book

Samuels, Selina (ed.) *Janette Turner Hospital*, London: Sir Robert Menzies Centre for Australian Studies/University of London, 1998.

(ii) Booklets

Beckett, Wendy, *Janette Turner Hospital's* Dislocations, Glebe: Pascal Press, 1994 [an aid to the study of Hospital's stories in school].

Perry, Susan, *A Text Response to Janette Turner Hospital's* Dislocations, Ballarat: Wizard Books, 1994 [another aid to the study of Hospital's stories in school].

Wilding, Michael, *Recent Australian Writing: Janette Turner Hospital's* Borderline *and Don O'Kim's* The Chinaman, *Working Papers in Australian Studies*, 29, London: Sir Robert Menzies Centre for Australian Studies/University of London, 1988.

(iii) Special issues of journals

Literature in North Queensland, Janette Turner Hospital issue, (ed.) Cheryl Taylor, 17.1 (1990).

Critique: Studies in Contemporary Fiction, (ed.) Donald J. Greiner, 48.4 (Summer 2007).

(iv) Articles

The following list includes all the major critical articles and sections of books dealing either wholly or significantly with Janette Turner Hospital that I have been able to trace.

Albertazzi, Silvia, 'Beautiful Travellers: Notes on Postmodern Fiction', *Commonwealth: Essays and Studies*, 11.2 (1989), pp. 53–62.

——'The Australian Landscape in Janette Turner Hospital's *The Last Magician*', in Susan Ballyn, Doireann MacDermott & Kathleen Firth (eds), *Australia's Changing Landscapes*, Barcelona: Promociones y Publicaciones Universitarias, 1995, pp. 15–21.

——'Violence, Angels and Missing People in Janette Turner Hospital's World', in Selina Samuels (ed.), *Janette Turner Hospital*, London: Sir Robert Menzies Centre for Australian Studies/University of London, 1998, pp. 31–8.

Barnett, Tully, 'The Many Modern Circles of Hell: Dante's Legacy in Janette Turner Hospital's Literary Thrillers', in Margaret Baker, Flavia Coassin & Diana Glenn (eds), *Flinders Dante Conferences 2002 & 2004*, Adelaide: Lythrum Press, 2005, pp. 190–9.

Bergmann, Laurel, 'Janette Turner Hospital's Radical Re-writing: Oedipal *Charades*', *Australian Literary Studies*, 17.4 (October 1996), pp. 364–72.

Bowen, Deborah, 'Borderline Magic: Janette Turner Hospital and Transfiguration by Photography', *Studies in Canadian Literature / Études de la littérature canadienne*, 16 (1991), pp. 182–96.

Brennan, Bernadette, 'Words of Water: Reading Otherness in *Tourmaline* and *Oyster*', *Journal of the Association for the Study of Australian Literature*, 3 (2004), pp. 143–57.

Callahan, David, 'Janette Turner Hospital and the Discourse of Displacement', in Wolfgang Zach & Ken Goodwin (eds), *Nationalism vs. Internationalism. (Inter)National Dimensions of Literatures in English*, Tübingen: Stauffenburg verlag, 1996, pp. 335–40.

——'Acting in the Public Sphere and the Politics of Memory in the Work of Janette Turner Hospital', *Tulsa Studies in Women's Literature*, 15.1 (June 1996), pp. 73–81.

——'Becoming Different in Janette Turner Hospital', *Ariel: A Review of International English Literature*, 28:2 (April 1997), pp. 23–34.

——'Aberrant Decoding and Witness in *Isobars*', in Selina Samuels (ed.), *Janette Turner Hospital*, London: Sir Robert Menzies Centre for Australian Studies/ University of London, 1998, pp. 39–51.

——'Rainforest Narratives: Janette Turner Hospital and the Ethics of Interference', *Antipodes*, 15.1 (June 2001), pp. 31–5.

——'Particles, Waves, and Stories: Janette Turner Hospital's *Charades*', *Critique: Studies in Contemporary Fiction*, 48.4 (Summer 2007), pp. 363–80.

Carr, Richard, '"Just Enough Religion to Make Us Hate": The Case of *Tourmaline* and *Oyster*', *Antipodes*, 18:1 (June 2004), pp. 9–15.

Clark, Maureen, 'Grim Wit and Family Outings in Janette Turner Hospital's *The Ivory Swing*', *New Literatures Review*, 37 (Summer 2000), pp. 1–13.

——'Power, Vanishing Acts and Silent Watchers in Janette Turner Hospital's *The Last Magician*', *Journal of the Association for the Study of Australian Literature*, 8 (2008), pp. 107–20.

Clutterbuck, Charlotte, 'A Shared Depository of Wisdom: Connection and Redemption in *Tiger in the Tiger Pit* and *Possession*', *Southerly*, 53.2 (June 1993), pp. 121–9.

Cowley, Julian, '"Violent times": Janette Turner Hospital's art of memory and the history of the present', in Sarah Sceats & Gail Cunningham (eds), *Image & Power: Women in Fiction in the Twentieth Century*, London: Longman, 1996, pp. 173–83.

Coyle, Fiona, 'A Third Space? Postcolonial Australia and the Fractal Landscape in *The Last Magician* and *Oyster*', in Jamie S. Scott & Paul Simpson-Housley (eds), *Mapping the Sacred: Religion, Geography and Postcolonial Literatures*, Amsterdam: Rodopi, 2001, pp. 111–30.

Craven, Peter, 'Beauty in Terror: Janette Turner Hospital's *Orpheus Lost*', *Critique: Studies in Contemporary Fiction*, 48.4 (Summer 2007), pp. 355–61.

Daniel, Helen, 'Introduction', Janette Turner Hospital, *Borderline*, London: Virago, 1990, pp. 1–6.

Davies, Bronwyn, 'Eclipsing the Constitutive Power of Discourse: The Writing of Janette Turner Hospital', in Elizabeth St Pierre and Wanda S. Pillow (eds), *Working the Ruins: Feminist Poststructural Theory and Methods in Education*, London: Routledge, 2000, pp. 179–98.

Davis, Donna J., 'Postmodern Issues in Janette Turner Hospital's Nature-Dominated Short Stories "The End-of-the-Line End-of-the-World Disco" and "Our Own Little Kakadu"', in Farhat Iftekharrudin, Joseph Boyden, Joseph Longo, and Mary Rohrberger (eds), *Postmodern Approaches to the Short Story*, Westport, CT: Praeger, 2003, pp. 65–75.

Davis, Joan, 'Come on in, the water's fine: Janette Turner Hospital's short prose fiction, "Isobars"', *Literature in North Queensland*, 17.1 (1990), pp. 109–13.

Gillett, Sue, '*Charades*: Searching for Father Time: Memory and the Uncertainty Principle', *New Literatures Review*, 21 (Summer South, 1991), pp. 68–81.

Greiner, Donald J, 'Ideas of Order in Janette Turner Hospital's *Oyster*', *Critique: Studies in Contemporary Fiction*, 48.4 (Summer 2007), pp. 381–90.

Herrero, Dolores, 'Globalization and terror as reflected in *Due Preparations for the Plague*', in *Culture and Power: Culture and Society in the Age of Globalisation*, Proceedings of the 10th Iberian Association of Cultural Studies Conference (Burgos, 2005), pp. 171–89. Revised and reprinted as '*Due Preparations for the Plague*: Globalisation, Terror and the Ethics of Alterity', *Kunapipi*, 28.1 (2006), pp. 25–43.

Howells, Coral Ann, 'Marian Engel *Bear*, Joy Kogawa *Obasan*, Janette Turner Hospital *The Ivory Swing*', *Private and Fictional Words: Canadian Women Novelists of the 1970s and 1980s*, London & New York: Methuen, 1987, pp. 106–38.

Huggan, Graham, 'Orientalism Reconfirmed? Stereotypes of East-West Encounter in Janette Turner Hospital's *The Ivory Swing* and Yvon Richard's *Les silences du corbeau*', *Canadian Literature*, 132 (1992), pp. 44–56. Revised and reprinted in Huggan's *The Postcolonial Exotic: Marketing the Margins*, London: Routledge, 2000, pp. 180–93.

Kinnane, Garry, 'Mutable Identity and the Postmodern', *Meanjin*, 57.2 (1998), pp. 405–17.

Langer, Beryl, 'Complicit Bystanders: Post-Colonial Bodies and Imperial Crime', in Leigh Dale & Simon Ryan (eds), *The Body in the Library*, Amsterdam & Atlanta: Rodopi, 1998, pp. 15–34.

Lovell, Sue, 'The Pygmalion Factor – Creativity in the Novels of Janette Turner Hospital', *Literature in North Queensland*, 17.1 (1990), pp. 78–85.

——'The Search for Agency in the Fiction of Janette Turner Hospital', in Sharyn Pearce and Philip Neilsen (eds), *Current Tensions: Proceedings of the 18th Annual Association for the Study of Australian Literature Conference*, Brisbane: Queensland University of Technology, 1996, pp. 204–13.

——'Janette Turner Hospital's *The Last Magician*: 'A Feminist's Nightmare'?' *Hecate*, 28.2 (2002), pp. 46–63.

——'The "Psychic Space" of Queensland in the Work of Janette Turner Hospital', *Queensland Review*, 11.2 (December 2004), pp. 11–23.

——'Janette Turner Hospital's *The Last Magician* in "An Expanded Field"', *AUMLA: Journal of the Australasian Universities Language and Literature Association*, 104 (November 2005), pp. 121–49.

Moss, John, 'Janette Turner Hospital', *A Reader's Guide to the Canadian Novel*, Toronto: McClelland and Stewart, 1987, pp. 180–7.

Müller, Anja I, 'Travels in No-Man's-Land: Closure and Transgression in Janette Turner Hospital's *Oyster*', in Liselotte Glage (ed.), *Being/s in Transit: Travelling, Migration, Dislocation*, Amsterdam & Atlanta: Rodopi, 2000, pp. 141–53.

Perkins, Elizabeth, 'The Fictional Daughter: Janette Turner Hospital's *Borderline*', *Literature in North Queensland*, 17.1 (1990), pp. 52–9.

Pons, Xavier, 'History and Her Story: the Deconstruction and Reconstruction of the Past in Janette Turner Hospital's *Charades*', *Caliban*, 29 (1992), pp. 145–55.

Ramsey-Kurz, Helga, 'Writing Back from Another Centre: *Charades* by Janette Turner Hospital', in Alwin Fill, Sonja Bahn-Coblans, Heidi Ganner-Rauth & Helga Ramsey-Kurtz (eds), *New-Found-Lands: Festschrift für Harro Heinz Kühnelt*, Tübingen: Gunter Narr, 1993, pp. 147–65.

——'The Charting of a "Private National Identity" in Janette Turner Hospital's *Charades* and *The Ivory Swing*', in Wolfgang Zach & Ken Goodwin (eds), *Nationalism vs Internationalism: (Inter)National Dimensions of Literatures in English*, Tübingen: Stauffenburg Verlag, 1996, pp. 341–50.

Rocard, Marcienne, 'Poétique de l'indétermination: Le Procès de Pygmalion dans *Borderline* de Janette Turner Hospital', *Annales du Centre de Recherches sur l'Amérique Anglophone*, 20 (1995), pp. 85–93, 235–6.

Samuels, Selina, 'Dislocation and Memory in the Short Stories of Janette Turner Hospital', *Journal of Modern Literature*, 20.1 (Summer 1996), pp. 85–95.

——'Introduction', in Selina Samuels (ed.), *Janette Turner Hospital*, London: Sir Robert Menzies Centre for Australian Studies/University of London, 1998, pp. i–v.

——'Janette Turner Hospital', in Selina Samuels (ed.), *Dictionary of Literary Biography: Australian Writers 1975–2000*, Farmington Hills, MI: Thomson Gale, 2006, pp. 153–63.

Schramm, Margaret K, 'Identity and the Family in the Novels of Janette Turner Hospital', in Mickey Pearlman (ed.), *Canadian Women Writing Fiction*, Jackson: University Press of Mississippi, 1993, pp. 84–98.

Shoemaker, Adam, 'Janette Turner Hospital and the National Dilemma', in Kate Burridge, Lois Foster & Gerry Turcotte (eds), *Canada–Australia: Towards a Second Century of Partnership*, Ottawa: International Council for Canadian Studies and Carleton University Press, 1997, pp. 427–36.

Slaughter, Joseph & Jennifer Wenzel, 'Letters of the Law: Women, Human Rights, and Epistolary Literature', in Marjorie Agosín (ed.), *Women, Gender, and Human Rights: A Global Perspective*, New Brunswick, NJ: Rutgers University Press, 2001, pp. 289–311.

Stead, Alastair, 'The Improprieties of Janette Turner Hospital: Strategic Punning in *Borderline* and *Charades*', in Shirley Chew & Lynette Hunter (eds), *Borderblur: Poetry and Poetics in Contemporary Canadian Literature*, Edinburgh: Quadriga, 1996, pp. 74–93.

——'Notes from Underground: *The Last Magician* and Janette Turner Hospital', in Selina Samuels (ed.), *Janette Turner Hospital*, London: Sir Robert Menzies Centre for Australian Studies/University of London, 1998, pp. 17–30.

Stoneham, Geraldine, 'Dislocations: Postcolonialism in a Postmodernist Space', in Jane Dowson & Steven Earnshaw, *Postmodern Subjects/Postmodern Texts*, Amsterdam: Rodopi, 1995, pp. 237–51.

Temby, Kate, 'Gender, power and postmodernism in *The Last Magician*', *Westerly*, 40.3 (Spring 1995), pp. 47–55.

Thompson, Christina, 'Janette Turner Hospital: Certain Uncertainties', *Scripsi*, 5.2 (1989), pp. 167–75.

Webb, Caroline, 'Forming Feminism: Structure and Ideology in *Charades* and 'The Djinn in the Nightingale's Eye'', *Hecate*, 29.1 (2003), pp. 132–41.

Webb, Jennifer, 'Endocolonialism and the Production of Gender', *SPAN*, 44 (April 1997), pp. 22–35.

West, Russell, '"Multiple Exposures": Spatial Dilemma of Postmodern Artistic Identity in the Fiction of Janette Turner Hospital', in Anne Luyat & Francine Tolron (eds), *Flight from Certainty: The*

Dilemma of Identity and Exile, Amsterdam & Atlanta: Rodopi, 2001, pp. 177–90.

West-Pavlov, Russell, 'Triangulating the Self: Turner Hospital, Hoffman and Sante', *Transcultural Graffiti: Diasporic Writing and the Teaching of Literary Studies*, Amsterdam & New York: Rodopi, 2005, pp. 115–36.

Zachariah, Matthew, 'Janette Turner Hospital's Passage to India: A Critique of *The Ivory Swing*', *Toronto South Asian Review*, 4.1 (1985), pp. 54–61.

(v) Reviews cited

Hospital's books have been reviewed in several countries, principally Australia, Canada and the United States, and many pages could be devoted to listing these reviews. Reviews in recent years tend to be placed on the internet, and can be easily located, while newspapers are increasingly putting their archives on line, albeit generally for subscribers. Earlier reviews can often be found listed on AustLit. Here I cite only those reviews actually cited in this study.

Adair, Tom, 'Vultures return to pick over the bones of lost childhood', *Scotland on Sunday*, 28 June 1992, p. 38. [*Charades*]

Birskys, Betty, 'Principles of Uncertainty', *Imago*, 1.1 (March 1987) p. 47. [*Charades*]

Burns, Graham, 'Lives in Truthful Disorder', *Age: Arts & Books*, 28 November 1987, p. 15. [*Dislocations*]

Cameron, Elspeth, 'Borders', *Saturday Night* [Canada], 101, April 1986, pp. 57–9. [*Borderline*]

Clancy, Laurie, 'Only the writing is certain', *Age*, 24 September 1988, Saturday Extra, p. 12. [*Isobars*]

Clutterbuck, Charlotte, 'Emptiness and Isobars – the Mapping of Isolation', *Southerly*, 51.1 (1991), pp. 159–65.

Coe, Jonathan, 'Sydney's Inferno', *London Review of Books*, 24 September 1992, p. 22. [*Last Magician*]

Dempster, Barry, 'Words that fly up', *Canadian Forum*, 66.764 (December 1986), pp. 38–9. [*Dislocations*]

Ellis, Markman, 'In the back of the outback', *Times Literary Supplement*, 13 September 1996, p. 22. [*Oyster*]

Frost, Lucy, 'The Distinctive Terrain of Janette Turner Hospital's Stories', *Australian Book Review*, 175 (October 1995), pp. 29–30. [*Collected Stories*]

Goulder, Gina, '*Dislocations*', *Literature in North Queensland*, 17.1 (1990), pp. 161–63.

Grove, Lee, 'Star-Crossed', *Boston*, 77.12 (December 1985), p. 125. [*Borderline*]

Groves, Robin, 'The Appreciation of Grace', *Australian Book Review*, 97 (December 1987/January 1988), pp. 10–11. [*Dislocations*]

Hall, Eleanor 'The World Today – Book *Due Preparation* [sic] *for the Plague* explores death, terrorism', at: www.abc.net.au/worldtoday/content/2003/s860328.htm.

Halligan, Marion, 'Countdown to the Millenium', *Australian Book Review*, 185 (October 1996), pp.40–1. [*Oyster*]

Howe, Valmai, 'Seduction and opals in the Outback', *Globe & Mail* [Toronto], 26 October 1996, p. D10.

Hussein, Aamer, 'Trial by triage', *Times Literary Supplement*, 3 July 1992, p. 25. [*Last Magician*]

Liddelow, Eden, 'Repeating the cataclysm', *Modern Times* (July 1992), p. 32. [*Last Magician*]

MacKendrick, Louis K., 'Clever by Far', *Essays on Canadian Writing*, 48 (Winter 1992–1993), pp. 55–9. [*Isobars*]

McNamara, Tim, 'Trapped between two poles', *Whig-Standard Magazine* [Canada], 2 October 1982, p. 19. [*Ivory Swing*]

Manguel, Alberto, 'Around the universe in 304 pages', *Quill & Quire* [Canada] (February 1989), p. 20. [*Charades*]

Merry, Bruce, '*Charades*', *Literature in North Queensland*, 17.1 (1990), pp. 156–60.

Miner, Valerie, 'The 1,001 Australian Nights', *Los Angeles Times Book Review*, 23 April 1989, p. 3. [*Charades*]

Morley, Patricia, 'Hospital may be great novelist', *Ottawa Citizen*, 1 October 1983, p. 42. [*Tiger*]

Mueller, Martha Ann, '*Dislocations*', *Queen's Quarterly*, 94.3 (Autumn 1987), pp. 692–4.

Ober, Doris, 'Powerful novel brings together a divided family', *San José Mercury*, 20 May 1984, p. 26. [*Tiger*]

Riemer, Andrew, *Sydney Morning Herald*, 4 May 2007. [*Orpheus*]

Rifkind, Donna, *Los Angeles Times*, 4 November 2007. [*Orpheus*]

Rivers, Bronwyn, 'Partridge Wings', *Australian Book Review*, 253 (August 2003), p. 50. [*North*]

Roberts, Paul, 'Hospital's latest nears new frontiers', *Quill & Quire*, 51 [Canada], (November 1985), p. 23. [*Borderline*]

Steacy, Anne, 'This Microcosm is her *Oyster*', *Books in Canada*, 25.9 (December 1996), pp. 20–1.

Sullivan, Jane, 'The thrills in Turner Hospital', *The Age*, 31 May 2003, Review, p. 3. [*Plague*]

Van Herk, Aritha, 'Fiction', *University of Toronto Quarterly*, 63.1 (Fall 1993), pp. 29–30 [entire review article pp. 26–48]. [*Last Magician*]

INDEX

Index

Index

Index

Index

Index

SELECTED FICTION BY JANETTE TURNER HOSPITAL

THE IVORY SWING

Juliet yearns for the 'ebb and flow of life lived avidly', for the pace and challenge of city living. The conflict between her love of her husband and children and her own passionate need for expression is intensified by her move from small-town Canada to Southern India.

The stifling restrictions on Juliet's freedom are magnified in the plight of her young widowed neighbour. The beautiful Yashoda longs to embrace the Western values that would release her from the strictures of Indian tradition. But the ancient mores are powerful and enduring, and challenging them inevitably leads to tragedy.

> 'The steamy, subtle, utterly impenetrable mysteries of India . . . a work both emotionally and stylistically deft.'
>
> Thomas Keneally

> 'A truly magnificent literary achievement.'
>
> *Booklist*

ISBN: 978 0 7022 3403 3

UQP

THE TIGER IN THE TIGER PIT

Like the rare Blue Wanderer butterfly, Emily Carpenter is never still for long. She flees emotional commitment, despite the longing of her eight-year-old son for family, and for the easygoing sheep farmer with whom she once found peace.

While Emily's eccentric mother works to reunite her scattered children, her once tyrannical father, made 'irritable as the tiger in the tiger pit' by old age and regret, does his own scheming. The scene is set for dramatic confrontation and unexpected revelations.

Janette Turner Hospital explores her fascination with the interweaving of time and place, and displays the superlative skills as a storyteller that have won awards and critical acclaim for all of her published books.

> 'One feels the rush of life in her pages . . . a writer of remarkable talent who writes about family relationships with rare insight and compassion.'
>
> *Publishers Weekly*

> 'Turner Hospital's gift for memorable characters and poetic prose come together in writing that is strong, wise and exciting.'
>
> *Ottawa Citizen*

ISBN: 978 0 7022 3402 6

UQP

BORDERLINE

A meat truck is intercepted at the Canadian–US border, and a group of illegal immigrants is removed. Felicity watches from her car, and talks with Gus who is also waiting in the queue. When they realise a woman has been left behind, they impulsively smuggle her across the border. La Magdalena will change their lives irrevocably.

In this, her third novel, Janette Turner Hospital transforms a thrilling and suspenseful story into a deadly resonant parable for our times, leaving her readers not just entertained, but enriched.

> 'Janette Turner Hospital is a stunningly stylish writer who turns almost every chapter into a virtuoso performance . . . this is a very clever, very fascinating book which should not be missed.'
>
> Brenda Little, *Australian*

> 'This book is brilliant in its several meanings: sparkling, intelligent, distinguished . . . Hospital is in complete and wonderous control of her material.'
>
> Shirley Streshinsky, *San Francisco Chronicle*

ISBN: 978 0 7022 3400 2

UQP

CHARADES

This vibrant, exquisitely crafted novel explores the elusive boundaries between existence and imagination, memory and truth. From the subtropical lushness of Queensland's Tamborine rainforest to the claustrophobic bedroom of a Boston physicist, Hospital's characters breathe an atmosphere of passion and suspense. Charade Ryan, an enigmatic story-spinning Scheherazade, searches for a way to unravel the long-held secrets of her family origins.

> 'A journey of strange and beautiful complexity through some of the finest prose being written anywhere today.'
>
> *Toronto Star*

> 'Janette Turner Hospital goes from strength to literary strength – ever brilliant in ideas, graceful in expression, resourceful in story – and in Charades throwing in, for good measure, a heady eroticism. I loved it!'
>
> Fay Weldon

ISBN: 978 0 7022 3388 3

UQP

THE LAST MAGICIAN

The last magician is Charlie, the photographer, who monitors and records everything as he seeks the silent Cat through physical and emotional infernos. Charlie, Cat, Robbie and Catherine shared a childhood summer in a Queensland rainforest. But a death intruded on their charmed circle, binding them to complicity and silence.

Decades later, festering memories seep through into the present, in the same way as the desperate underside of a corrupt Sydney breaks through into tidy lives and well-kept secrets.

This superb novel is richly textured and intellectually challenging, a breathtaking read from our most elegantly seductive writer.

> 'Spellbinding reading, an adventure of the mind and heart that enthralls from first page to last . . . Haunting, disturbing, subversive.'
>
> *Newsday*

> 'The real magic at work here is the writer's . . . an ambitious, intense and satisfying book.'
>
> *New York Times Book Review*

ISBN: 978 0 7022 3401 9

UQP

NORTH OF NOWHERE, SOUTH OF LOSS

I live at the desiccating edge of things, on the dividing line between two countries, nowhere, everywhere, in the margins.

Janette Turner Hospital's stories have won widespread international acclaim for their dazzling style, intellectual depth and crackling energy. Her characters oscillate between estrangement and a sense of belonging, as Hospital herself has suffered geographical displacement from the Far North of Australia to the Deep South of the United States.

These insightful stories transport us to such delightfully varied locations as Brisbane and Paris, Cairns and Atlanta, reflecting Hospital's own nomadic existence.

> 'Her stories are like brief cyclones wrapped around an unexpected center of calm.'
>
> *Los Angeles Times Book Review*

> 'Sensuous, speculative fictions about the experience of dislocation . . . her stories develop like poems or meditations.'
>
> *New York Times Book Review*

ISBN: 978 0 7022 3333 3

UQP